COLD
DAWN

Also by John Newhouse

De Gaulle and the Anglo-Saxons
Collision in Brussels
U.S. Troops in Europe

COLD
DAWN
THE STORY OF
SALT

John Newhouse

HOLT, RINEHART AND WINSTON
NEW YORK   CHICAGO   SAN FRANCISCO

Copyright © 1973 by John Newhouse

All rights reserved, including the right to reproduce
this book or portions thereof in any form.

Published simultaneously in Canada by Holt, Rinehart
and Winston, of Canada, Limited.

Library of Congress Cataloging in Publication Data

Newhouse, John.
Cold dawn: the story of SALT.

"A substantial portion of the material in this book appeared
originally in the New Yorker, in slightly different form."
Includes bibliographical references and index.
1. Strategic Arms Limitation Talks. 2. Atomic
weapons and disarmament. I. Title.
JX1974.7.N47   327'.174   72-91556
ISBN 0-03-001631-2

Published, June, 1973
Second Printing, January, 1974

Printed in the United States of America

Contents

The folly of mistaking a paradox for a discovery, a metaphor for a proof, a torrent of verbiage for a spring of capital truths, and oneself for an oracle, is inborn in us.—PAUL VALÉRY, *Introduction to the Method of Leonardo da Vinci.*

Preface

Cold Dawn is an account of the background and conduct of the talks between the United States and the Soviet Union on limiting strategic arms. The story is, of course, contemporary, culminating in the historic agreements reached in Moscow on May 26, 1972. Those agreements concluded SALT's first phase, which covered a period of thirty months. The second phase of this continuing and enormously difficult negotiation is likely to last at least as long.

Although the ongoing nature of the talks complicates an already complex subject, a more important difficulty is the sensitive and understandably secret character of the talks. Most international negotiation is conducted behind a veil, but superpower talks on weaponry are particularly sensitive to light. In relating this kind of contemporary history, the writer must rely on the willingness of those directly involved to speak frankly of what they know. He must sift their comments carefully, taking account of their personal biases, of the vested interests of the agencies they represent, and, in some cases, of personality conflicts that might distort their perceptions of reality or simply tempt them to even scores. To the degree possible, information acquired from one part of the government must be discreetly verified in another.

Most of this book draws upon information obtained in innumerable private conversations, and the individuals concerned, except in rare cases, cannot be identified. At all levels of government, many people—some still in public service, others not—contributed to my knowledge and understanding of SALT and of such related and controversial issues as the decisions to deploy anti-ballistic missiles. I am indebted to them all. They do not, of course, bear any responsibility for the book's conclusions or its point of view. The responsibility is mine.

I would also like to record my appreciation to William Shawn. His interest in SALT and, hence, in serializing this book in *The*

New Yorker greatly encouraged me in taking on so formidable a task. Finally, I'd like to thank the editor of the book, Mrs. Marian S. Wood, for her considerable and uniformly helpful efforts.

John Newhouse

COLD
DAWN

1   Piercing the Veil

Sometime between the great world wars, a Whitehall civil servant took to admonishing visitors with a few words framed on the wall behind his desk; they said: "If you know what you think you don't understand the problem." The name and exact vintage of this professional skeptic are not reliably recorded, but one doubts that he and his contemporaries grappled with problems as labyrinthine, or as treacherous, or as rich in paradox, contradiction, and abstraction as those covered by SALT, the Strategic Arms Limitation Talks. If the term itself is by now among the world's best-known acronyms, its substance is available only to initiates—to the assorted bureaucrats and scientists who are professionally involved. And many of them are confused, their thinking shifts and oscillates, because the analysis flowing from SALT mocks, if it doesn't overwhelm, tidy, clear-cut points of view.

Still, thinking coherently about SALT is one of those civic duties. Politicians and editorialists—not all of them prone to exaggerate—tell us that SALT is the most fateful negotiation in human history, although they are hard put to explain what exactly is at issue and why. The agreements reached in Moscow in May of 1972—possibly the first in a series—drew massive congressional endorsement. It's hard to imagine a SALT agreement being rejected any more than the limited test-ban treaty or the nonproliferation treaty could have been rejected. Yet the insight on SALT available to the concerned public and its elected representatives is much less than was the case with either of those other agreements, both of which dealt with less sensitive, more modest issues.

SALT, then, is perverse; it enlists our curiosity, yet discourages comprehension. It is not, however, beyond the grasp of the nonspecialized and the noninitiated. Moreover, thinking about SALT —understanding what is involved and what is happening—is richly rewarding less because of its self-evident importance than because SALT is probably the most fascinating, episodic negotiation since the Congress of Vienna. SALT is likely to go on indefinitely.

Thus, even though progress may be slow, the affair prone to bog down occasionally, SALT could develop a cumulative impact on the world system comparable to that of the Congress of Vienna, whose achievement was to spare Europe any major bloodletting for 100 years. Such is the hope.

Piercing the veil of SALT to a point where the fascination begins means acquiring three insights: why the United States and the Soviet Union are engaged in this wholly unique enterprise; why SALT is opaque; what the essence of SALT really is.

The immediate question turns on why Washington and Moscow are even negotiating on strategic arms. The answer, as yet unclear and incomplete, will determine whether SALT will produce further agreement and, if so, whether it will actually stabilize the power balance—that is, blunt each side's incentive to seek strategic advantage.

"The Congress of Vienna," Castlereagh told the British House of Commons, "was not assembled for the discussion of moral principles, but for great practical purposes, to establish effectual provisions for the general security."[1] Castlereagh's stricture could apply as well to SALT. Yet such is the complexity of SALT that few senior officials involved in the process—or middle-level bureaucrats for that matter—appear to agree on why the superpowers opted for SALT; indeed, opinions clash on whether SALT is even desirable. Of course, governments, like people, rarely take their major decisions for a single obvious reason. Then, too, the motives animating official actions may be easily obscured by the actions themselves, or by the rhetoric clothing the actions. SALT, like most actions of consequence, illustrates this tendency.

Still, there is a kind of agreed-upon rationale for SALT. The senior official finding himself before a seminar on arms control and asked why bother with SALT might answer something like this:

The talks were launched, not from a common impulse to reduce armaments, but from a mutual need to solemnize the parity principle—or, put differently, to establish an acceptance by each side of the other's ability to inflict unacceptable retribution in response to a nuclear attack. (The assumption here is that neither side will initiate a first strike if the other's retaliatory capability is strong enough to survive its impact. Mutual deterrence, then, rests on the awareness by each side of the other's retaliatory—or

second-strike—capacity.) Thus, each *may* recognize that an unlimited arms race would undermine deterrence—and, hence,
stability—conceivably by allowing one side or the other to
acquire a margin of superiority that in turn would create risks
of a first strike. But additionally, a failure to set limits could mean
sustaining indefinitely the push for more and better nuclear arms,
with costs driven constantly upward—possibly at the expense of
other priorities. Here, too, stability, the equivalent in the nuclear
age of Castlereagh's "general security," could be degraded.

For all kinds of reasons traceable to internal politics, foreign
policy, and competing defense priorities, both great powers want
to stabilize spending on arms. Each is obliged to maintain large
general-purpose (as distinct from strategic) defense forces. Each
confronts internal pressure to reorient priorities. If the entire
U.S. defense budget were stabilized, or even modestly cut, the
resources liberated for other purposes over the next few years
would be negligible; it follows that any rise in the proportion of
resources earmarked for defense would retard some programs
aimed at improving society and preclude others.

Each side, our senior official might continue, makes coldly
analytical assumptions about the other's purposes and goals. Each
assumes the other is negotiating because parity has been achieved.
Each also suspects the other may be engaged in a "hold-and-
explore" gambit—trying to buy time in order to catch up or
jump ahead, either "quantitatively" (in number of weapons) or
"qualitatively" (in destructive potential of existing and follow-on
systems).

The Russians, he would add, are in the talks partly because they
have caught up with the United States in strategic weapons. Their
efforts, after the Cuban missile trauma, to match the Americans
by achieving a balanced second-strike force have succeeded. Now,
the Soviet leaders, like America's, hope to head off another major
offensive weapons cycle. They know that to succeed they must
inhibit ballistic-missile defense, an insight acquired from the
Americans. Baldly, this means that defending people is the most
troublesome of all strategic options, for stability demands that
each of the two societies stand wholly exposed to the destructive
power of the other. Acceptance of this severe and novel doctrine
illustrates the growing sophistication of Soviet thinking and some

willingness to break with fixed attitudes, including the old Russian habit of equating security with territorial defense. And it points up the American interest in raising the Russian learning curve—in creating a dialogue that will encourage, however gradually, a convergence of American and Russian thinking about stable deterrence. Thinking about deterrence is mind bending even for initiates. It takes time and some knowledge of the weapons as well as the issues.

The gap in such thinking is not just between the U.S. strategic community and the Russians, whose concern with these concepts is more recent. It is also between the Americans and their European allies, and between those Americans directly involved ("in-house") and those observing from the sidelines of academia.

Both sides are at the negotiating table at least in part to get a better grip on their own internal policy issues. SALT forces decisions through the two bureaucracies (if not in the same way for each); within the U.S. system, it obliges competing elements to settle differences and take what might become self-limiting steps. Briefly, SALT offers a way for both sides to do some things that each may want to do anyway. Doing some of them as part of a bilateral agreement is easier than trying to do them from within, unilaterally. In the bureaucratic idiom, it is a "high-confidence" way of taking various steps because the other party—the adversary—"signs off" on the same piece of paper and because both sides are agreed on what they are talking about. That alone is novel, as well as crucial.

Our senior official, especially if he were representing the State Department or the Arms Control and Disarmament Agency (ACDA), might conclude his answer to the question—why SALT? —with a word on parity. The alternative to parity, he would say, is a quest for superiority, a goal robbed of its strategic value by the undoubted continuing ability of each side to destroy most of the other's society. Parity, as such, may have even more significance for the Russians. It represents a cherished objective—the claim to power the equal of America's, and with this power, expanding political horizons; Europeans worry that the United States is even less likely to use its nuclear weapons to defend them against Soviet force should the need arise. Europe and other parts of the world are thus put on notice that Soviet nonnuclear forces, also growing, can back a venturesome, possibly aggressive, diplomacy with minimal risk of a nuclear confrontation with Washington. Parity, then, is as much a political as a strategic value.

Just as governments rarely do anything for one reason, different parts of the official apparatus will agree to take an action often for quite different reasons. At least some part of the Soviet system is thought to have favored a leisurely SALT negotiation as a means of sniffing out the anxieties of European NATO governments about the talks and, if possible, of maneuvering these anxieties into open splits between the United States and its allies. This is just one of the numerous collateral motives of which each side, rightly or wrongly, suspects the other.

The pace and style of the Congress of Vienna eventually taxed Talleyrand's patience with what Harold Nicolson, in his fine portrait of the Congress, characterized as "Castlereagh's caution and Metternich's unbearable habit of twisting the issues into small cat's-cradles of string."[2]

> "Prince Metternich," wrote Talleyrand himself, "has shown at this sitting the full extent of his mediocrity, of his taste for petty intrigues and an uncertain and tortuous course, as also of his marvelous command of words that are vague and void of meaning."[3]

One wonders how Europe's consummate diplomat would have reacted to SALT. Like the Congress of Vienna, SALT is a political negotiation concerned with finding an equilibrium in which the great powers feel secure. Unlike the Congress, whose pivotal issue was purely political (the control of Poland and Saxony), SALT is an anarchy of technical issues and asymmetries, frequently so complex as to frustrate efforts to agree on common definitions and terms of reference. The essence of SALT is political, but technical issues are used on all sides to shore up political and strategic biases.

Understanding SALT means getting behind this and other veils: the secrecy of the process; the theological approach that has overtaken the Americans, or many of them; the mythology of SALT; the ambiguities arising from the savagely conflicting attitudes within what might be called the defense and arms-control communities in the United States, as well as the deeper ambiguities emerging from the Soviet performance on SALT-related matters.

The security is remarkable. Rarely if ever has so prominent a negotiation been so closely held. At the outset, both delegations solemnly agreed to forbear seeking propaganda advantage by leaking any of what went on in the proceedings. During the lengthy negotiations that led to the first accords, members of both delegations faithfully observed this rule of secrecy, although some of their colleagues in Washington did, from time to time, lift the curtain on some part of the talks; these derelictions often led to a brief tit for tat, with the Soviet Embassy in Washington offering its version in response to an Administration-inspired account of the American position, or vice-versa in the case of an Embassy leak.

Both delegations deplore leaks, whatever the source. On this, as on other issues, they have acquired an identity of view arising from their proprietary attitude toward SALT. A Washington-based journalist, Robert Toth of the *Los Angeles Times*, is probably unaware that he was jointly censured by the delegations during SALT III (the third round of SALT) in Helsinki. Someone in Washington told him that the Russians had just accepted an American proposal to limit ABM (antiballistic missile) defense to the two capitals, Moscow and Washington; the Americans had indeed put forward such a proposition, and, to their subsequent and considerable chagrin, the Russians did accept it. The Americans, however, were having sober second thoughts about this notion, and thus most of those involved were particularly upset by Toth's story, which appeared in the *Los Angeles Times* on November 26, 1970. All leaks seem to annoy the Russian delegation.

The forbidding nature of the talks also contributes to their secrecy. A reporter finding himself the chosen conduit for a SALT leak very well knows that newspaper space limitations will not allow him to present his prize (usually earned, by the way) in an account that even serious readers of the *Washington Post* and *The New York Times*—the normal outlets for SALT leaks—can easily comprehend. It is hard to reduce any SALT-related story to 1000 or 1200 words and do more than impress the reader with the jumble of acronyms, abbreviations, and strategic jargon of which SALT seems to be confected. The attention span of many readers is unfairly taxed by such stories; news editors understand this, and have little fondness for SALT.

Genuinely revealing articles about SALT, because they are irregular and selective, do not allow a close newspaper reader to acquire an ongoing and coherent view of what the talks are about. The leaks, whether from U.S. sources or the Soviet Embassy, are naturally self-serving. On the American side, they may be stimulated by the White House, the State Department, or some part of the Pentagon. The leaks from the Soviet Embassy have originated either with Ambassador Anatoliy F. Dobrynin or, more often, with his Minister-Counsellor, Yuri M. Vorontsov, a gifted diplomat and one who has been involved with arms-control matters since 1958.

This haphazard pattern of communicating with the public on SALT is yet another element adding to the elusive quality of the subject. The pattern also tells something about life along the Potomac. The current leadership conceals many of its activities and attitudes, not only from the public but, to the degree possible, from the bureaucracy as well. Not only are the State Department and other agencies often kept in the dark, but the expert staff toiling under Henry Kissinger's direction in the Executive Office Building next door to the White House is sometimes no better informed. This celebrated bureacracy, erected by Nixon and Kissinger to strengthen their hold on national-security matters, works at an exhausting pace to prepare and hold open options for presidential decision. But it is not often consulted on what the President and his chief adviser ultimately decide to do. It has no access to the President himself and must rely for guidance on what Kissinger tells it, which may be much, little, or nothing—depending on the issue and the moment.

On SALT, as on other security issues, this system both inhibits and generates news copy. The White House passion for control and for secrecy is a constraint on other parts of the government. But the system also arouses bureacrats toiling elsewhere, who, finding their arguments overruled or ignored, are less reluctant to take the case to the press. Even now, the exact source of some of the most prominent SALT leaks—and in one case, the most damaging—are unknown. Even establishing a rational motive for some of the leaks, and thus possibly tracing them, has proved difficult.

What this White House system has generated is a relentless

flow of analysis. The interstices of every aspect of every SALT-related issue are explored and reexplored. It is an endless and, one suspects, somewhat exaggerated procedure. The question of force planning is sometimes posed in terms of how much is enough. The same question can be asked in regard to SALT: How much analysis can the SALT process usefully accommodate? How much of it can the leadership really use? Is the bureaucracy sometimes sent off chasing hares? Kept busy and out of the way? Rightly or wrongly, some bureaucrats feel misused in this way.

Not long ago, a distinguished professor of government attended a conference on SALT. He prepared himself by spending the better part of two days talking with an initiate—also a conferee—and reading documents. At one point during the conference, the expert turned to the novice and asked him if he didn't feel about SALT the way the small boy felt about penguins after reading a book about them—in short, that he had learned more about SALT than he wanted to know. The professor replied: "I've learned more about SALT than there is to know."

It was a nicely subtle point. The analysis is all very useful and a source of comfort to senior officials; but whatever its undoubted utility, the analysis contributes little perspective on SALT—to establishing what precisely Washington seeks from the negotiations. Obviously, the issues of SALT do require exhaustive analysis. Too often, however, the vast analytical machine is set to grinding out assessments of alternatives that nobody contemplates (and that may already have been rejected), or of contingencies too remote and abstract to merit serious high-level attention. In short, beyond a certain point, analysis becomes an end in itself—a substitute for internally agreed-upon goals.

However treacherous, the terrain on which Castlereagh, Metternich, Talleyrand, and Alexander I maneuvered in the Vienna Congress more than 150 years ago was neither alien nor abstract. The substance of SALT is a mix of weapon systems (the hardware of the nuclear age that nobody intends to use) and strategic doctrine (the theology of the specialists in the nuclear age).

On the American side, SALT is directed by a small group of senior officials, called the Verification Panel. Like most such groups, it was created and is chaired by Henry Kissinger. Through his staff, he controls a Verification Panel Working Group, composed of highly competent and, for the most part, senior bureaucrats. The Working Group runs the operational side of SALT. In generating the "inputs," it focuses the analytical talents of hundreds —sometimes as many as a thousand—specialists from the Departments of State and Defense, ACDA, the Joint Chiefs of Staff (JCS), the intelligence community, and outside nongovernmental institutions.

This structure is to the metaphysics of deterrence what the post-Nicaean fathers of the Church—the Scholastics, say—were to Christian theology. So much of the substance and vocabulary of SALT are at least as remote from reality, as most of us perceive it, as early Christian exegesis. The Greek term *homoousion* (consubstantial), when it emerged from the First Council of Nicaea, must have befuddled the far-flung clergy and faithful just as the acronym MIRV (mutiple, independently targeted re-entry vehicle) gave pause to even knowledgeable Washingtonians, for whose eyes the term was first declassified and insinuated into the *Washington Post* on January 29, 1967.

As in the case of the early Church, contending schools form around antagonistic strategic concepts. The most relevant of these are known as assured destruction and damage limitation, and each can claim broad support and intellectual respectability. Debates between the two schools recall those between the Thomists and the essentially Franciscan followers of Duns Scotus. The Thomists prevailed, as have the proponents of assured destruction, who assert, for example, that ballistic-missile defense of population is immoral because it may degrade your adversary's ability to destroy your own cities in a second strike. His confidence undermined, he might then be tempted in a crisis to strike pre-emptively; in short, knowing you are effectively protected from his second-strike assault and fearing your intentions, he may choose to strike first. Thus, stability, a truly divine goal in the nuclear age, becomes the product of secure second-strike nuclear offenses on both sides. This offensive capability is known as assured destruction; it is the supreme dogma of the ascendent branch of the defense and arms-control communities.

The antagonists of assured destruction believe, in greater or lesser degree, that to renounce the means by which damage to society can be limited is a heresy. Thus, the damage-limitation school argues for the deployment of offensive forces capable of measurably reducing an adversary's own offensive weapons, or for the defense of metropolitan areas with antiballistic missile systems, or for both.

The abstractions of Church doctrine are matched, if not exceeded, by the abstractions of the internal SALT debate. Soviet tests of multiple re-entry vehicles for the SS-9—a land-based missile of stupendous destructive power—generated a long epistemological debate within the upper reaches of the Nixon Administration about what is and what is not a truly MIRV'd missile system. The issue turns on the distinction between MRV's, or multiple re-entry vehicles, and MIRV's, multiple, individually targeted re-entry vehicles. MRV's, like pellets from a shotgun, follow a single ballistic-missile path and cannot be aimed at separate targets. The more-advanced MIRV's release individual warheads at varying times and angles, and thus can be assigned multiple targets. Establishing this distinction is far from simple; and for sheer arcana, for level of abstraction achieved, for depth of passion aroused, this debate on the implications of the Soviet tests recalls nothing so much as the querulous hair-splitting out of which Church dogma emerged.

Heresy has a long half-life. Most of those that have split the Church persist in one form or another today. Strategic heresy is no exception. Measured by what it did, as shown in the May accords, the Nixon Administration must be said to have accepted parity and acquiesced in assured destruction, a more modest concept than damage limitation, which has first-strike implications. Yet measured by what he said, the President specifically rejected parity in favor of "sufficiency"—a less compromising term, as can be seen from his suggestion, made in his first presidential press conference, that the difference between superiority and sufficiency was largely semantic.

The President is not alone. Assured destruction may be the fashion, but, throughout the government, one finds people for whom the term represents a temporary constraint—dictated chiefly by limits on spending—that will yield sooner or later to the politically and strategically more congenial criteria of damage . limitation. Briefly, assured destruction is for some scholastics of strategy a façade. For others, like Robert McNamara, it is the only rational option. In their view, the superiority on which any significant damage-limiting capability must rest has become chimerical. Ironically enough, McNamara is the prophet of record for both schools. In a celebrated commencement address at Ann Arbor, in June, 1962, he said: "The principle military objective in the event of nuclear war should be the destruction of the enemy's forces [not his population]."[4] In January, 1967, testifying before the Senate Armed Services Committee, his *volte face* was shown to be complete: "I think we could all agree that if they struck first we are going to target our weapons against their society and destroy 120 million of them."[5]

If SALT, like the Church, is agitated by tenacious internal controversies, it is also beset by ambiguity. Could, for example, certain mutually agreed-upon constraints—say a MIRV ban—be verified by "national means," or would they require provisions for on-site inspection? As with questions of dogma, there is no way by which either side can be fully vindicated. The technicians, alas, can prove or disprove anything.

Another splendid example of the ambiguity is the issue of "Tallinn upgrade," a hardy perennial of the internal debate. Indeed, even after seven years of sometimes stormy controversy, Tallinn was, in the words of one senior White House bureaucrat, "the major unresolved issue inside our system."

Tallinn is a high-performance Soviet air-defense system based on the SA-5 missile. The Americans named it after the Estonian capital city near which the components were first observed. Deployment began shortly before the Russians started installing another system—code-named Galosh and clearly designed for ballistic missile defense—around Moscow. With the advent of Galosh, the Americans began to fear that the Tallinn system might also be ultimately designed for defense against missiles or, at the least, to serve dual purposes. Tallinn, guarding the approaches to Leningrad and to the industrialized European Russia in the south, is an area that requires defending against bomber attacks. But the location of the system also coincides with the flight paths of many American missiles, and this strengthened the suspicion that it was destined for an ABM capability. As the SA-5 and its radars began to be deployed in large numbers around the Russian perimeter, the Air Force argued—with some support from DIA (the Defense Intelligence Agency)—that it was illogical for the Soviets to commit such large resources against a diminishing American bomber threat unless Tallinn was to have some ABM capability. (Deployment of Tallinn roughly coincided with McNamara's cancellation of the RS-70, a supersonic bomber pushed by the Air Force as a replacement for the aging B-52s.) Equally visceral support for the affirmative case came from DDR&E (Defense Department Research & Engineering), the Manichæans of the defense community.

For a time, the concern over Tallinn's dual role, or its upgrade potential, was shared in greater or lesser degree, by many scholastics in many parts of Washington. But by 1967 and 1968, the NIE's (National Intelligence Estimates) on Tallinn were shifting. Analysts in the State Department, ACDA, and the CIA argued that, while Tallinn had a theoretical potential—and probably not much at that—to shoot down "old" (single-warhead) missiles, it could never cope with the real threat, multiple warheads abetted by sophisticated penetration aids. Thus, rather than trying to upgrade a primitive system, the Soviets, if they were serious about ballistic-missile defense, would start from scratch with something more modern. In the face of this, the Air Force's Strategic Air Command (SAC) and DDR&E continued to argue that, rather than start from scratch with a new ABM system, which would be detectable and would involve long lead times, the Soviets might well forego quality in favor of a speedy and possibly clandestine upgrade of Tallinn's existing radar and missile infrastructure. This, it was further argued, would give them, virtually overnight, an ABM network far more extensive than anything the United States could develop over a reasonable period of time. So went the Tallinn upgrade argument and so it still goes, still alive despite the treaty limiting ABM's, and, oddly enough, second only to the prospect of MIRV'd SS-9's as a source of anxiety to some SALT scholastics.

The staying power of this and other issues recalls the First Council of Nicaea: it lasted fifteen years and produced agreement on sensitive issues. SALT, if it is to be a high achiever, must also endure. Hopefully, it, too, will settle sensitive issues, not just solemnize modest accords, many of whose provisions give little pain to either side. Hopefully, SALT will constrain the various technologies from which new or improved generations of weapons could spring.

Probably most of the ecumenical councils or synods of the Church were concerned in one way or another with the distribution of power, temporal as well as ecclesiastical. Still, the analogy should not be pushed too far. SALT is wrapped in doctrinal issues and conditioned by the distribution of power. But peel away the theological wrappings and the essence of its positive side—the perceived need for stable nuclear deterrence—is revealed. Here again, it is the Congress of Vienna, not the Church councils, that stands comparison to SALT.

The initial temptation was to leave SALT to the technicians. That temptation has been resisted. Like war, the historic task of setting limits on stretegic weapons—of inhibiting man's push toward the outer reaches of a self-destructive process—exceeds the competence of bureaucracy, splintered as always by agency biases. Bureaucracy cannot decide what is negotiable and what is not.

Equally to be avoided, or repressed, was the notion that all the elegant analysis (or, for that matter, the reality of the number of weapons deployed) would not matter because the horrendous consequences of a nuclear strike could never be calculated. In the event, mere men would react, but whether rationally or irrationally cannot be known and, in any case, no President will allow a computer printout to dictate his fateful decision. In fact, these things —the balance of strategic forces, the analytical processes—do matter. Presidents and senior officials do have the responsibility for deterrence. Inevitably, and rightly, they take the view that the best way to discourage the use of these weapons, whether by design or miscalculation, is to deploy them in sufficient number and variety to make credible their use in response to an attack.

Preparation for the odyssey through SALT requires an introduction to the issues—the grist of the talks; a recognition that the skirmishing between interest groups in Washington, and doubtless Moscow, too, dominates the enterprise; and a glimpse of the key players on both sides, some of them well known, others not at all. The major issues are few in number. The trouble is that each conceals lesser, related issues. These, plus the bewildering problems of just defining terms, produce complications. What, for example, is a first-strike weapon? Or at what point can a radar have more than a space-tracking or air-defense function; at what point does it serve to enable defensive missiles to intercept attacking missiles?

Verification implicitly links and dominates the other issues and provides a context for the talks. Verification relies on so-called national means. Each side, in effect, must verify from afar what the other is doing. Neither can reliably estimate what the other may be producing—except for land-based ICBM's and nuclear submarines, which require elaborate construction facilities. Neither can make on-site inspections: The Soviet Union adamantly rejects such intrusion, and the United States doesn't much like the idea either, even though it once had strong declaratory backing in Washington.

Only at the testing and deployment stages is verification possible. The issue then turns on the degree of reliability. Perhaps no problem has focused more analysis and internal debate in Washington than this one. Castlereagh, in despair and frustration, could have called it an exercise in "political metaphysics."

The Americans can neither propose nor accept anything that cannot be verified with reasonably high confidence. The problem is less severe for the Russians. Their detection systems, like America's are constantly improving and may have achieved comparable performance. Their advantage is that of a closed society competing against an open society. It is a major advantage. Their aversion to on-site inspection is doubtless genuine, but, apart from a passion for secrecy, their position owes something to the small benefit they would obtain from having direct access to what the United States does, not much of which is concealed.

Probably nothing the United States does is more closely held than the techniques and performance of its verification machinery. Even here, though, a fair amount of information finds its way into technical journals. We know that accuracy expectation for optical photography is a ground resolution of 10 to 12 inches from an altitude of 60 miles; that the width of the strip photographed during a satellite transit may be up to 75 miles. We know that observations may be telemetered to earth in an hour; but, because this means an unacceptable loss of definition, we know that the CIA and the Air Force rely on five or six capsules of film (weighing a few hundred pounds each) ejected in sequence from each vehicle. These, we know, are recaptured by specially modified aircraft as they descend by parachute. Finally, we know that satellite photography is weather-dependent; Russian weather is more uncertain than American, with long periods of overcast.

Probably the most revealing statement on verification was made to the Arms Control Subcommittee of the Senate Foreign Relations Committee in April, 1970, by Herbert Scoville, Jr. Before retiring in 1969, Scoville had been Assistant Director of ACDA for Science & Technology. Prior to taking that job in 1963, Scoville had spent many years in charge of the CIA's scientific intelligence and evaluation of military intelligence. A few fragments of what he had to say about what is easy to verify and what is more difficult are worth citing.

On fixed land-based ICBM's:

[These] require extensive launch-site construction in order to provide the necessary hardening to make them resistant to blast from a nuclear explosion. This construction requires many months, and therefore ample time is available to permit its detection. . . .

Submarine-launched ballistic missiles (SLBM's):

Submarines which have large numbers of long-range missiles and which can operate for protracted periods at long distances from their home ports require large and distinctive facilities for their construction. . . . After the submarines are launched they require many months for fitting out, during all of which they are subject to observation. To have a reliable operational capability they must be shaken down and cruise in the open oceans . . . for the Soviets to increase their . . . rapidly growing SLBM force without U.S. knowledge to a point where it would significantly effect U.S. security would not seem possible.

On MIRV's and MRV's:

Since a single large warhead can be replaced, without changing the external configuration of the missile, by several smaller warheads either with [MIRV] or without [MRV] a capability to be individually targeted, it is hard to visualize how the U.S. could verify by national means whether a deployed missile has or has not multiple warheads. In fact, even on-site inspection to make this determination would be difficult. It would require the right to inspect any deployed missile including those on submarines, on sufficiently short notice to prevent substitution of the reentry vehicle. The inspection would require access into the interior of the reentry vehicle or at very least, the use at close range of some scientific technique, such as X-rays, to determine the number of warheads present. Such inspection would almost certainly not be acceptable to the U.S.S.R. If the Soviets required similar inspection to verify that the U.S. was not secretly deploying MIRV's, it is doubtful that the U.S. could accept it.

Therefore, if MIRV's are to be controlled, every effort should be made to limit testing as well as deployment. . . . What are the opportunities for the U.S. to verify a ban on MIRV and MRV testing? . . . Since the type of MIRV which could threaten the fixed land-based missile force is one which has a very high capability for destroying hardened ICBM sites, that is, a reliable MIRV with high accuracy and high yield, I believe verification is possible. In order to achieve such a capability it will be necessary to test at full range and at as near operational conditions as possible. Such tests can be monitored to determine the number of reentry vehicles. No nation would replace existing reliable missiles and consider initiating a nuclear war with a missile which had only been partially tested. . . .

On ABM's:

ABM's to cope with the sophisticated type threat of which the U.S. is capable are complicated and large systems. They require large radars which have a high visibility, have a long leadtime for construction and which, furthermore, must radiate energy continuously if they are to be of any value. In addition, an ABM system requires large numbers of high performance defensive missiles if it is not to be saturated. Extensive training exercises must be carried out to develop operational competence. All these factors greatly facilitate the verification of a freeze on ABM's. If, however, the limitation did not ban a nationwide net of large radars . . . and keep the number of missiles to low levels, then verification would be much more difficult since additional defensive missiles could be secretly produced and then rapidly deployed. Once ABM radars with nationwide coverage are in place it will be much harder to verify any ABM limitations.

A serious problem in the ABM area could be the confusion between systems designed for defense against aircraft with those designed for defense against ballistic missiles if the former were not controlled.[6]

Scoville is among those who feel that the broader the agreement, the easier verification becomes. Amrom Katz, a Rand Corporation expert on verification, has for many years taken a more somber line. In a brief paper called "Hiders and Finders," Katz wrote that conversations with

> groups of people at the Rand Corporation, in the Air Force and elsewhere have turned up an overwhelming preference for hiding over finding. There seems to be an *a priori* assessment that hiding is easier than finding . . . I invariably ask whether one would rather be a hider or a finder. It usually appears quite obvious to those who have given these matters thought that hiding missiles, or bombs, or warheads, to take a class of interesting examples, permits one more options than finding them, and people seem to want to play a winning game.[7]

Dean Rusk observes that the "political aspect of verification is at least as important as the technical. If the public and the Congress can be assured of a reasonable degree of verification they'll feel reasonably secure about the agreement."

A SALT agreement may be stabilizing or destabilizing. Much depends on the motives of the parties: whether one or both seek to observe the agreement and build upon it; or whether one or both seek to work around it and perhaps even cheat. Verification, as Rusk suggests, is more a political than a technical judgment. Verification and stability are sibling values. And just as there is no absolute degree of verification, neither is there any absolute stability. "What we seek," says Katz, "is meta-stability. A sailboat that can survive a hard gust of wind has it. A round stone perched on a peak is unstable. Put the same stone in a dimple and it has considerable, though not complete, stability." Henry Kissinger, in *A World Restored*, puts it this way, "The foundation of a stable world order is the *relative* security—and therefore the *relative* insecurity—of its members." Almost as if anticipating his involvement with the treacherous issues of verification and surprise abrogation, Kissinger warned that "the danger to the equilibrium is never demonstrated until it is already overturned.[8]

Talleyrand, whom Kissinger admires much less than Metternich and Castlereagh, also understood: "The general equilibrium of Europe," he wrote, "cannot be composed of simple elements; it can only be a system of partial equilibrium. An absolute equality of power between all the states, not only can never exist, but also is not necessary to the political equilibrium and would perhaps in some respects be hurtful to it.[9]

All SALT issues arise from instabilities, real or potential. Some instabilities are no less real for being rooted in suspicion and fear instead of hard fact. What is stabilizing for one side—something it is doing—may seem wildly destabilizing to the other. Although each side seeks stability, neither is willing to accept a heavier weight of relative insecurity—a sense of strategic inferiority—than the other.

Stability's handmaiden is MAD—an acronym for mutual assured destruction and one coined by enemies of the concept. SALT, then, is supposed to persuade each side to abandon steps that might weaken or jeopardize the other's assured destruction capability. That is what SALT is all about in the eyes of in-house scholastics.

Washington's criteria for defining assured destruction are arbitrary and conservative. Back in the mid-1960s, the Pentagon hit on roughly 25 per cent of the Soviet population and 45 per cent of Soviet industry as a cut-off point in targeting weapons. Beyond that point, defense planners reckoned that more than double the number of weapons would be needed to gain even marginal increases in levels of destruction. About 400 one-megaton weapons, or the equivalent, was worked out as the amount of second-strike power needed for such destruction.

In a useful book called *How Much Is Enough?* two former in-house scholastics, Alain C. Enthoven (who ran Systems Analysis in the Kennedy-Johnson years) and K. Wayne Smith (who for a time ran the SALT Working Group in the Nixon White House), explain the link between assured destruction and the size of U.S. forces:

> . . . the main reason for stopping at 1,000 Minuteman missiles, 41 Polaris submarines and some 500 strategic bombers is that having more would not be worth the additional cost. These force levels are sufficiently high to put the United States on the "flat of the curve"—that is, at a point where small increases in target destruction capability would require enormous increases in forces, and therefore in cost. The answer to the question of how many strategic offensive forces are enough rests heavily on such flat-of-the curve reasoning.[10]

Fair enough. But there remains the question of whether three different forces are needed for the job. America has such a triad. Its components are the Minuteman force, the Polaris submarines, and the B-52 bombers. Each of these, in a retaliatory situation, is judged capable of meeting the criteria of assured destruction. This, to say the least, is a conservative posture.

The first thing to be said about the triad is that it came about more by accident than design; the second, that it is useful; the third, that it is in declining fashion. A Washington commonplace suggests that the triad is the product of a struggle between the armed services, each determined to have a strategic role. That is a partial explanation. The United States had only bombers in the 1950s. For insurance, the planners decided to build missiles. Uncertain of being able to build into any one of them the qualities of reliability, high accuracy, and quick reaction time, Washington developed several. By the early 1960s, America had a triad.

With time, Washington has grown to admire the triad. Political and military leaders especially like the redundancy in command and control, which they see as a clear gain for stability. Each element of the triad has its own command and control links, and these are tied to each other. America's most secure—hence stable —system, quite obviously, is the submarine. Yet communicating with the boats when they are submerged is something of a problem. Washington says little about this so as not to invite countermeasures, and the problem is not, in the words of an in-house expert, "really serious." Still, it does encourage sentiment in favor of having at least one other system. But there is another argument in favor of diversity. If, for example, all U.S. strategic forces were put to sea in the form of submarines, the Soviet Union would expend far greater resources on antisubmarine warfare techniques. Thus, a gesture aimed at stability might cause instability.

Some argue that it was a mistake to keep the bombers, which are very expensive to operate and maintain. Bombers are slower to react than missiles; their ability to penetrate the Soviet defense system is also less certain. But the great advantage of bombers is precisely their slowness: they can be recalled. The bomber makes virtue of flaw; it is not menacing as a first-strike weapon. Bombers, in short, are stable.

What then is unstable, or least stable? A stable strategic weapon should be capable of delayed response; it should be invulnerable; and it should be unambiguously deprived of what is called a first-strike, or damage-limiting, capability. Put differently, it should not be able to disarm some portion of the other side's forces, or diminish them appreciably. Measured by these standards, the least-stable element of America's triad is the Minuteman force. Although looked upon not long ago as the backbone of the deterrent, it is the fixed, land-based missile, not the bomber, that is likely to go the way of the cavalry. It won't happen next year or the year after, but almost certainly before the end of the decade.

Minuteman has been compromised. It is unstable, or will be, because its invulnerability is in doubt. At some point, nobody can say when, the Soviet Union should be able to wipe out the Minuteman force, or most of it, in a first strike. The weapon for this is the SS-9, the Soviet behemoth, also called the Scarp. The SS-9 (as well as an even bigger missile that may replace it and that is just entering the testing phase) is a fixed, land-based ICBM. It began to be deployed in the late 1960s. At first, it made no strategic sense, at least not to American scholastics. With the SS-9 the Russians seemed to be rejecting the American experience: Instead of moving as the United States had, away from the awkward, slow-reacting, liquid-fueled missile, they began deploying one; instead of moving, as the United States had, toward smaller warheads with higher accuracies, they did the opposite, arming the SS-9 with a warhead of unimagined power—up to twenty-five megatons; instead of deploying cheaper, more reliable quick-reacting solid-fueled missiles, like America's Minuteman, the Russians, it seemed, had opted for a white elephant that probably cost them about twice the price of a Minuteman. Washington was persuaded that Moscow had been sold a bill of goods by some part of its military bureaucracy. Even now, American experts regard the SS-9 as technologically regressive; its destructive power is out of all proportion to any rational strategic mission, at least as seen from Washington.

Still, not for a long time has Washington looked upon the SS-9 as a white elephant. Indeed, when it dawned on people there that two could play at the game of MIRV, they began to see the SS-9 in a different light. It became startlingly clear that, say, 430 SS-9's armed with three five-megaton MIRV's as accurate as a Minuteman could, for practical purposes, destroy Minuteman. About 300 SS-9's with six MIRV's each would achieve the same result. In more technical terms, a five-megaton weapon with Minuteman's accuracy would be nearly certain to destroy a hardened Minuteman silo. When, in August, 1968, the Russians began testing MRV's (the less-sophisticated multiple re-entry vehicles), the handwriting was on the wall. It would not be long before they had a MIRV program, although it would be quite a while before they had a real MIRV, still longer probably before their MIRV's would acquire accuracies comparable to the United States version. But few if any experts still doubt the Soviet Union's ability to make a first-strike weapon of its superbrutes, of which there are now 288, with 25 more to come. This perception gave a great boost to SALT, especially since the large-scale deployment of the SS-9 roughly coincided with the arrival of Mr. Nixon.

A fine irony runs through this interaction between the SS-9 and Minuteman. It is the threat of the aesthetically contemptible Russian missile to Minuteman—probably the most proficient offensive weapon ever built—that shapes in greater or lesser degree the thematic elements of SALT. These are: (1) parity, or comparability, as it is sometimes called; (2) crisis stability; (3) mobility, which means the changeover from fixed-site ICBM's (in silos) to shifting-site ICBM's (on railroad cars, trucks, or barges; (4) ballistic-missile defense (the ABM); (5) MIRV.

Parity, as noted, has been achieved. Each side can inflict unacceptable second-strike damage to the other. Although the balance of forces is not symmetrical, it is comparable. Which side has the offensive edge depends on what is deemed critical. Here judgment becomes subjective.

America has more and better strategic bombers; its numerical edge is 250. The Russians have more ICBM's—about four times as many as they had five years ago. Potentially, their edge is 564: 1618 to America's 1054. American ICBM's, on the other hand, are more reliable and more accurate. And then, of its 1000 Minuteman missiles, all of which were built to fire a single warhead, Washington is "MIRV'ing" 550. The new version, called Minuteman III, will carry three MIRV's. Deployment is proceeding; by 1974, the American ICBM force may have nearly 400 more warheads than Russia's (although some of the re-entry vehicles are not MIRV's but decoys). The Russians, on the other hand, have a "throw-weight"—that is, payload—advantage. Their warheads are larger. A throw-weight advantage in single-warhead missiles doesn't bother American planners, who feel that accuracy, not yield, is the critical element of this calculus. Yet when the Russians, too, deploy MIRV's America's warhead advantage will be wiped out. Moreover, besides their MRV-MIRV testing program for the SS-9, the Russians are testing MRV's for their 900 SS-11's, another regressive ICBM but considerably smaller than the SS-9.

America's absolute advantage is at sea, where for the moment it deploys more and better submarines. When Mr. Nixon went to Moscow in May to sign the SALT agreements, the United States had forty-one submarines to Russia's thirty. The Soviets are building twelve more, can produce about ten per year, and before long should have a significant numerical edge. Numbers, however, are misleading. Thirty-one American boats will have a MIRV capability; from ten to fourteen warheads are stacked like cordwood on the Poseidon missile. The other ten boats retain the Polaris missile, each of which has three warheads.

The sea for the United States is a congenial strategic environment. Its boats have easy access to their operating areas and can remain on station for extended periods. It has maintenance facilities at Holy Loch, Scotland, and Rota, Spain, and these permit keeping as many as thirty boats on station at a given time.

For the Russians, operating at sea is onerous. Transit time of submarines from port to their stations along the coasts of the United States is exceedingly long. Maintenance is a problem.

Until recently, they have rarely done better than three boats on station at one time, but that is slowly changing. Also, their submarines are noisier, hence easier to keep track of. At considerable expense, the Americans track them, using a network of submerged acoustic receivers, sonar buoys, and other systems.

Geography, in the Russian case, favors land-based missiles. The land is Russia's natural strategic environment. Yet Moscow, too, has perceived—perhaps reluctantly—that the SLBM (submarine-launched ballistic missile) is perhaps the only weapon that over time will satisfy in full the requirements of stable deterrence. Neither side really thinks that technology will throw up a more efficient destructive tool than the MIRV'd ballistic missile. And while the Russians toy with other systems, both sides are freezing future offenses around the companion technologies of MIRV and ballistic missiles.

Nothing about so volatile a matter as arms is certain. Still, the push toward a primarily "blue-water" strategic mode would seem irreversible. Neither side can afford to rely chiefly on bombers, still less on fixed land-based missiles. One day, though, both may give up the luxury of triad by putting most big weapons to sea, while keeping a small but reasonably secure land-based force as a hedge against antisubmarine warfare.

This is a hard scenario for the Russians. They start far behind the Americans. Most of their submarines, like America's, carry sixteen ballistic missiles, but unlike America's, theirs have just a single warhead. They have not managed to achieve the equivalent of Polaris. Yet Washington can deploy a MIRV'd Poseidon, a vast improvement on Polaris, and is moving briskly toward a new submarine, called Trident, and a new SLBM, called ULMS (underwater long-range missile system), an acronym that is becoming nearly as familiar as MIRV. The virtue of ULMS lies in its probable range, about 4500 nautical lines. By nearly doubling the range of Polaris and Poseidon (about 2500 nautical miles), ULMS will increase the operating area of the submarines by a factor of ten. The difference lies in the distance over land that Polaris and Poseidon missiles have to fly to reach targets in the Soviet Union; because of this distance, these submarines are limited to a rather narrow band of ocean. For the subs to have about ten times more ocean in which to operate offers enormous advantages. ULMS, for example, would be a hedge against any major breakthrough in antisubmarine warfare techniques. Even the gloomiest worst-case planners have trouble projecting a Soviet antisubmarine warfare capability that might seriously menace wide-ranging ULMS-equipped submarines.

While the quality gap in SLBM's grows apace, Moscow is obliged to rely on numbers—to build submarines as rapidly as possible, while trying to design better ones. At great cost and difficulty, the Russians have developed a longer-range SLBM, but its bulk limits the number that can be installed on a submarine to twelve. Equally important, it is a single-warhead weapon, whereas Trident, when deployed, will carry either twenty or twenty-four MIRV'd ULMS. Not for very many years will the American and Russian SLBM forces stand comparison.

To compare American and Russian systems, whether SLBM's or ICBM's, is to talk about apples and oranges. Yet much of what goes on at SALT is an effort to measure parity, or comparability. The Americans dwell on Russia's three-to-two advantage in ICBM's. Russians note America's warhead advantage, but do not press the point; their own MIRV's lie ahead. Americans point to the Russians' submarine buildup, noting that even if they tried, they could not match the Soviet rate of construction before the end of the decade (if then). If only for internal purposes, each probably exaggerates the other's strengths. Russia's is a more visible superiority, easier to exploit politically. America's, for the moment, is real.

The equalizer could be the SS-9 and its monstrous new sibling. Minuteman's vulnerability introduces another thematic element— crisis stability, as it is called. The issue is a product of worst-case thinking about what one side might do during a political crisis if it had the means of limiting damage to itself by destroying a major part of the other's strategic forces. The nightmare proceeds something like this: During a political crisis, the Soviet Union wipes out all or most Minuteman missiles in a surprise attack, even though America's SLBM's and bombers would remain available to destroy most of urban Russia. The question is, would Washington do that? Moscow would be betting against America's willingness to commit national suicide by avenging the loss of 1000 missiles scattered around the middle and northwestern United States. The alternative would be to settle the crisis on Russian terms and keep intact the larger part of American society.

Scenarios of this kind seem grotesque to all but those who have the responsibility for deterrence. They are pressed, especially by the military, to hedge against the possibility of nuclear war by assuring that their side would emerge less crippled than the other. The higher and more realistic duty is to excise the source of instability. This leads to the third thematic element in SALT: ICBM mobility.

If Minuteman is the least-stable system in the arsenal, what, if anything, should be done about the Minuteman force? The options have been four: (1) dismantling all or part of it; (2) superhardening the silos; (3) defending it; (4) putting it on mobile launchers.

Abandoning Minuteman is the least feasible short-term course. Washington would require reciprocity; Moscow would say no. In theory, Washington could dismantle the system and compensate by building a great many more submarines and bombers. One day this may be done, but not now. Neither ULMS nor the new B-1 bomber is out of the design stage. Neither can be deployed much before the end of the decade. The United States cannot now build more submarines because current capacity is exhausted by the program of shifting over from the Polaris to Poseidon missiles.

Superhardening is probably futile. Sinking silos in natural layers of hard rock would be a wildly expensive hedge, but rather easily overcome. The Air Force could, say, quadruple the hardness of the silos; Moscow in turn could improve SS-9 accuracies by a factor of two—not so difficult—and Minuteman would be just as vulnerable as before.

Defending Minuteman was for many scholastics the most-attractive option. It meant deploying ABM sites around Minuteman bases, a step ruled out by the May, 1972 SALT agreements. The single Safeguard site allowed under the ABM Treaty cannot, as designed, defend a Minuteman base. Those who favor Minuteman defense have for years urged a cheaper and more reliable system than Safeguard, one that would be built around a concept known as "dedicated hard site." A hard-site defense would mean deploying ABM's and radars smaller and more numerous than Safeguard's, and designed solely to protect ICBM's. The issue has been shelved for now, thanks to SALT, although research and development on the hard-site technology continues.

The last option, mobility, is yet another thematic element of SALT. A mobile ICBM force with no fixed launching points would be more secure than even a heavily defended one; but a mobile force would be destabilizing if the missiles could not be counted by the other side. Stability relies on each knowing what the other has.

Herbert Scoville uses the mobility issue as an argument for SALT. "If, as a result of SALT, it were agreed that mobile ICBM's would be totally banned, then the ability to detect the deployment of even a single such missile would be sufficient to verify whether the agreement was being abided by. It would not be necessary to count precisely the number of mobile missiles deployed, which might be very difficult unless one had instantaneous observation of the entire Soviet Union."[11]

To date, SALT has failed to ban mobile ICBM's. The United States pressed such a ban; the Soviet Union turned it down. Neither has yet deployed mobile ICBM's, although the Soviets have some short-range missiles mounted on trucks in eastern Russia. The option of mobility is one they will yield reluctantly, if at all: Land-based systems allow the Russians to exploit their natural advantages; moreover, they do have a lot of unused railroad capacity in sparsely settled eastern Russia.

America could exercise the mobility option, although less painlessly than the Russians. Minuteman was originally designed as a rail-mobile ICBM; it was shifted into silos for many reasons, not least of which was the greater accuracies that can be achieved with fixed missiles. The Washington bureaucracy has been split on the mobility issue, with the weight of opinion now against it. The State Department and ACDA, predictably, are opposed; the Office of the Secretary of Defense (OSD), on balance, is in favor; the Joint Chiefs are opposed, partly because the Air Force would rather superharden than go mobile; putting Minuteman on rails or wheels would oblige the Air Force to prove that so costly a version of the system was sufficiently "cost effective" (vis-à-vis sea-based missiles) to make it worthwhile. Keeping Minuteman in silos avoids this issue; thus, however vulnerable it may become, Minuteman is cost effective.

Most of Kissinger's staff members also disliked the mobility option and threw onto the scales two astringently worded nontechnical considerations. Conservationists and others, they suggested, would be appalled by mobile missiles rolling through national parks, where at least some of them would probably be deployed. And besides, they pointed out, SDS or some black-power group or antiwar activists could easily hijack a mobile missile. Kissinger used this horrific prospect, along with the misuse of parkland, to squash the case for putting Minuteman on wheels.

Finally, the dramatic main theme of SALT thus far has been the interplay of ABM and MIRV. In city defense against missiles (ABM) and in proliferating re-entry vehicles (MIRV) lie the true enemies of stable deterrence. Each can sap the opponent's confidence in his own forces; the first does this by degrading his ability to strike the other's cities, the second by menacing (or seeming to menace) the forces themselves. The logic of deterrence is bizarre; it argues for targeting weapons at "countervalue"—against people—instead of "counterforce"—against other weapons.

Metaphorically, ABM and MIRV may be seen as sides of a coin, each complementing the other; or as the chicken and egg, each justifying the existence of the other; or as two hot particles in the compression chamber of deterrence, where they agitate the entire SALT process. In fact, ABM and MIRV drive the process by openly shaping some issues, tacitly posing others.

A former White House scholastic says that the ABM–MIRV interplay "leaves you with four basic SALT options, or variants of these: (1) high ABM and high MIRV; (2) low (or zero) ABM and high MIRV; (3) ban MIRV, but not ABM; (4) ban both." Washington and Moscow picked the second option by agreeing to limit ABM and refusing to hobble MIRV. In that perhaps inevitable choice lies the significance of SALT to date, the dilemma of SALT tomorrow.

There are good and bad ABM's, good and bad MIRV's. Good ABM's, which do not yet exist, would defend only missile sites. Bad ABM's defend cities; hence they are destabilizing. Good MIRV's are deprived of the blend of accuracy and yield that impart first-strike capability. Bad MIRV's have the capability.

Most, though not all, scholastics think that ABM is much worse than MIRV. Defending cities, they feel, is not just illusory (won't work) but is truly dangerous; defend your cities and you arouse fears on the other side that you seek the option to strike first. Thus, any and all means of defending cities must be eliminated; accomplish that and both sides are shorn of the incentive to preempt, since neither can defend itself against the other's forces. In two and one-half years, SALT *has* accomplished essentially that.

Not the least of the ironies of SALT is that defending cities against missiles really *is* a mug's game, and both sides know it, yet fear it; MIRV's, conversely, do work—just as well as single warheads—yet arouse fewer anxieties. MIRV, some argue, is not per se a source of instability, since its first-strike potential can threaten the other side's land-based missiles, but not its submarines, or its bombers. So it would seem, with everyone agreed, if deterrence were less metaphysical. In fact, a MIRV capable of knocking out hardened targets is destabilizing, simply because governments think it is.

MIRV is a wondrous technology. The low-thrust final stage of the missile is a bus. The bus, pushed along by a single guidance and propulsion system, carries all of the re-entry vehicles. These it releases one at a time by changing velocity and direction. Incredibly, these adjustments actually define the path of the re-entry vehicle to its target. The bus follows a meandering course, now zigzag, now rolling over and releasing a cloud of chaff, now perhaps rolling again to fire another decoy, now shifting direction and releasing a real warhead. This is America's way of doing it. The Russians may have another. Washington doesn't really know, not yet anyway.

Systems analysts like MIRV, and not just because it can be separately targeted. MIRV can penetrate defenses more easily than its forerunner, the MRV. Polaris MRV's are released simultaneously by a spring and can be discriminated by reasonably sophisticated radars. MIRV's, because they leave the bus sequentially, are more difficult to discriminate and destroy.

The question is, or should be, does anyone need MIRV? There are only two reasons for deploying MIRV: to penetrate ABM defenses; to improve, or achieve, a damage-limiting capability. With a lid now on the ABM, the first reason would seem a spent force. The second is irrelevant if Washington's disavowal of the counterforce option in favor of countervalue is genuine. The President and other leading officials have assured Congress, both by letters to individual members and in testimony before committees, that America will not seek greater accuracies through improved guidance for MIRV. On at least one occasion, funds requested for precisely this purpose were denied.

With present accuracies, MIRV's do not increase America's so-called hard-target kill capability (the capacity to destroy the other side's hardened sites).

David Packard, while Deputy Secretary of Defense, assured a congressional subcommittee that Poseidon achieves a mere 6 per cent increase over Polaris in effectiveness against hard targets, while Minuteman III is only 65 per cent as effective against these targets as the non-MIRV'd Minuteman II. The reason, of course, is that MIRV's are necessarily smaller than single warheads.[12]

Bravo. The trouble is that the Russians are at least as fearful of America's MIRV, which is deployed, as Americans are of their's, which is not. Russians are asked to accept U.S. bona fides —to reject their pessimistic assumptions and worst-case scenarios, while America, as a matter of prudential planning, deploys MIRV's against a nonexistent Russian ABM capability.

Do the Russians believe that the Americans can or would stifle the dynamic of MIRV technology? Do they accept that the American's MIRV program is static or that Packard's statement is genuine? Or could the Russians be at least as impressed by statements from other quarters that MIRV does, in fact, give the United States a counterforce option? General John D. Ryan, Chief of Staff of the U.S. Air Force, has said of Minuteman III: "This missile, with a multiple, independently targetable re-entry vehicle will be our best means of destroying time-urgent targets like the long-range weapons of the enemy."[13]

And in Washington's Naval Museum, down at the old Navy Yard, there is a display of Poseidon. The description concludes with a bit of foolish hyperbole: "Poseidon will have double the payload of the Polaris A III. It will be twice as accurate. As a result its effectiveness against a hardened target will be some eight times greater than the latest version of Polaris."

A subcommittee of the House Committee on Foreign Affairs held hearings on MIRV in 1969; one subcommittee document described the system like this: "Besides being a potentially attractive means of penetrating an adversary's ABM defenses, MIRV, with sufficient accuracy, is well suited to being a 'counterforce' weapon, that is, a system capable of destroying the adversary's strategic offensive forces."[14]

And back in the spring of 1968, with MIRV still in the research and development stage, Alain C. Enthoven, then the head of Systems Analysis, told a Senate subcommittee: "I . . . think the MIRV's have improved the damage limiting capability of our forces." And later: "We do have a hard target killing capability, and I think that MIRV's contribute to this capability because they can be cross-targeted and can be laid down in patterns."[15]

In the same hearings, John S. Foster, Jr., DDR&E's Director said: "Recently . . . we found ways of improving the accuracy of Minuteman and Poseidon so as to be able to get much greater kill capabilities even though the warhead yields were reduced, and so in fact we are beginning to get a rather effective damage limiting capability."[16]

The Russians know as well as anyone that improving Minuteman III accuracy by a factor of two would give each warhead about a 95 per cent chance of destroying one of their underground missile silos. The slightly less accurate and considerably smaller Poseidon warhead, to have the same capability, would have to be upgraded by a factor of four—much more difficult though not wholly infeasible.

A distinction should be drawn between Poseidon and Minuteman III. Poseidon is arguably a second-strike weapon and a very good one; only at great difficulty and expense could Poseidon develop a counterforce punch. Even then, its reliability to play the part would be in doubt because it is too small (Navy propaganda to the contrary notwithstanding). Minuteman III is a different case. It is larger and easier to improve; hence, more suspect.

The Administration argues that to halt all or part of the MIRV program, as some propose, would reduce America's bargaining strength with the Soviets. With the Soviet buildup proceeding, the argument continues, Washington needs something to bargain with in Phase II of SALT. Since Russia now has many more missiles, America's only strategic advantage lies in its superior number of warheads, a dividend of MIRV.

MIRV is a less convincing bargaining chip than the Safeguard ABM, if only because neither side seems serious about limiting MIRV's. Safeguard did help to promote the May agreement limiting ABM's because the Russians wanted to avoid a competition in modern ABM's and sought to discourage America's program by making a deal. Nothing in their actions to date, however, suggests any interest in abandoning their development of MIRV. Washington disavows a first-strike MIRV; Moscow disavows nothing. Unlike ABM, it appears that MIRV's beget other MIRV's—that the surge for qualitative advantage is, or will be, self-sustaining. MIRV may fuel the Soviet incentive to compete more strenuously, possibly even to reject the parity principle on the grounds that Russia hasn't fully achieved it. V. V. Larionov, a Soviet scholastic, writes: "What appears 'sufficient' to one side can look like a desire for superiority to the other side."[17]

America stumbled into MIRV. The deployment decision was not informed by clear strategic purpose. Now, in a sense, America is stuck with MIRV. Many scholastics feel that, whatever happens, Minuteman III should be canceled. Quite clearly, this will not happen, even though there seems little sense in spending $6 billion to modify a weapons system that one day will be vulnerable, hence unstable. Indeed, if Minuteman is vulnerable, putting MIRV's on more than half of them should only increase any temptation Moscow would have to eliminate the force in a crisis situation. In short, the MIRV's merely increase the "bonus" the adversary gets by striking first. That, at least, is how some wargamers view it.

Setting some kind of limit on MIRV should be a priority issue during the second phase of SALT. The first phase dealt chiefly with ABM and numbers of offensive missiles. Although MIRV bobbed up occasionally, once even moving Washington's internal struggle on SALT to a dramatic peak, both governments, for different reasons, avoided meeting the issue head-on. So by tacit agreement it was left hanging.

Secrecy and abstraction tend to dismay, yet need not deter, those who want to know whether, and if so why, SALT may alter the course of great-power diplomacy in a way that will insure against nuclear war. Stripped of its wraps SALT emerges as a colossal multitiered negotiation. At the outer, most obvious tier, it is a negotiation between rival powers. At another level, it is a negotiation between Washington and its chief NATO allies, whose feelings about SALT are mixed; while applauding efforts to stabilize deterrence, they are wary of the political consequences of formal parity and frankly worried that SALT may foreshadow a great-power condominium whose writ would go far beyond the issues at hand. At yet another level—so far, the least consequential—SALT is, in the United States, a negotiation between the executive and the Congress: Key committees and individuals are consulted, but only rarely do they learn enough to have a rounded view of what is happening and why; most important SALT decisions are taken without reference to the Congress.

Finally, and most importantly, SALT is an internal negotiation. It is within the two capitals that the critical bargaining—the struggle to grind out positions—lumbers endlessly, episodically on. The marrow of SALT is found in the contesting views and clashing organizational interests of government agencies.

These internal struggles, however secret, have some visibility, more so, of course, in Washington than in Moscow. And they are not unconnected. Each side tries to influence the other's debate—by utterance, by example. In the case of the Russians, even more direct means are used. The Dobrynin-Vorontsov team, with a large embassy staff in Washington, strenuously lobbies the Soviet SALT case on Capitol Hill and somewhat less so with key members of the local press corps. The embassy also keeps up broad contacts with arms-control buffs in academia.

What goes on in the talks is conditioned, of course, by the internal drama. Probably the most-conspicuous but least-significant polarity is that between some parts of the defense-related bureaucracy and much of the scientific community. Many bureaucrats fear that a Russian numerical superiority in offensive missiles, even if strategically meaningless, may embolden Moscow. Other governments, especially in Western Europe, might then be faced with renewed Soviet intimidation. Thus, a Russian edge, in this view, could be destabilizing, could lower the nuclear threshold in times of emergency and crisis. Conversely, these bureaucrats find comfort in a margin of U.S. superiority. Something a little "better" than absolute parity, they think, is useful both in terms of reassuring NATO and impressing the Soviet Union that the United States is not to be shoved around. A decade later, the example of the Cuban missile crisis, when the United States had overwhelming superiority, remains a vivid example to both American and Russian planners.

Such conjecture convinces few scientists except for those who move into parts of the government, like DDR&E, where many of them adopt fiercely hawkish attitudes. Their colleagues who work on weapons development outside the government by and large take a different view. Unlike bureaucrats, most of them inhabit a reasonable world where problems are actually solved, where issues can be reduced to precise measurement and reliable projection, not left to fallible judgment.

As self-professed muses of the apocalypse, most scientists insist on rational standards of political conduct for the nuclear age. They ascribe reasonable intentions to governments, including adversary regimes, believing that the responsibility of possessing nuclear weapons is perforce a sobering and a moderating one. They are less concerned with irrational conduct than with the continuing deployment of weapons of progressively greater destructive power. The bureaucrats, for whom the weapons are a fact of life, are more concerned with building around them a new and stable equilibrium. Their impulse is to hedge against what they cannot ignore—the possibility of irrational conduct or the awful prospect of another nuclear face-off arising out of some unforeseen political crisis. They hedge by using extremely conservative criteria for force planning. So does Russia.

Both groups harbor extreme elements, not all of them bureaucrats and scientists. (Each has its academic consultants and even congressional allies.) At one end are the ritual disarmers, eager to promote or acquiesce in *any* agreement to reduce nuclear weapons, the very existence of which they see as a threat to all life. At the other extreme are the "worst-case" force planners, armed with their fantasies and their circular, pocket-size bomb-damage-effect computers—the working tool. Fearful of what Moscow may be contemplating, or even doing—testing clandestinely an especially lethal weapon on the far side of the moon, to cite one of the more-picturesque anxieties—the super-hawks are convinced that nothing less than absolute superiority in the number and quality of our weapons will fully deter a society led not long ago by a man who didn't flinch from sending millions of his compatriots to their death. Probably more important, many of them have built careers on developing weapons and seeding fresh technological ground.

Within both the scientific and bureaucratic communities, many SALT buffs cling to fixed notions and points of view. Even though SALT is, par excellence, a study in the infinite variety of truth, these specialists refuse to concede merit or intellectual respectability to conflicting views. Indeed, while suitably impressed by the gravity of SALT (if one is to believe what they say), they are, in numerous cases, not above rigging the assumptions and fudging the data on which their cases rest. Thus, they seek to deceive the leadership, the Congress, and, who knows, perhaps themselves. Advocacy, alas, often relies on a stiff dose of self-deception. "A problem for the policy officer," says Dean Rusk tersely, "is to know whether a scientist is speaking as a scientist or as a politician."

What then of more reasonable men working within the narrow perimeter of the feasible and the prudent? Their job is to forge links between arms control and security—sides of a coin, really—at no great cost to either consideration. Here lies the significant polarity, the truly relevant clash of viewpoint and organizational interest. Here, too, by the way, strategic options may be framed to fit a point of view, moderates having no monopoly on detachment or intellectual probity. They do, however, dominate the great internal debate on SALT. Stable deterrence—the only security allowed us in the nuclear age—will emerge, if at all, from the interplay between communal skirmishing and the purposes of men with power who are determined to hold it.

People say that SALT, like other less-important negotiations, suffers from too much politics, bureaucratic and otherwise. The answer is that SALT is, after all, a political matter, only secondarily a technical one. For Moscow and Washington to negotiate may, though not necessarily, reflect a joint willingness to accept a series of self-limiting steps. If so, their bureaucracies must also acquiesce; agreement relies on both political impulsion and a bureaucratic consensus that the effects of agreement are not prejudicial to security. This explains why few if any arms-control pacts affect either great power's ability to wage war.

Still, agreement comes hard. Negotiations on the partial test-ban treaty were spread over five years of hard bargaining; the truly self-denying comprehensive ban on testing is still not in sight. The Nonproliferation Treaty merely obliges the great powers to forebear doing what neither would do in any case— spread about their nuclear hardware. It took ten years to negotiate. Only the treaty banning weapons of mass destruction from sea-beds fell into place quickly. It took just fourteen months for Moscow and Washington to agree to deny themselves the use of the ocean floor as a launching platform; this, again, was an easy one, since nobody harbored any such plans.

SALT is unique precisely because it actually goes to the knuckle of security. Thus, while it is too important to be left to technicians, it does, as an internal political matter, require reasonably broad support from the agencies directly involved in national security. Washington bureaucrats nervously eye the government's ap-proach to SALT. They assay the domestic political currency to be banked by a SALT agreement. The allure of agreement, many fear, could push politicians to reject or ignore the best technical assessments and, thus, to accept risks that collide with the bu-reaucracy's estimate of how much self-denial the national interest can tolerate. Any proposal, let alone agreement, that stretches security tolerances, as these are perceived by some critical faction or combination within the government, would release counter-currents that could—probably would—spoil the unique opportu-nity of SALT.

Narrow organizational interests aside, much of the conflict pro-ceeds from two attitudes driven far apart by some SALT-related issues, less so by others. The first favors restricting the develop-ment and deployment of strategic weapons. The second—normally more "hard line"—fears that any agreement that is other than narrow and unrestrictive could undermine security by encourag-ing cheating and accelerated competition in areas not covered by the agreement.

It is really a question of emphasis and priority. Both attitudes animate essentially moderate men seeking a stable balance of power. One group, sensing that accommodation with Moscow is a slow process, resists efforts to force the pace; it favors a cau-tious, prudential course. The opposing viewpoint frankly fears that the race for qualitative advantage is already halfway to the point of no return. The moment for significant risk-taking, it argues, is long overdue.

Much of the drama of SALT flows from this doctrinal division in the bureaucracy. Much of the confusion arises from overlapping points of view. Contesting elements may ally themselves on a given issue, oppose each other on another. The nearest thing to a constant is the tendency, on whatever issue, to defend organizational interests.

These, too, need definition. In the broadest sense, the order of battle pits the State Department and ACDA against the Pentagon. The former find a solid role in negotiating arms-control agreements; the latter, in most of its parts, is understandably less sympathetic to self-denying measures. The White House normally likes to keep presidential options open, but what it does depends on the style of the President. Under Lyndon Johnson, the tendency was to stand aloof and let the bureaucracy thrash out most SALT-related issues, even if this sometimes risked stalemate—a no-decision contest. Under Richard Nixon, the fondness for options runs much deeper, and the tendency is to exploit existing divisions the better to exercise control.

The CIA, less and less a center stage figure in SALT, strives to protect its role against encroachment by other parts of the intelligence community and by DDR&E. SALT or no SALT, the CIA is chiefly responsible for keeping the other players up to date on the numbers and performance characteristics of Soviet systems. It also has the primary analytical task of estimating whether the various elements of a SALT package can be verified and, if so, with what degree of confidence. Here especially is where the CIA finds sharpening competition, since verification is the critical measure of any part of any SALT proposal. The competition is important. The CIA's technical judgments are based on, yes, intelligence—that is, on hard, or reasonably hard, information. DDR&E, in the role of a CIA competitor, stands rational bureaucratic procedure on its head, but that is indeed what has happened. And DDR&E assessments of Soviet capabilities, more often than not, rely less on intelligence than on extrapolation from technology. (Tallinn upgrade is only one of numerous cases.) In fact, the CIA and DDR&E procedures are both essential. Future trends in Soviet weaponry cannot be ignored. To exaggerate or distort them, however, can—does, in fact—mightily confuse Washington's analytical approach to SALT. Then, too, DDR&E's obvious organizational interest lies in making the best possible case for procuring the advanced systems it is nudging along. Thus, DDR&E can usually be counted on for the gloomiest estimate of future (and current) Soviet capabilities.

"Get a pony and ride it." That is the tribal whoop of many of the scientists and engineers who are either building careers in DDR&E or using it as a springboard to other things. It means: scramble aboard some weapons-related project in its infancy; establish an office; crank up a staff; start coordinating with the procurement and materièl sections of the relevant military service. Operating with a scope and degree of autonomy that is the envy of other civilian departments answerable to the Office of Secretary of Defense, DDR&E flourishes in a world where the emphasis is on novelty and versatility, never quantity and simplicity; where, too often, performance of a system is measured in terms of how many functions it can perform. It is a world where the best is never an enemy of the good. And never mind about the traditional combat elements of the services who must actually use the hardware and who, more and more, grumble that such values as reliability and economy are the victims of DDR&E's passion for the exotic.

DDR&E is just one of several Pentagon elements with a heavy interest in SALT. Others include, of course, the services, especially the Air Force and Navy; the Joint Chiefs of Staff; the Office of the Secretary of Defense, which includes numerous units under the direct supervision of the Secretary of Defense and the Deputy Secretary. Besides DDR&E, the most important of these are Systems Analysis and International Security Affairs (ISA).

All OSD units tend to reflect the attitude of the Secretary. They are, by and large, his people. McNamara, after becoming a passionate advocate of strategic-arms limitation, was vigorously supported by Systems Analysis and by ISA. Systems Analysis, McNamara's most conspicuous innovation, is just about what its name suggests—an analytical tool for tailoring forces to established needs within a rational budgetary framework. ISA, which monitors the Secretary's interests in foreign policy and other areas of national security, acquired remarkable influence and reach under McNamara. In fact, ISA played not just a key role, but *the* key role in 1968 when the Johnson Administration ground out America's first SALT proposal.

With the advent of Nixon and his first Secretary of Defense, Melvin Laird, ISA was shunted from center stage, while Systems Analysis, although somewhat diminished in scope, fared better. On SALT and related issues, a lively competition developed between DDR&E and Systems Analysis. Much less than in the past was it a question of doctrinal difference; rather, the issue turned on who did the work. Systems Analysis had the nominal job of protecting the Secretary's interests on the SALT Working Group; but DDR&E, resourceful as always, probably deployed about as much influence and had perhaps equal impact on Pentagon SALT positions. Other than sometimes communicating a frankly suspicious view of the affair, Laird himself rarely took a direct hand in SALT operations.

The Joint Chiefs of Staff take an uncluttered view of SALT. They don't like it, but can live with it—that is, so long as the process limits itself to simple agreements that doesn't alter the status quo by much and might even constrain Moscow. Theirs is the predictable bias that what kind and how many strategic systems America deploys is America's business, nobody else's—least of all Moscow's. Nonetheless, the performance of the Joint Chiefs on SALT is, on balance, rated good by White House scholastics: this is probably because the Chiefs have felt more comfortable with the Nixon Administration than was the case with its predecessor.

The services themselves react to SALT strictly in terms of its potential effects on pet projects or budgets or both. The Army now has the least interest and never really had much. Long ago it fought a losing battle with the Air Force for control of medium-range ballistic missiles; America no longer deploys such weapons. The Army's only chance for a major share of the strategic action always seemed to lie in operating a broad ballistic-missile defense of metropolitan America. As the ABM lost its congressional following and became little more than a bargaining counter in SALT, the Army's expectations fell.

Air Force and Navy positions are remarkably symmetrical and

fiercely competitive. Each deploys a major strategic system that is being modernized with MIRV's. The Navy, of course, is converting thirty-one of its forty-one missile-firing submarines by replacing Polaris missiles with the MIRV'd Poseidon system. The conversion takes from eighteen months to two years per boat, and should be completed in 1975. The Air Force is MIRV'ing more than half its Minuteman force. The cost of 550 Minuteman III will be about $6.1 billion, as compared to the $10.6 billion spent for 1000 Minuteman I and II. This conversion program disturbs many scholastics. It seems a disproportionately large investment in a questionable system.

Concern about all defense spending is on the rise, not just in the Office of Management and Budget (the former Bureau of the Budget) but throughout most of the government and in Congress. In turn, the Air Force and Navy are becoming more more jittery about cost. Each worries about cutbacks in its respective conversion programs, although Poseidon, despite its heavier cost, is less controversial and strategically more respectable than Minuteman III. Each service seeks to encourage doubts about the other's chief strategic system. Paradoxically, each will also support many of the other's funding requests, a kind of logrolling intended to promote the fortunes of major new weapons. Both services are animated by an eternal pressure for a new, or follow-on, generation of weapons. In the case of the Air Force, whose institutional heart was never captured by guided missiles, it is the drive for a supersonic strategic bomber—the B-1—to replace the elderly B-52 force. And the Navy, of course, is pressing to replace Poseidon, itself barely into the deployment stage, with ULMS. But the real gleam in the Navy's eye is Trident, the new submarine still on the drawing board that will carry ULMS. The Navy is not moved by the argument that the existing submarine fleet could also accommodate ULMS.

ULMS and Trident are embedded in SALT; they disturb the Russians by sharpening Moscow's sense of technological lag, by highlighting America's striking virtuosity in sea-based strategic weapons. As yet, the B-1 is not a SALT issue, although it may become one. The B-1, however, is controversial in Washington, where opinions normally in conflict on most things look upon ULMS as the best—that is, the most stable—weapon an uncertain future can offer. The B-1, on the other hand, arouses relatively little enthusiasm outside the Air Force and a good deal of open hostility in many parts of the town. As airplanes go, the B-1 would indisputably be a great one—the best in the world and much the costliest, about $31 million per copy, not even counting its elaborate avionics or its offensive and defensive missiles (and their nuclear weapons). Calculating these and other costs suggests that the anticipated fleet of 250 B-1's might well be second only to Trident as the most expensive system ever built. With such costs would go undeniable performance advantages. Here, though, is a case where numerous systems analysts, other scholastics, and scientists feel that the best is truly the enemy of the good. Supersonic speed is no defense against Soviet surface-to-air missiles (SAM's). Ivan Selin, a former head of Systems Analysis, feels this keenly. He says that the critical characteristics of a long-range bomber should be its range and payload, both of which are penalized by the dubious virtue of supersonic speed. The Air Force, he also points out, estimates the added cost of going supersonic at about 30 per cent; in fact, says Selin, 50 per cent is a lot closer and, he asks, for what? Selin and numerous other experts would prefer what some call the "Systems Analysis" airplane. As described by Dr. Marvin Goldberger, a Princeton physicist and former Chairman (1961–64) of the Strategic Weapons Committee of the Department of Defense, it would look like this: "a large, subsonic, non-penetrating [cannot penetrate Soviet air defenses] essentially cargo plane that carries long-range weapons. These might be ballistic missiles or subsonic cruise missiles. . . . Such planes could be freed entirely from reliance on tankers. . . . The concept of a non-penetrating bomber has, of course, been studied by the Air Force and they are not enthusiastic about it. Part of their attitude, I suspect, is subjective—such a plane is not very exciting."[18] Without Air Force support—and there is none—such a concept will not move beyond the conversation stage.

The Congress is rarely inclined to second-guess military judgment, although it has on occasion authorized funds for weapons the executive refuses to procure. So surprise was general when, in September, 1971, the Senate Committee on the Armed Services delivered a somber warning to the military. Its Chairman, Senator John Stennis of Mississippi, issued a committee report on the military authorization for fiscal year 1972: the report spoke of "deeply troubling" cost tendencies and noted:

> If the geometric cost increase for weapon systems is not sharply reversed, then even significant increases in the defense budget may not insure the force levels required for our national security. If we can afford a permanent force structure of only one-fifth as many fighter aircraft or tanks as our potential adversaries —because our systems are about five times more expensive than theirs—then a future crisis may find us at a sharp numerical disadvantage.[19]

In time, an informal coalition may be able to moderate the sybaritic tastes of the services; such a coalition would have to include, besides the Budget and Treasury people, key congressional groups, some parts of the Pentagon's civilian bureaucracy, and farsighted elements in the services themselves. The impact of such a coalition may ultimately depend on whether the White House can overcome its normal reluctance to interfere in the internal affairs of the military. Nixon and Kissinger, for all their stress on solid defense options emerging from rigorous analysis, have not yet been willing to challenge those cost tendencies that the Stennis Committee found "deeply troubling."

On past and current form, it is doubtful that some novel coalition will shut off the pressure for qualitative improvements in strategic weapons, or "modernization," as it is called. In-house scholastics know that there is even less incentive for this in Moscow than in Washington. Russians, it seems, do worry about the implications of a long-distance race for quality; but for the Russians, their technological lag is of far greater concern and certainly a disincentive to talk about these things with the Americans.

Most parts of the government came to favor a SALT agreement of one kind or another, for one reason or another. Each, however, has had its motives questioned by some rival. In general, the State Department, ACDA, and the CIA would prefer broad agreement, broader certainly than anything acceptable to most of the Pentagon. Nixon's White House, tugged by numerous considerations, has had the most ambiguous SALT style. Originally skeptical, the

President and Henry Kissinger eventually decided to pursue agreement. Now, besides charting the negotiating path, they control the SALT process, including the shape and variety of options it throws up. This assures endless skirmishing with the agencies involved and the SALT delegation. The skirmishing, however predictable, has been fierce; it has nourished White House suspicions of the bureaucracy, set off personality conflicts, and inspired *ad hoc* bureaucratic alignments against the White House, which, in turn, have reinforced White House wariness.

The State Department and ACDA have been close allies on SALT. This owes something to the remarkably close rapport and identity of view that developed between Gerard C. Smith, who headed the U.S. SALT delegation through Phase I, and Raymond I. Garthoff, until recently the Executive Officer and Senior Adviser to the delegation. Smith, of course, was Director of ACDA. Garthoff belongs to the State Department's Bureau of Political-Military Affairs (PM), the section chiefly responsible for SALT.

The State Department–ACDA harmony is also doctrinal. Each decided long ago that deterrence, not defense, was the only rational strategic policy, or, put differently, that the hazards, costs, and implausibility of damage-limiting options dictated acceptance of the assured-destruction concept that drifted slowly across the Potomac from Mr. McNamara's Pentagon in the second half of the 1960s. McNamara never had the slightest difficulty with his colleague, Dean Rusk, on an arms-control matter. ACDA counted for little then, if only because there was nothing so important as SALT to deal with, but Rusk's relations with the ACDA leadership, especially with the Deputy Director at the time, Adrian Fisher, were also remarkably close. The views of Secretary of State William Rogers were generally sympathetic to the ACDA and PM positions. And, while he was Undersecretary of State, Elliot Richardson was an occasional ACDA ally. Moreover, unlike Rogers, Richardson was a persuasive voice in the White House, thanks to an excellent working relationship with Henry Kissinger. The departure of Richardson marked still another decline in the State Department's influence on SALT.

The Nixon Administration began life leery of both SALT and assured destruction. Time, experience, events, and politics induced what, for practical purposes, has amounted to an acceptance of both. Yet, as is often the case, the blurring of doctrinal differences between rival institutions has not diminished the intensity of the conflict. Few presidents, of course, have much admired the State Department. Few if any, though, have so effectively diminished its role and influence. Yet, differences between the White House and the principal military voices—the Joint Chiefs and OSD—have exceeded its doctrinal differences with the State Department and ACDA on SALT. Still, the White House mistrusts the vested interest of the State Department and ACDA. In the meantime, SALT is very much a high-water mark for ACDA, an agency never in the past taken seriously.

State and ACDA tend to be more venturesome than the White House (though not always), less concerned about verification, and more confident that agreement on SALT will discourage, not encourage, cheating. With less to lose, they are less reluctant than the White House to take on the Joint Chiefs or OSD. Still, a good indication of the ornery nature of the process is the occasional alliance of State, ACDA, the Pentagon and the SALT delegation against the White House for tactical purposes having little if anything to do with the substance of the talks. Such gestures express a sense of rebellion against tight White House control. Kissinger, it bears repeating, keeps the SALT bureaucracy on a short leash.

Then as now, the SALT delegation replicated the SALT bureaucracy. Smith, as ACDA Director, was the leader. The other four delegates represented OSD, the Joint Chiefs, the State Department, and the scientific community. Smith's role was one of several reasons that the delegation was regarded with suspicion, and occasionally with open hostility. Smith had the respect of the Washington community; he was a competent negotiator with a good grasp of the issues. His only apparent weakness, however, was critical: To direct both ACDA and the SALT delegation is compromising, certainly in the view of the White House or any agency that takes exception to ACDA's position on any SALT issue. However unfairly, Smith was seen as ACDA's man at SALT, chiefly concerned with extending the range of what might be negotiable. As such, he lacked the full confidence of the White House (and the Pentagon). Arguably, then, it was a mistake to have placed the head of ACDA in charge of the talks; it was not a mistake that the preceding Administration intended to make when it was gearing up for SALT.

Still, the choice of Smith may have been inevitable; it had a certain logic, after all. Moreover, in a system designed to permit the President and his senior adviser to control the action on security, perhaps nobody of stature could have gained the confidence and authority for which Smith must have longed. Because he was persistently denied the responsibility he thought he should have, Smith quit at the start of Nixon's second term.

Kissinger is said, both in printed portraits and in Washington gossip, to venerate Metternich—a suggestion he himself ridicules. His first, and perhaps best, book—*A World Restored*— dealt with Europe after Napoleon and was largely devoted to the Congress of Vienna and the great figures assembled there. The book shows his admiration for Metternich to be complete (although Castlereagh, too, emerges in heroic proportion). Some in Washington demur, asking: "Would Metternich have sent the head of ACDA to negotiate a new equilibrium with the Russians?" The answer, of course, is that Smith, like his Soviet counterpart, Vladimir Semenovich Semenov, has had no such authority. The critical negotiation during the early rounds of SALT was held by Kissinger and Dobrynin in Washington, not by Smith and Semenov in Vienna. Smith wasn't even informed. Kissinger does have a classic and consistent aversion to mixing bureaucracy with policy. As he wrote in *A World Restored*, "the spirit of policy and that of bureaucracy are diametrically opposed. . . . It is dangerous to separate planning from the responsibility [for] execution."[20] Why then was Smith chosen? Some ranking figure with relevant experience and solid Republican credentials had to go to Helsinki and Vienna. The only reason it should not have been Smith is that he runs ACDA.

No part of the SALT bureaucracy is above suspicion of bias. That includes the intelligence community. The Defense Intelligence Agency (DIA), along with the intelligence arms of the military services, are seen, rightly enough, as sharing the biases of their principals. The CIA is not an arm of a policy organization and thus suffers no guilt by association; yet, the CIA has, by its analytical work, shown a strong bias in favor of the venturesome approach to SALT. It was precisely this bias that helped to start the CIA off on the wrong foot with the Nixon Administration. The clash was on verification, a problem of which the CIA takes a cheerier view than any competitor. It finds that most parts of any currently imaginable SALT package could be verified with reasonable confidence. Put differently, cheating would be detected on any scale large enough to make cheating worthwhile. The White House is less sanguine; it finds the CIA bias "Ivy League," as someone there put it. The White House has also suspected the CIA of abetting those who favor a broad SALT agreement in order to promote funds for the additional systems that could be needed to monitor the various constraints and prohibitions. A broad agreement, depending on what was covered, might require certain detection systems not presently "on the shelf."

Some acquaintance with the instrumental figures of SALT hastens understanding. A few of them, like Presidents Johnson and Nixon, are well known; others, scarcely at all. Some are no longer in government. One of them, Career Ambassador Llewellyn E. Thompson, is dead. Some key Russians can be identified; others cannot because we don't know who they are. And on both sides, old faces are being replaced by new and less familiar ones.

Of the two Presidents, Lyndon Johnson was the stronger advocate of SALT, even showing at times an excess of zeal. Richard Nixon was at first mistrustful, tending to look upon SALT as something to be done only if the Russians proved helpful on other matters, like Vietnam or the Middle East. But for assorted reasons Nixon eventually came to press as hard for a SALT agreement as Johnson had pressed for the talks themselves.

Johnson's zeal was matched by his senior ministers, Rusk and McNamara. McNamara was obviously closer to the issues involved in launching talks with the Russians; in Rusk, he had an unfailingly strong ally. Never were they in disagreement on any major point.

Rusk was no scholastic. He had little patience with the complex detail of weapons-related issues and the finer theological points of deterrence. "Once you involve yourself in a lot of detail," he said recently, "you are dead." Rusk says he tried to divorce people from their "picayune anxieties" in order to move them on to the "broadest possible ground, where agreement is possible." The blanks, he believed, could be filled in later. Recalling the Washington Naval Treaty of 1922, Rusk draws a parallel with Hughes, who "brushed aside the admirals on the issue of the size of the guns, and got a simple formula." The formula, among other things, established naval parity between the United States and Britain.

In Washington, Rusk was known as a passionate advocate of arms control. McNamara, although Secretary of Defense, achieved the same reputation on a national—indeed, international—scale. Even now, Russian diplomats speak admiringly of McNamara's early initiatives aimed at starting talks.

McNamara may be judged a tragic figure, at least as a victim of the harshest ironies of the 1960s. He seemed more than anyone, except perhaps President Kennedy himself, to embody the new sense of purpose and moderation, plus the stylish pursuit of excellence, that was asserted by the New Frontier. McNamara's story limns the dispiriting saga of Washington in the late 1960s—with all the hope and purpose faded, the moderation overrun by immoderation, the excellence disfigured by exaggeration and miscalculation.

The McNamara whose dominant side inclines to moderation and reasoned judgment became the prisoner of a spurious data base on Vietnam that he himself helped to inspire; following the logic of the one-dimensional data for which he thirsted, he gave America's commitment to the war a great burst of energy. Early critics called it McNamara's war. He grew to detest it.

He aimed to establish civilian control of the Pentagon and to make the defense budget "cost effective," a dual process in some measure set in motion by his predecessor, Thomas Gates. He did establish a good deal of control, more than any predecessor. He operated largely through instruments of OSD—Systems Analysis, which he created, and International Security Affairs. Yet he never brought DDR&E, after Foster began running it, into line with the prevailing spirit of moderation and cost effectiveness.

On the managerial and procurement side, McNamara's was a mixed performance, although in a sense remarkable. For a civilian nonprofessional to say no to a weapon that marries the freshest insights of technology to the military's best judgment of its own needs is very rare. McNamara said no to the Air Force on the B-70 strategic bomber, then to the RS-70, a modified version of the same airplane. He said no to the Air Force's request for a new ICBM bigger than Minuteman.

Yet it was he who insisted on the unfortunate TFX; other not very cost-effective systems, the C-5A and F-14 for example, have their roots in the McNamara Pentagon. One of his innovations, concurrency, is being buried as swiftly as possible. Concurrency, which was intended to cut production delays and other forms of waste, reduced the testing phase of a new weapon by narrowing the gap between development and production, chiefly through paper studies. The concept of total package procurement, as it became known, promised to lock things into place by avoiding the cost pushes associated with delays and testing. It didn't work, and the longer testing phase, rightly enough, is back in fashion, accompanied by the slogan: "Fly before you buy." McNamara's concurrency did funnel great authority into DDR&E, which became an empire within the Pentagon.

It was in nuclear strategy that McNamara seems to have done best. Yet even here, the record is clouded by decisions rooted in uncertainty or miscalculation. He did turn the Air Force away from counterforce and toward deterrence. He chopped off Minuteman deployment at 1000. He kept warheads small. He taught public opinion that security no longer lies in superior numbers of weapons. He struggled to start talks with Russians on limiting strategic arms, especially defensive arms. Curiously, this is where the ambiguity begins. McNamara, to his credit, effectively blocked the push for a massive ABM program. But while he seems to have had no choice but to initiate some ABM deployment, he chose the option of defending cities without giving the more modest and strategically respectable option of defending Minuteman a fair run. He made the decision to deploy MIRV—not merely to continue its development and evaluation, but to deploy it as a hedge against a potential threat, not a real threat. The threat never materialized.

One of the continuities of SALT was Llewellyn E. Thompson, who died on February 6, 1972, in the very latter stages of the first phase. Along with Rusk, he was an ally of McNamara's in seeding the unique enterprise. Thompson was that rare, invaluable figure, a man who had the confidence of the White House, the bureaucracy, and the Russians. Had the talks started earlier, he would have been the leading figure on the American side. Because of the discretion with which he dealt both with his own government and with the Soviets, his contribution, though major, is not calculable.

Another figure, then as now, at the center of those events is Paul H. Nitze. At sixty-five, Nitze has accumulated more experience with the affairs of U.S. security than anyone alive. Nitze worked closely with McNamara, first as head of ISA, next as Secretary of the Navy, finally as Deputy Secretary of Defense. Earlier, he had been a colleague and confidant of Dean Acheson in the State Department. He was the national security adviser to President-elect Kennedy following the 1960 election. Nitze earned the lasting respect of Europeans for his work in the Four Power contingency planning during the Berlin crisis of 1961 and 1962. Nitze is one of the five American delegates to SALT; he is the key Pentagon figure in the talks. For a long time, he has advocated hard-site defense of Minuteman. Nitze is tough-minded and combines the experience gained as a policy-oriented senior State Department official with a strong grasp of weapons technology acquired in the Pentagon. Withal, he is a cultivated, worldly man, fond of discussing music and the progress of the arts with Soviet delegates Semenov and Shuchkin, also worldly men.

The Joint Chiefs' man on the SALT delegation is Air Force Lieutenant-General Royal B. Allison. Allison, who played a useful, and perhaps critical, role in the summer of 1968 when the Johnson Administration was preparing for SALT, had the confidence of the then Chairman of the Joint Chiefs, General Earle G. Wheeler. He became a link between divergent civilian and uniformed elements dealing with SALT.

Another of the continuities was represented in the person of Dr. John S. Foster, Jr., Director of DDR&E. Among scholastics, Foster is just "Johnny," much as Robert Kennedy was just "Bobby" to the political community. Although not directly involved in SALT, Foster managed by the range and weight of his activities to exercise considerable influence on Pentagon attitudes toward the talks.

Foster, now forty-nine, became the third Director of DDR&E in 1965. His predecessors were Dr. Herbert York and Dr. Harold Brown. Brown, the SALT delegate representing the scientific community, is president of the California Institute of Technology. York and Brown also preceded Foster as Directors of the Livermore Laboratory in California. Each has a long history of supporting arms-control agreements. Foster never showed much sympathy for arms control; for example, he testified against the partial test-ban treaty in 1963. He was the despair of many of his fellow scientists and bureaucrats. Equally, those among them who see more pitfalls than opportunities in SALT relied on Johnny Foster to defend their viewpoint.

Across the Potomac, Raymond L. Garthoff of the State Department has accumulated more direct experience with SALT than anyone. His importance to SALT's first phase was perhaps matched only by his anonymity—at least, beyond the bureaucracy. Within it, Garthoff is universally known as a gifted and versatile civil servant. Like most gifted people, he is also controversial. Those who admire the prevailing State Department–ACDA view of SALT saw Garthoff as not just the chief executive officer of the delegation, but its pivotal force. Those who take a warier view of SALT and see the State Department and ACDA caught up in a rhythm of negotiation for its own sake worried about Garthoff for the same reason. He probably was the delegation's pivotal figure.

Garthoff is a tall, balding man—looking younger than his forty-four years—with a somewhat ironic, professorial style. His career seems almost to have been a preparation for SALT: a Sovietologist, Garthoff is a specialist in Soviet military affairs (about which he's written four books), fluent in Russian, and a veteran of the inner working level of every important arms-control negotiation since the partial test-ban treaty. Garthoff even has a NATO string to his bow, and was, in fact, recalled from the U.S. NATO Mission in Brussels in 1968 to help prepare for SALT. Had the talks gotten underway in 1967, as Washington first hoped, Garthoff would have been a delegate. With the departure of Elliot Richardson, Garthoff, though lacking defined authority, had more to say about SALT than anyone in the State Department. In another administration, he might even have been the *eminence grise* of SALT. None of the eminences of the current Administration is gray.

An equally arresting personality is Morton H. Halperin. Though not for the moment "in-house," Halperin has been at times a major force in the SALT process. Indeed, in 1968, Halperin—then a deputy to Paul Warnke in the Pentagon's ISA—became the crucial figure in SALT. Rarely has a single individual played so large a role in maneuvering a sensitive, highly controversial initiative through the bureaucracy. Halperin, too, is gifted, versatile, and, of course, controversial. Although his interests (and publications) are wide ranging, arms control is his passion. Other interests, notably China, Japan, and bureaucratic politics, are in large part a function of his involvement with arms control.

Halperin has crammed a remarkable sum of experience into thirty-five years. He left behind him when he joined ISA in 1966 a considerable teaching career at Harvard (where he and Kissinger were faculty colleagues), and a trail of a half-dozen books and endless articles to his credit.

Halperin, joining Kissinger before Nixon's inauguration, helped establish the present structure of the National Security Council, and became a senior staff aide within that structure. It did not work out and he left in September, 1969. Halperin and Kissinger admire each other, but are motivated by sharply differing instincts and values. They probably were destined to clash. Halperin now follows government from the nearby Brookings Institution. Nobody doubts that one day he will be back.

Excepting Kissinger, the most important White House influence on SALT has been Laurence E. Lynn, Jr. Lynn, who has now left, is a thirty-five-year-old economist. In 1969, he acquired the chief responsibility for SALT preparation and related matters. He invented the celebrated Verification Panel. Lynn had Kissinger's confidence to a degree possibly never matched by any colleague or successor. Although totally different in intellectual formation, Kissinger and Lynn were kindred spirits on strategic issues. Like Kissinger, Lynn is greatly admired by those who have worked with him, whether they agree or disagree with his views. And like Kissinger, he is a controversial figure within the defense and arms-control community.

Henry Kissinger is so dominant an influence that it is sometimes hard to remember that he is the President's agent. He has no equivalent in this century, if only because the power and influence of the United States are incomparably greater than in the day of Colonel House, or even Harry Hopkins. Kissinger's favorite statesmen were nineteenth-century figures. None of them—not Metternich, not Castlereagh—deployed the power to shape events that he now has. Yet Kissinger can be, sometimes is, overruled by the

President. He doesn't win every battle; he has at times been out-voted within the Administration and outmaneuvered by a bureau-cracy less intimidated now than at the start. Few would deny the remarkable gifts and energy that allow him to manage the strands of national security and foreign policy. Yet he has made mistakes, traceable to miscalculation, or possibly to fatigue in some cases. Since power uses men, he may make more.

Kissinger has also made enemies, but in Washington those who dislike him most are those who know him least. Those of his staff who resigned primarily on policy grounds retain great admiration —even fondness, in some cases—for a leader who used them, but rarely consulted or advised them.

Congress is unused to a figure who seems to be playing every instrument in the band; for such a figure to be beyond the reach of congressional committees, as is the case with presidential assis-tants, is hard to swallow. The situation fosters tension and can only deepen a growing institutional conflict between Congress and the executive in security affairs.

Still less does bureaucracy approve of the White House predilec-tion for managing foreign policy the way de Gaulle managed it— by secrecy and surprise. In fairness to Kissinger, his magisterial style owes less to personal preference than to the President's. Kissinger's mistrust of bureaucracy is less relevant than Nixon's. The President insisted on establishing control through a single, trusted, omnicompetent individual. He is served well, and Kissin-ger is a salutary influence in Nixon's White House. His own view of bureaucracy was first recorded in 1954, in *A World Restored*.

> The essence of bureaucracy is its quest for safety; its success is calculability. Profound policy thrives on perpetual creation, on a constant redefinition of goals. Good administration thrives on routine, the definition of relationships which can survive medi-ocrity. Policy involves an adjustment of risks; administration an avoidance of deviation. . . . The effort to administer politically leads to total irresponsibility, because bureaucracies are designed to execute, not to conceive.[21]

Fourteen years later, on the eve of his great moment, Kissinger spelled things out a bit:

Because management of the bureaucracy takes so much energy and precisely because changing course is so difficult, many of the most important decisions are kept to a very small circle while the bureaucracy continues working away in ignorance of the fact that decisions are being made, or of the fact that a decision is being made in a particular area. One reason for keeping the decisions to small groups is that when bureaucracies are so unwieldy and when their internal morale becomes a serious problem, an unpopular decision may be fought by brutal means, such as leaks to the press or congressional committees. Thus, the only way secrecy can be kept is to exclude from the making of the decision those who are theoretically charged with carrying it out.[22]

Morton Halperin and his Brookings colleague, Leslie Gelb, disagree: "When the creative leaders turn to new problems, it is up to the bureaucracy to keep the wheels of policy turning. If the bureaucracy is ignored and is not persuaded by the President's policy, bureaucrats will undermine that policy—when no one is looking."[23]

Somewhat ironically, the SALT talks began with bureaucracy, in the main, more adventurous than Nixon and Kissinger and less tied to routine and orthodox defense-planning criteria. Although the pattern shifted as the White House began to press hard for agreement, Phase II of SALT may well find a large part of the bureaucracy once again out in front of the leadership.

As chairman of the delegation, Gerard C. Smith, directed a fair-sized portion of the SALT bureaucracy and tackled his work with similar *élan*. His role, of course, was limited by the nature of the system. Smith had long experience with nuclear diplomacy. He was adviser to John Foster Dulles on nuclear matters and, later in the Eisenhower Administration, chairman of the State Department's Policy Planning Council, where he helped originate the ill-fated multilateral force (MLF).

Smith is wealthy and public-spirited, in manner discreet and reserved. Whether pressing for acceptance for the MLF or an agreement on SALT, he has gained a reputation for industry.

Smith's Russian colleague, Vladimir S. Semenov, has been a Deputy Foreign Minister since 1955. The larger part of his experience is in Germany; he is, in fact, a German scholar and speaks no

English. Semenov was the senior Soviet political adviser in Berlin at the time of the 1949 blockade and hence acquired a reputation as the key man in the effort to starve Berlin into submission. He became High Commissioner of East Germany in May, 1953; one month later, he had to authorize the use of troops to put down the uprising. An auto crash obliged him to return to Moscow in 1954, and he became Deputy Foreign Minister the following year. In the one article he has written (in April, 1969), he strongly advocated peaceful coexistence with capitalist powers and a simultaneous build-up in the power and influence of the Soviet Union. He is generally regarded as an advocate of agreement on arms control.

Colonel-General Nikolai Vasil'evich Ogarkov was listed as the second-ranking member of the delegation until he failed to appear at the fourth round of SALT in the spring of 1971. However, as First Deputy Chief of the General Staff, an office he has held since August, 1968, Ogarkov continues to be a strong influence on the Soviet SALT position, certainly stronger than Semenov. Both men became candidate-members of the Central Committee of the Soviet Communist party in 1966. But Ogarkov, unlike Semenov, was promoted to full membership in the Twenty-Fourth Party Congress of March, 1971, which may explain his abrupt withdrawal from the delegation. Ogarkov was replaced by the lesser-ranked Lieutenant-General Konstantine Trusov, a member of the General Staff with various technical responsibilities. The United States delegation, which had never heard of Trusov, was titilated by his name.

The Russian delegation is organized like the American. It has five delegates representing various constituencies and a large number of advisers and experts, plus an interpreting staff. The Soviet scientific delegate is Aleksandr N. Shuchukin, a prominent specialist in radio electronics. He is credited by his government with the discovery of the principle of impulse radio communications. Shuchukin, now seventy-two, also holds the rank of major general in the engineering-technical service of the Soviet armed forces.

In appraising the Russians, it must be borne in mind that the Dobrynin-Vorontsov team in Washington has functions that may be as important, if not more so, than those of the Soviet SALT delegation. Nor surprisingly, the delegation is known to see a competing influence lurking in the Soviet Embassy in Washington.

Finally, the cast of personalities should not leave out the man who invented the acronym SALT. He is Robert Martin, who works with Garthoff in the Bureau of Political-Military Affairs in the State Department. In the spring of 1968, when the prospect of talks suddenly brightened, bureaucrats began having to write cables about limiting strategic arms. Any combination of words labeling the process was inevitably cumbersome. Martin, who was then a member of the Political Section of the U.S. NATO Mission in Brussels, finally gave up and concocted SALT. His Ambassador, Harland Cleveland, resisted the term for a while; so did a number of Washington officials, finding it too cute. ACDA disliked it. The issue arose at a meeting of senior officials; the CIA finally insisted on formal adoption of "SALT" because its filing system was already being organized around the term.

Those who assume that everything in Moscow is decided at the top are wrong. As in Washington, large interest groups, or constituencies, shape Soviet strategic decisions. Moscow, too, has its internal budgetary skirmishes; there, too, weapons technology can establish, instead of serve, the choices of the leadership. There, too, an internal dynamic—a blend of these competing interests and the impulse of technology—drives force planning. The urge to catch up or exceed the United States—to play the great power game—provides a context.

We know too little about the internal Soviet debate, and ignorance feeds Washington's wariness about SALT. Ideally, the prospect of evasion or surprise abrogation of an agreement should be measured at least in part in terms of the interests of rival groups. A good illustration is the Soviet air defense command, which has existed as a separate command since 1955 and is never starved for funds. With how much struggling did it resist giving up all but a meaningless ABM capability, as well as apparently foregoing the more advanced ABM technology that lies within the grasp of both great powers? Could anyone have expected the much-indulged air defense command to lose this battle? The newest of the five Soviet military commands is the Strategic Rocket Forces, once called the country's strong right arm by Khrushchev. A freeze on land-based missiles and the push toward the sea may darken the future of this command. A ban or limit on MIRV testing and deployment would hurt more. SALT agreements can weaken the relative strength of one command vis-à-vis the others, perhaps even call into question its existence.

Washington worries that SALT agreements might give Moscow an incentive to conceal its activities. So far, the Russians have had little such incentive. They have neither the tradition nor the procedures to make disclosures of the kind the United States makes through congressional presentations, budgetary messages, and so forth. Yet they have an interest in at least partial disclosure, in giving the world an impression of what they are doing. Glimpses of the hardware are offered in "drag-by's" during May Day parades. They rely chiefly on Western disclosures to impress the world with the size of their forces. Pentagon presentations of the strategic balance help the Soviet Union to proclaim its great power position. The military balance published annually by the Institute for Strategic Studies in London, plus Jane's reviews of fighting ships and aircraft do the same thing.

Washington's anxiety is sharpened by the undoubted and growing power of the Soviet military bureaucracy, whose influence on defense policy exceeds that of any Western counterpart. Since Stalin's death, the influence of the military has grown; since Khrushchev's fall, it has risen even more sharply, again with reference to defense matters. Primarily, political questions are settled by the party leadership without reference to the military; at least, we think this to be the case, although some Sovietologists feel that military influence may have been decisive in forcing the decision to invade Czechoslovakia in August, 1968.

SALT gives us a better focus on the interplay of civilian and military interests in Moscow. Actually, there is little such interplay, as Americans know it. There the polarity is greater, the debate never really joined. In Washington, ACDA and OSD bureaucrats, although disagreeing, may jointly draft SALT positions under White House direction. Nothing comparable takes place in Moscow. There, civilian bureaucrats may press some defense-related foreign-policy measure only to see the military veto it on feasibility grounds. The civilians are hard put to protest because they lack factual military knowledge, even about Soviet strategic forces.

The point has been dramatically illustrated at various SALT sessions. Once during the second round, in Vienna, Gerry Smith was presenting charts comparing the size of Russian and American missiles and silos. In replying, his Russian counterpart, Mr. Semenov, confused Minuteman silos, quite small, with SS-9 silos, very large. He seemed unacquainted with the elementary fact that Soviet ICBM's are much larger than America's. He was openly set straight by his colleague, Colonel-General Ogarkov. Later in the same round, Ogarkov, then listed as the second-ranking member of the Soviet delegation, took aside a U.S. delegate and said there was no reason why the Americans should disclose their knowledge of Russian military matters to civilian members of his delegation. Such information, said Ogarkov, is strictly the affair of the military. Since then, the Americans have occasionally sought to exploit this polarity by pointing to some recent Soviet weapons development, about which Washington knew little, in order to see whether their civilian colleagues across the table, who also knew nothing, might be able to learn something from Moscow that would shed more light.

Such gambits have had little if any success. Early in 1972, an American deeply involved in the talks said: "Even now [in the last round], Soviet civilian members of the delegation are no better informed than they were at the start about the locations of their ICBM's, the number of missiles in a field, the relevant information about their radars. They rely to a great degree upon what we tell them during the plenary meetings and working group sessions."

The ignorance of the Soviet delegation complicates the work of the American. The problem is how to to deal in precise terms with a negotiating team that is often poorly instructed because it is denied knowledge of the numbers, characteristics, and locations of the weapons deployed by its own government.

In *A World Restored*, Henry Kissinger wrote: "The memory of states is the test of truth of their policy. The more elementary the experience, the more profound its impact on a nation's interpretation of the present in the light of the past. It is even possible for a nation to undergo an experience so shattering that it becomes the prisoner of its past."[24] Russian attitudes toward SALT are conditioned partly by history. Accumulated humiliations affect the Russian view of the world and the judgment of how much military power the state requires. Suspicion is fed by the anxieties of people whose land, lacking frontiers, has been overrun countless times.

The Russian word for security, *bezopasnost'*, conveys both a broader and more acute meaning than the English equivalent. It means lack of danger, total safety. Russians are haunted by China and Germany. America is an adversary thrown up by ideology and the realities of power. The German phoenix, if it touches the Russian viscera, is no longer an objective menace. China is both a visceral anxiety and a perceived menace.

Moscow is tugged in many directions. No less than Washington does the leadership seem to recognize the need for stability. The question is whether stability is merely useful or an end in itself. Stability as a goal may collide with the Soviet Union in the role of mother Russia caught up in an imperial rhythm—embarked on a venturesome, high-risk diplomacy somewhat reminiscent of 1815. Then, with Napoleon apparently swept from the board, Alexander backed aggressive diplomacy with boasts of being able to put a million men into the field, while simultaneously putting forth patently disingenuous proposals for mutual force reductions among the European powers.

"Better the French as enemies than the Russians as friends," was a reflection that took hold swiftly at the Congress of Vienna. Castlereagh and Metternich, with little else to agree on, swiftly developed a joint apprehension about Russian imperialism. Nicolson wrote:

> The Russian generals and diplomatists . . . having convinced themselves that Russian arms alone had liberated Europe from an odious tyranny, being intoxicated by the military prestige which Russia had unexpectedly acquired, began on every occasion and in every country to indulge in self-assertiveness and intrigue. "Well, so far as that goes," boasted a Russian general when discussing the impending Congress, "one does not need to worry much about negotiations when one has 600,000 men under arms."[25]

Today, Soviet Ambassadors in Western Europe discreetly and at the highest levels cite the SS-9 and the general Soviet military buildup as evidence of their primacy. Just read, they suggest, what Mr. Laird and other Americans say about our missiles. Even the Americans now see that we have the biggest missiles and the greatest number; they understand our determination. Don't bind yourself too closely to them. Except for the *sotto voce* style, it sounds curiously like the stadium football claque chanting "We're Number One."

Both diplomatically and militarily, the Soviet Union is raising its sights. A more freewheeling and less-cautious style links civilian and military bureaucrats to complimentary purpose, although the former are more sensitive to the criteria of stable deterrence; both hope to avoid the risks that may arise from bolder diplomacy.

The Soviet military are less constrained. They are uneasy, to put it mildly, about such unnatural concepts as parity, which arms-control buffs banter about. Their claim to the dominant role in strategy is the more remarkable for being comparatively recent. To take just one of many examples, a Lieutenant-Colonel C. Ivanov wrote in a major military journal shortly before round one of SALT that, while the party's role is pre-eminent, political leadership must rely on the judgments of military science if its decisions are to be effective.[26]

The late Marshal N. I. Krylov, formerly Commander of the Strategic Rocket Forces, was taking his distance from the Foreign Ministry when he wrote at the same time: "Moscow could not agree with the U.S. position that there could be no winner in a nuclear war."[27] Krylov also warned against "complacency" arising from the new weapons balance.[28]

The more moderate and subtle Larionov adopts a hermetic style in appraising the attitude and role of the military. Connoisseurs know that the only available means of commenting on the Soviet military is to comment on the American military. Thus, he writes: "One cannot discount the fact that professional military men, who on the whole are not accustomed to the notion of 'surplus forces,' act in the United States as the most competent experts in evaluating the degree of sufficiency."[29]

The Washington-based Soviet scholastic Yury Vorontsov professes a strong bias in favor of SALT, which, he says, "is the most important thing we have to do together. It's closer to the essence of what we both regard as our security. Thus, it cannot be compared to negotiations which, like Berlin, involve other countries. SALT resists comparison with other negotiations."

Moscow, too, has strategic schools forming up around competing viewpoints. The term "assured destruction" is not used, but thinking on these lines has acquired respectability. Nor has the term "damage limitation" entered the Soviet strategic literature, but the concept suits the preference of the Soviet military, or a good part of it.

Moscow rarely offers more than a glimpse. And, as with other things, Russian strategic thinking contains all the internal contradiction that flows naturally from a system bred from the Soviet dialectic. Reconciling *détente* diplomacy with a general military buildup is just not a problem. All or most of the big constituencies concerned with defense and foreign policy are in the main satisfied. For example, the military argues to advantage that for the Party to accept and pursue a high-risk diplomacy requires the solid authority that only military power can provide, and whose dimension is best determined by professionals.

Major competing viewpoints, whether diplomatic or military, are linked by a common hubris and self-righteousness; by a common fear of external conspiracy; by a common anxiety rooted in a sense of inferiority. So we find some Soviet diplomats, while frankly acknowledging the buildup, saying, in effect: "Whereas you Americans had for years a crushing military superiority in nuclear weapons, you must now accept us as your equal, perhaps even your superior. You Americans took the line that since you were good and peaceful people, the superiority was safe with you. Now you will have to accept a similar claim on our side."

Such talk has a faintly hollow ring. Bigger missiles in superior numbers, a navy growing in size and versatility, a huge and superbly equipped army—all this provides a potent political weapon. Still, the honors in an open race for strategic advantage should go to the fastest horse on technology's track—the United States. Nobody knows that better than the soldiers and diplomats of the Soviet Union.

Understanding SALT requires skepticism as well as persistence. Undeterred by the secrecy and the theology, one must also penetrate the SALT mythology. This means accepting first that SALT is not necessarily a good thing. A "soft" (superficial) agreement might be "counterproductive," as the bureaucracy says. It could very well breed hostility at home and troubles abroad—especially with allies fearful of the consequences of what they would see as a spurious condominium settling over their heads matters as vital to their security as to America's. A soft agreement would set off pressure to work around the constraints, thus nullifying whatever dividends it might otherwise return. Put differently, in return for a marginally more-stable strategic environment, we might get a less-stable political environment.

One SALT scholastic, while part of the White House Working Group, drew up a mock memorandum for the President at the end of a long day in which paradox and contradiction had borne in heavily on him. His lapidary document, never sent of course, contained three alternative views of SALT as perceived by some contesting elements in the bureaucracy. It said: "SALT is (1) a snare and delusion (the Pentagon); (2) man's last best hope (ACDA); (3) none of the above (the Working Group's attitude)."

SALT is a model of irony and paradox. Dispassionate insiders understand that a soft agreement could be about as useful as a ban on bows and arrows, given the wondrous refinements that lie within the research-and-development capabilities of both great powers. Both bureaucracies, finding themselves constrained by an agreement limiting numbers of systems, could hasten the impulse, always lurking, for big leaps on the qualitative side. Individual services could be relied upon to lobby more vigorously for new weapons and for improvements of existing systems not covered by the agreement. They would argue forcibly that failure to hedge against the agreement would be to mortgage the future. In short, if SALT fails over time to constrain "quality," it might fuel the race for offensive superiority—better accuracies, yields, ranges—within a specified outer limit on numbers of weapons. Equally, an agreement limiting known types of defensive systems—ABM's—would be of little value if the two sides set about developing more exotic and proficient counterparts based on lasers, or something called a particle generator, or both. "Exotic," by the way, is the agreed term for the novel defensive systems that may lie around the corner. Happily, the treaty limiting ABM's has virtually closed the door on such exotica.

Just as misleading as the argument that any reduction in arms is salutary is the related notion that strategic spending follows an unbroken spiral, carrying aloft with it the federal budget. Indeed, the duel for strategic advantage and the Vietnamese war are widely believed to have put the U.S. economy in the grip of soaring inflationary costs. Although the war did help to produce this effect, the budget for strategic arms has been remarkably stable.

Nonetheless, spending for strategic weapons focuses much more public concern and analytical attention than the far heavier spending for general-purpose forces. Typically, the concern generates more heat than light. Actually, over the past decade, the budget for strategic arms has, on balance, declined, has shown more dips than rises. It normally consumes about a fifth of the total defense budget. That, in fact, is the current level—nearly $19 billion, more than half of which is taken up by such indirect costs as research and development, intelligence and communications, pay raises, and the like.

The Kennedy Administration began life in 1961 encumbered with a famous missile-gap myth nourished by numerous leading Democrats, not least the then Vice-President who, besides having run the Senate, had presided over an Armed Services Subcommittee on Preparedness. Although Kennedy and McNamara were swiftly disabused about the gap, they approved a major buildup of strategic forces. They have since been blamed for overreacting. This is partially unfair and misleading. Failure to proceed with the buildup of Minuteman and Polaris, much of it already programmed, would have generated horrendous difficulties with the Congress and bureaucracy. In fairness to Kennedy and McNamara, they set limits on the buildup and obliged the services to scale down their expectations. A glimpse of the heavy pressure they faced is offered by a chance meeting Kennedy and McNamara had with the then Commanding General of the Strategic Air Command, Thomas Powers. In March, 1962, Kennedy and McNamara were in California; the President was speaking at Berkeley. It was decided that together they would visit Vandenberg Air Force Base for a briefing on Minuteman by General Powers. At one point, Powers spoke of the day when 10,000 of the quick-reaction, solid-fueled Minuteman missiles would be deployed. Kennedy, although no less an admirer of Minuteman, swiftly admonished the General that never while he was President would anything like 10,000 of them be procured.

By the mid-1960s, strategic spending and the size of America's deterrent forces had leveled off. Washington, although rhetorically committed to a damage-limiting capability, was tacitly accepting the more-modest criteria of assured destruction. The Minuteman force would be held to 1000. The number of Polaris nuclear submarines would not exceed 41, or 656 missiles, since the boats are equipped with 16 each. The veteran B-52 strategic bomber had peaked at 639 in 1962. Worn-out airplanes were not to be replaced and the number had dropped to 460. Add to all this 54 Titan missiles, then as now obsolete but still in service.

At this stage, it became a question of adapting, not increasing, the size of U.S. forces. The trend to lower levels of strategic spending continued through fiscal year 1967, even though the Soviet Union was then launched on its major strategic buildup. Spending increased slightly in fiscal years 1968 and 1969 as the pace of the modernization program quickened. Yet in fiscal 1970, as a study by the Brookings Institution points out, "the administration reduced spending on strategic programs by $2 billion, while continuing both the MIRV and ABM programs."[30] Strategic spending rose again in fiscal year 1973 by $1.2 billion, with most of the increase absorbed by the Navy's Trident and ULMS development.

Stated briefly, the United States has not increased the size of any part of its strategic forces in several years. It has—and is—making qualitative improvements, chiefly by MIRV'ing the major portion of both the sea-based and land-based missiles, plus hardening missile silos.

Running through public and congressional discussion of SALT has been the expectation that an agreement would put an end to strategic extravagance. We see now that SALT will have little if any immediate or short-term effect on spending. The same Brookings study of the defense budget says that SALT "would not have much effect in reducing U.S. strategic spending over the next three or four years, since a wide range of qualitative improvements could and probably would be pursued, and older systems would continue to be replaced. But an agreement could keep the budget from rising much above $20 billion."[31]

Only if and when SALT begins to hobble "quality" will the desired effect—in this case, reducing spending—be achieved. Both the Brookings study and an unclassified internal White House paper calculate the cost of the most likely improvements in strategic systems over the next ten years. The first study estimates $50 billion, the second $55 billion. These are crude projections, ignoring the vagaries of world politics, or the possible research and development costs of other innovations now contemplated by a relative handful of people.

Whether the strategic budget shows a rising or a stable trend in the next few years will depend on whether systems now under serious study will be produced and deployed, if so, when, and, in the event, whether they will reduce or increase operating costs. In any case, short of a political disaster and the collapse of SALT, strategic spending should not rise sharply. Moderate elements in the government seek to adapt strategic force budgets, not expand them; to absorb technological change at current spending levels, not to be victimized by it. Here performance with regard to spending on strategic weapons has been reasonably good. Such is not the case with regard to hardware for general-purpose forces; there, the performance in some instance is deplorable. This is probably because the smaller sums spent on America's nuclear deterrent represent a far more-conspicuous—hence disturbing—item in the clouded public view.

Another popular notion not to be taken for granted suggests that an action-reaction cycle paces the arms race. Such wielders of military power as Napoleon and Robert McNamara have said that states design weapons to counter those of their adversaries, real or imagined. Self-evident, but narrow, truth is contained in this reflection, which must be hedged. The famous action-reaction cycle is exaggerated, misleading, and, in some cases, irrelevant to the procurement of various systems. Although arms development is obviously related to what others do, much of what the great powers deploy is inspired by internal politics and the celibate impulse of technology. So-called gaps that generate catch-up "crash" programs are sometimes not gaps at all. Instead, they are in large part the product of pessimistic assumptions by bureaucrats and soldiers of both sides who find gaps lurking in their extrapolations. It is as if force-planners in Washington and Moscow were wedded to the higher interests of technology in a silent unacknowledged compact. A State Department scholastic deeply involved in SALT describes the action-reaction cycle as "very exaggerated." He says that "in general, what one side does is used to fuel and fortify what the other wants to do anyway."

The Soviet Union's passion for secrecy has also energized American programs, as much perhaps as the actual weapons it has deployed. Nor is the spending pressure traceable to a conspiratorial monolith popularly known as the "military-industrial complex." It is much more the consequence of single-minded bureaucrats pursuing independent organizational interests. Each military service tends to deal in this area as if the others didn't exist, just as each occasionally backs another's pet project the better to secure solid backing for its own. What is true of the services is also true of related departments, like the Pentagon's DDR&E and Systems Analysis. In short, each group seeks to stake out and consolidate its share of the action in strategic arms, its lasting role in the great game of deterrence. But the pattern is uneven and fortuitous, the structure far from monolithic.

The Scylla and Charybdis of deterrence, as seen by many in the arms-control and defense communities, are the MIRV and ABM technologies. Some people tend to favor or tolerate the one, while deploring the other. What may be said is that these technologies have dominated strategic force planning for many years. The development and deployment of ABM and MIRV by the United States, which has a commanding lead in both technologies, was in part inspired by the so-called action-reaction cycle; but they are also the product of these other tendencies—most importantly an uncertainty about Soviet purposes reinforced by internal bureaucratic politics in Washington. Robert McNamara says flatly that Washington's MIRV deployment decision was taken in response to the Soviet installation of the Galosh ABM system around Moscow, a gesture that might have foreshadowed nationwide Russian ABM coverage and thus greatly complicated the ability of American missiles to reach their targets. On the other hand, one of Mr. McNamara's principal aides at the time, Paul Warnke, told a Senate Foreign Relations subcommittee that "we made the decision to deploy MIRV's in the late 1960's when we feared that the so-called Tallinn air defense system might prove to be a large area ABM deployment."[32] A year earlier, Adrian S. Fisher, the Deputy Director of ACDA throughout the Kennedy and Johnson years, told the same subcommittee the same thing: "It [MIRV] was originally justified on the ground it was necessary to prevent—to saturate the Tallinn system which was then thought to have an ABM capability."[33] And Johnny Foster told the Senate Subcommittee on

Preparedness in 1968 that the Poseidon Program (our sea-based MIRV) "was started mainly because of the uncertainty of the Tallinn threat."[34]

In fact, Soviet deployment of Galosh was an incentive for the MIRV decision. Much the same could be said of Washington's anxious reaction to Tallinn. As will be seen, however, there were other causes not directly related to what the Russians were doing.

The ABM deployment decision is endlessly fascinating and more complex even than MIRV. McNamara and some who served with him at the time assign the responsibility (i.e., blame,) to political pressures—chiefly those coming from Capitol Hill. Dean Rusk and Adrian Fisher take precisely this view. But they were not consulted, or even closely informed. It's quite true that the pro-ABM sentiment of assorted congressional guardians of national security, prodded by the Joint Chiefs of Staff, did put President Johnson and hence McNamara under great pressure to deploy something. But the picture, typically, is far more complicated. The eventual deployment decision, as we shall also see, has tangled roots; it should not be accepted historically as the dilemma of a beleaguered Secretary of Defense no longer able to hold out against political forces who should have understood, as he did, that ABM deployment would achieve nothing except a compensatory increase by the Soviet Union in its offensive capability.

Here again, partial truth on so elusive a subject obscures other, possibly deeper, truths. And catching a clear glimpse of SALT, as well as understanding the May agreements, will require insight into the curious, if all too human, forces that have animated both the ABM and MIRV programs.

2   Origins

To identify the end of any period of experience and the start of another is arbitrary. The chronicler can reach into the distant past for deep perspective, or he can identify an event, or series of events, that directly set in motion what was to come. The era of American nuclear supremacy was predictably short-lived. The era of nuclear parity began well before the Soviet Union closed the gap.

SALT has its origins in the mid-1960s, when Washington, in some confusion, was trying to reconcile its commitment to a damage-limiting strategy with the knowledge that such a strategy would not work. The best glimpse of the dilemma is offered by McNamara's posture statements of the period. Every January, the Secretary of Defense opens the military appropriations process with an exhaustive presentation to Congress of defense needs and purposes. Posture statements are awaited by the defense community with the kind of expectation with which feeders of the world await the new edition of the *Guide Michelin.*

In January, 1964, McNamara put assured destruction and damage limitation on an equal footing:

> . . . a damage limiting strategy appears to be the most practical and effective course for us to follow. Such a strategy requires a force considerably larger than would be needed for a limited "cities only" strategy. While there are still some differ-

ences of judgment on just how large such a force should be, there is general agreement that it should be large enough to ensure the destruction, singly or in combination, of the Soviet Union, Communist China, and the Communist satellites as national societies, . . . and, in addition, to destroy their warmaking capability so as to limit, to the extent practicable, damage to this country and to our allies.[1]

In a sense, this was the last hurrah for damage limitation. Washington clung to the idea of being able to limit damage to society—it still asserts a modest capability of the kind—but after 1964 the language of these annual statements became more ambiguous, the assertions gloomily hedged by the acknowledged difficulties of appreciably limiting damage to the United States and its allies. Johnny Foster, a tireless advocate of damage limitation, recalls that "the term 'assured destruction' was first used in 1964."[2]

Unlike instant massive retaliation, a fanciful doctrine of the 1950s, the option of limiting damage did not head straight for the discard; it is alive today, if only in a largely rhetorical sense, and in the years since 1961, it has remained close to the center of fashion. But by 1964, the recognition that the United States was in the autumn of its strategic supremacy had set in. A number of things seemed to empty damage limitation of credibility, if not desirability.

Recognition came hard. Washington's assessments of Soviet strategic capabilities tend to cover four-year cycles during which it miscalculates and overcorrects. In the post-Sputnik period, 1957–61, it exaggerated Moscow's performance and asserted an alarming but nonexistent missile gap. In the ensuing four years—1961–65—it underestimated Moscow's intentions. From 1965 to 1969, it misread the direction of the Soviet strategic program and overreacted to the infant Chinese program.

By the mid-1960s, Moscow was moving toward invulnerable second-strike forces along the American model. Missile silos were being hardened; a buildup of offensive forces had begun. Curiously, what fluttered Washington most was the lesser event of China's formal entry into the nuclear fold: in October, 1964, China set off a low-yield atomic bomb; this was followed by a slightly larger detonation in May, 1965. Construction of a large ballistic-missile launch facility at Shuang-ch'eng-tzu also began in 1965.

These events coincided with ominous rumbles from Lin Piao, then China's defense chief, most notably his famous "Long Live the Victory of People's War" of September, 1965. McNamara, in his 1965 posture statement, called Chinese medium- and long-range ballistic missiles "a most disturbing long-term prospect."

The more-critical portents lay in the expanding Soviet program; these were fully predictable. A classified study by the Rand Corporation, conducted in 1961–62, looked ahead to a time when damage limitation would no longer be feasible. When the Russians inevitably began to build up their own forces, it said, America would not be able to rely on its strategic offense to limit damage. Some mix of civil defense and ballistic-missile defense (ABM's) would be needed if the United States were to achieve even a modest damage-limiting capability, it concluded. But the impact of the Rand study was not immediate. As Alain Enthoven and Wayne Smith, point out:

> Despite the inevitability of the day when the Soviets would have a secure retaliatory or "second-strike" force, the U.S. was proceeding with large and costly programs that could be justified only if we were trying for a first-strike capability—that is, an ability to destroy in a first strike the Soviet ability to retaliate. . . . Because of Soviet progress in missile development and deployment, it should have been clear even in 1961 that such a first-strike capability for the middle and late 1960's would be unattainable, regardless of how much we were willing to spend.[3]

For its part, Moscow made no effort to hide its intentions. Indeed, after the Cuban missile crisis of October, 1962, John McCloy, operating on assignment from President Kennedy, found himself hosting Soviet Deputy Foreign Minister V. V. Kuznetsov at his Connecticut home. Kuznetsov assured McCloy that Moscow would observe the agreement to remove Soviet missiles and bombers from Cuba, but warned: "Never will we be caught like this again."

As Washington began reacting in the period between 1964 and 1966, two contradictory impulses were set against each other. One was to limit strategic arms, the other to hedge against strategic leaps by Russia and China. The first impulse was expressed in various rather awkward and self-conscious arms-control proposals and in some useful studies of the problem; the second in decisions to deploy both MIRV and ABM systems. SALT is rooted in the interplay of these contesting impulses.

Arms control is a rhetorical objective of big governments, but rarely an operational one. Arms control becomes a serious matter only when directly linked to national security. SALT, for example, could never have been seeded by the Arms Control and Disarmament Agency: ACDA's influence within the Washington system is just too narrow. It was when the Defense Department was able to show that various goals could be better achieved by limiting some systems and canceling others that restricting strategic arms became respectable, even important.

McNamara recalls "becoming convinced around the time of the partial test ban treaty [1963] that we should accept more of the risks arising from arms limitation." About that time, he began making statements warning against the dangers of an uninhibited arms race and stressing the virtues of mutual deterrence.

In 1964, the United States took its first halting steps toward limiting strategic arms. In January, President Johnson wrote to Khrushchev about liquidating some old bombers. On March 19, Adrian ("Butch") Fisher, ACDA's Deputy Director, formally put forward a "bomber bonfire" scheme at a session of the Eighteen Nation Disarmament Conference (ENDC) in Geneva, proposing that an equal number of American B-47's and Soviet TU-16's should be removed from the operational inventory at the rate of 20 per month over a period of two years. Since both aircraft were obsolescent, the Americans were suggesting very little. Moreover, Washington had already scheduled the destruction of the B-47's and had even made public its intention of doing so. In short, the United States offered to take a step jointly that it was going to take on its own. The proposal accomplished nothing, other than to give conference wits some fresh material; someone put up a variant suggesting that the Americans and Russians jointly deposit these old bombers, one by one, in Lake Geneva.

Of no greater consequence was Washington's famous "freeze" initiative. In August of 1964, the United States suggested freezing the "number and characteristics" of strategic nuclear offensive and defensive vehicles. Besides limiting numbers, Washington advo-

cated a ban on novel systems. Predictably, the proposal foundered on its provisions for on-site inspection. (For example, resident
inspectors would be stationed at production sources.) Moscow
called the idea "obstrusive" and, of course, rejected it.

A senior American official closely involved in this affair says that
the idea of mutual inventory controls by inspection was really
no more acceptable to Americans than to the Russians. In effect,
he said, by its proposal, the United States sought to satisfy the
rhetorical commitment to arms control while using verification as
the means of assuring that nothing would happen. Looking back,
this official now says that both the Americans and the Russians
had a kind of "let's get together for lunch" attitude toward the
subject at that time; each side knew the other was not entirely
serious about it.

In Washington, serious people, especially in ACDA and the CIA,
kept busy trying to design effective, if not ideal, agreements. The
question was how to inhibit production, this presumably being
the best way both to limit deployment and to preclude clandestine
deployment of strategic weapons.

The cheerless experience of the 1964 *tentatives* generated thinking about fresh approaches. Starting in 1965, in-house arms-control
experts began to ask themselves a different question. Instead of
focusing on how to control production, they wondered what
might be done to limit deployment that would avoid the barrier
reef of on-site inspection. Why not, they concluded, just limit
those things, like big ABM systems and land-based missiles, that
could be counted by satellite cameras. Holding verification to
national rather than on-site means might maneuver the issue onto
negotiable ground. Cheating, it was agreed, would be possible, but
probably not worthwhile except on a scale large enough to be
observed. Thoughts on these lines were informally recorded on
bits of paper.

These bits of paper were sufficient to move the Joint Chiefs to
protest: Arms-control buffs, they declared, were ignoring the
problems of cloud cover over Russia, as well as of camouflage and
other techniques of concealment. Such objections, however, flew
in the face of CIA experience in monitoring Soviet missile deployments. Gradually, the attitude of the Chiefs began to change, at
least with regard to monitoring fixed and unimproved weapons. As

the ACDA–CIA case developed coherence, the Chiefs shifted ground, contending that while verifiable limits might be set on fixed, single-warhead ICBM's, no such scheme could be extended to cover upgraded—that is, MIRV'd—systems.

Meanwhile, even as McNamara was beginning to urge restraint and managing to hold strategic programs at current levels, the other impulse—to counter whatever Moscow (and Peking) might hatch—was gathering force. What the United States did, partly in response to that impulse, was to opt for MIRV and ABM systems, which doubtless made a certain amount of sense at the time. MIRV, in fact, seems to have gone forward with few demurrals, let alone organized opposition, from any side. But hindsight shows these deployment decisions to have been of dubious merit and, indeed, vulnerable to criticism. Enthoven, who ran Systems Analysis at the time, and his colleague, Smith, write:

> The fact that an assured-destruction capability is so basic to U.S. national security dictated that requirements calculations be made on the basis of *extremely conservative* assumptions. This conservative bias produced two major results. First, it led to the buying of very large forces. In fact, between 1961 and 1969, U.S. assured-destruction capability in being remained consistently higher than the levels judged adequate by the Secretary of Defense and the President.[4]

And Lyndon Johnson, in an unguarded moment, could say in the spring of 1967, some sixteen months before the first flight tests of the Poseidon and Minuteman III MIRV's:

> I wouldn't want to be quoted on this—but we've spent $35 or $40 billion on the space program. And if nothing else had come out of it except the knowledge we've gained from space photography, it would be worth ten times what the whole program has cost. Because tonight, we know how many missiles the enemy has. And, it turns out, our guesses were way off. We were doing things we didn't need to do. We were building things we didn't need to build. We were harboring fears we didn't need to harbor.[5]

At that moment, ABM's and MIRV's were years away from deployment; indeed, the ABM deployment decision had yet to be taken. These, too, were "things we didn't need to do," based upon fears "we didn't need to harbor." In 1968, for example, Washington determined that its forces "had an assured capability to destroy nearly 50 percent of the Soviet population and nearly 80 percent of its industrial capacity in a retaliatory attack—much higher than the . . . levels . . . used for planning purposes."[6]

Another novelty of 1965 was the entry into the strategic lexicon of the Greater-Than-Expected Threat (GET). The term, or concept, signifies an enemy capability that exceeds the "high end" of the range of threat in the National Intelligence Estimates (NIE's). Acceptance of the concept meant laying down an orderly process of planning how to hedge against it. The question was how to hedge: whether by deploying new or additional systems, or by continuing research and development of new systems but not deploying them unless or until the improbable GET began to emerge. McNamara, in his 1966 posture statement, said:

> To hedge against the possibility of . . . a greater-than-expected threat, we now propose to accelerate the development of the Poseidon missile (which was initiated last year) and move forward on the development of new penetration aids. The timing of a decision to produce and deploy the Poseidon and the new penetration aids would depend upon how this threat actually evolved.[7]

The threat against which Poseidon was supposedly designed failed to evolve. Yet Washington decided to deploy it. Similarly, Washington decided to deploy both Poseidon and Minuteman III. (They were not publicly called MIRV's then, but rather penetration aids.)

The Greater-Than-Expected-Threat was supposed to represent both the offensive and missile-defense potential of the adversary. In fact, it was Soviet ABM activity, real and imagined, that inspired the concept. Precisely which Soviet activity contributed most to American anxieties is not entirely clear. It is a point on which people's memories are not fully reliable, on which judgment tends to be subjective. As noted, some officials were disturbed most by the Galosh ABM system around Moscow, others by the fear that the Tallinn air-defense system was really designed, or also designed, to knock down attacking missiles.

On November 7, 1964, the Russians paraded Galosh in Moscow. The Tallinn system was already under construction. Two months later, in his 1965 posture statement, McNamara revealed America's intention to develop "a new, larger submarine launched missile designated the Poseidon." Understandably, he said nothing about independently targeted warheads, noting euphemistically that the system's "larger payload would permit it to carry a much greater weight of penetration aids, and thereby to penetrate heavily defended urban/industrial targets."[8]

Such, indeed, was the role envisioned for MIRV's. An Air Force study in 1958 had looked ahead to ballistic-missile defense, suggesting a number of hedges and noting that the ultimate solution might be multiple re-entry vehicles (MRV's).[9] With time, America's ABM research encouraged the designers of long-range missiles to plunge into the MRV technology. Briefly, by the early 1960s Washington was pitting two technologies—ABM and MRV/MIRV—against one another.

Americans had flattered themselves that the Russians, in building up their forces, would follow the strategic path they had traced, and to a degree the Russians did—hardening their ICDM's and developing a Polaris-type nuclear submarine. But by deploying Galosh—doing something America hadn't done and didn't plan to do—the Russians startled the Americans. Galosh, a technologically deplorable system, may have been one of the most counterproductive weapons ever built. It encouraged Washington to overreact to Tallinn. In turn, American fears of both systems fueled the argument in Washington to deploy both MIRV and ABM. In effect, Galosh and Tallinn established a rationale for MIRV and imparted strong, if irrational, pressures for ABM deployment.

What the Americans saw in 1965 was, they feared, just the top of the iceberg. The existence of Galosh, of large missile- and space-tracking radars, and, withal, of Tallinn seemed to betray a broad Soviet ABM research-and-development program that, in time, would produce refinements leading to extensive protection of all urban Russia.

Galosh and Tallinn set off fierce controversy within the national-security bureaucracy. The clash of opinion showed up in the National Intelligence Estimates, and in notes appended to these documents. The NIE's are the responsibility of the U.S.

Intelligence Board, whose members include, besides the CIA, the DIA (Defense Intelligence Agency), the State Department's Bureau of Intelligence & Research, the National Security Agency (NSA), the Atomic Energy Commission, and the FBI. (The last three agencies take part only on matters of direct concern to them.) But the three services also have a role, and they append notes to the NIE's, even though the cover list of the documents does not name them. A former Pentagon official says that the NIE's on Galosh and Tallinn were taken seriously by many people less for their analysis than for what they revealed about agency positions. For rigorous analysis, he says, you would talk directly to CIA experts.

From 1964 to 1966 the CIA was predicting a major expansion of Galosh, a view shared by most Pentagon analysts. Fear of an improved long-range Galosh interceptor missile took hold and, in the words of a former ACDA bureaucrat, "began to drive the MIRV issue." CIA views started to change—and the tone of the NIE's as well—when the expected big ABM-type radars failed to appear elsewhere in Russia. Galosh, it seemed, would be confined to Moscow.

McNamara recalls that "MIRV was entirely a reaction to Galosh, not Tallinn, which," he also recalls, "was never taken seriously. MIRV . . . was directed against an extended Galosh, despite estimates that the system probably would not be expanded. It was then," he adds, "that MIRV developed its impulsion. We began to explore its feasibility as an ABM penetrator. We would not have been able to cover Soviet targets without such a penetrator."

Others disagree. A former colleague of McNamara's, then in Systems Analysis, says that at this time (between 1964 and 1965) a large part of the bureacracy felt that Tallinn had "possibilities," but not Galosh. Then, in 1966, an NIE appeared which said flatly that Tallinn was nothing more than an air-defense system. Dissenting notes were appended.

Ivan Selin, who was then in Systems Analysis and later ran it, says:

The NIE's always contained disagreement on Tallinn. The Navy said it was just an anti-aircraft system. The Army said it had

ABM potential. The Air Force waffled—didn't want to suggest that its missiles couldn't penetrate. [The Strategic Air Command later took the darkest possible view of Tallinn.] The CIA, the only disinterested agency, always took a negative view of Tallinn's ABM potential, while the DIA [a JCS-oriented organization] tended, by and large, to go along with the Army and Air Force views. All points of view were predictable and reflected the interests of the agencies involved.

A very-much-involved ex-senior official now says that the NIE's for the most part ascribed a sizable ABM potential to Tallinn; although these estimates did change, the shift was never enough to make any difference. He, too, agrees that the argument was subjective, never really analytical. Many of the agencies felt that in deploying so many of Tallinn's SA-5 missiles (about 1000) against a declining bomber threat, the Russians were either "incredibly stupid," or planning to upgrade the system to an ABM role. For the Russians to be that "stupid" seemed unlikely. This attitude appears to have missed the point, for the Russians, besides having a strong predilection for air defense, were doubtless far from convinced that America's bomber threat was actually declining.

Whether Galosh or Tallinn supplied the larger push behind MIRV doesn't matter much now. What does matter is the almost certain inevitability of Poseidon and Minuteman III. Deploying MIRV's suited most points of view, aroused little opposition, solved a few problems cheaply, and last, though not least, fuzzed the conflict between the competing strategies of assured destruction and damage limitation.

At first, MIRV was seen and even labeled as a penetration aid— "penaid" in the jargon. Penaids were and are part of the multiple re-entry package. They include coated balloons that, when released, show up on radar screens like warheads. The re-entry vehicle may also release a cloud of light objects called chaff, which, at high altitudes, also deceives defensive radars. Closer in, other decoys can baffle such relatively primitive radars as those of the early Galosh system.

The shift toward assured destruction inspired ultraconservative planning assumptions. Nothing could be left to chance. McNamara demanded "high confidence" in meeting the assured destruction criteria. He decided against allowing decoys to figure into scenarios in which enemy ABM's might be a factor. His systems analysts were convinced that penaids would "use up" part of an opponent's ABM; chaff and other decoys might saturate its data-handling capability, thus collapsing the system's "brain." Such a tactic, however, would be less reliable than McNamara's preference for "exhausting" the system by shooting more warheads (MIRV's) at it than it had launchers.

During this period, McNamara's grip on the Pentagon was being jostled by the services and various baronial figures in Congress. The Army was trying to maneuver approval for a thick urban ABM system. The Navy wanted more of everything: more nuclear submarines, carriers, and a fleet of missile-firing surface ships. The Air Force, then the most politically adroit of the services, was pushing for a larger ICBM than Minuteman, the land-based variant of Poseidon, and for a new strategic bomber and superhardened missile silos. The military's shopping lists pointed to a damage-limiting strategy and the dizzying costs that would go with it. For McNamara and his colleagues in the Office of the Secretary of Defense, the virtues of restraint were fortified by the deepening commitment in Vietnam and the spiraling costs that would go with it.

MIRV was put to the service of restraint, and became a strong bureaucratic instrument for discouraging other new systems and higher numbers of systems. McNamara's analysts showed that multiple, independently targeted warheads could perform both damage-limiting and assured-destruction tasks as well or better than other weapons and far more cheaply. Expanding Soviet industry, argued the Air Force and Navy, dictated an expanding assured-destruction target list—hence, more offensive weaponry. Systems analysts replied that MIRV's would considerably extend target coverage without increasing the number of missiles. In answer to the Joint Chiefs' worst-case scenario—the destruction of Minuteman and a portion of the B-52 force—the analysts proved that Poseidon alone could perform the entire task of achieving assured destruction. To the argument that failure to buy a range of new weapons would deny the United States a damage-limiting capability, the analysts calculated that MIRV's with improved accuracies would score well against hardened targets. What then of the soft urban targets and the Greater-Then-Expected Threat? A Galosh missile, DDR&E and the Joint Chiefs had argued, could knock out three incoming MRV's from a Polaris submarine because these are so closely spaced. MIRV's, because they are more widely spaced and separately targeted, silenced that concern, too.

MIRV, it seemed, was the *rara avis* of the arsenal—competent, versatile, cost-effective, and no threat to stability. Some scholastics, who now see MIRV in a more ominous light, had no reservations at the time. Moscow, they felt, could easily measure how many warheads the United States had by monitoring flight tests of MIRV. These would disclose the number of re-entry vehicles, which, when multiplied by the number of missiles, would give the Soviet Union a precise count of America's total offensive missile capability. It is the unknown, not the known, that fosters instability.

McNamara also struck a blow for stability by deciding to outfit Poseidon with ten to fourteen small MIRV's; in doing so, he chose to reject another version of the system that, using just three much bigger ones, would have packed a wallop so enormous as to inspire Soviet fears of a first-strike weapon. Minuteman III, the other MIRV'd system, pleased Systems Analysis because its warhead was sleek and easy to decoy; the warhead for Minuteman II was, for technical reasons, much more difficult to decoy effectively.

Stated briefly, MIRV abruptly emerged as the most-efficient way of delivering a payload. McNamara was always inclined to compare United States and Soviet forces in terms of numbers of warheads; he normally calculated a U.S. advantage ranging from three or four to one (with bombers included). Even with the Russians trying to catch up, MIRV would permit him both to continue claiming the advantage and to hold out against pressure, coming from the services and elsewhere, to expand the strategic inventory.

By this point, it was axiomatic in the circles around McNamara that instead of deploying new weapons against the Greater-Than-Expected-Threat, the United States should hedge against it with research and development. MIRV became an exception to the rule. The ABM, in a sense, became another.

ABM was always a weapon in search of a role. Neither the Sentinel system approved for deployment by Johnson and McNamara, nor the very similar Safeguard system adopted by the Nixon team has been coherently linked to a rational mission. The Nixon people hit on the right ABM role—defending Minuteman—but sustained a design that eludes the role. In 1971, Donald Hornig, who had been Johnson's science adviser, made the point: Although Presidents may change, Secretaries of Defense may come and go, the philosophies enunciated by political leaders may change, the design of our ABM system hardly changes at all.[10]

Almost certainly, the misdirected ABM program has been a useful bargaining instrument at SALT. Little more, if anything, could be claimed for it. In fairness, it is just as true that many of the arguments raging around ABM deployment in the mid-1960s had intellectual merit.

The notion of ABM crept into favor as the prospect of civil defense disappeared. Detection of Galosh, the Chinese explosions, and the Russian buildup set the stage. Three separate roles for an American ABM swam to the surface: (1) a thick population defense against Russian missiles; (2) a thin population defense set up clearly against Chinese rather than Soviet missiles, which would also offer protection against an accidental launch from anywhere; (3) defense of Minuteman sites. The first two options fitted a damage-limiting strategy, but threatened stable deterrence (by possibly sapping Moscow's confidence in its own second-strike forces). The third, or hard-site, option (defending Minuteman) was nicely suited to assured destruction, since it would protect a major part of America's deterrent.

Hard site made sense but got short shrift. Predictably, the thick defense against Russia drew the heaviest support—from the military, from DDR&E, and from the services' allies among committee chairmen on Capitol Hill. McNamara and some of his associates, notably a few systems analysts, were fiercely opposed to the thick system, but impressed by the argument for a thin area ABM as a defense against China and accidental launches. At this early stage, the hard-site option had few partisans.

It was decided to deploy the thin anti-China system, grandly called Sentinel. The twisting, random course of this affair shows off brilliantly the interplay of clashing Washington interests as well as the all-too-familiar pattern of how unresponsive a major decision can be to the merits of what it involves. Whereas MIRV seemed at least in line with the logic of the new U.S. direction, the decision to develop Sentinel showed floundering. At best, it seemed a small, hopefully harmless, gesture—one that might shut off pressure for larger ABM deployment.

In a bureaucratic sense, the ABM issue may have been the toughest McNamara ever dealt with. "At one point," he recalls, "almost everyone in the building [the Pentagon]was for ABM, except Cy Vance and me." (Vance was then Deputy Secretary of Defense.) The Joint Chiefs were putting a $10 billion price tag on the thick system. McNamara felt that $40 billion was a more realistic figure; he was dead set against deploying any specifically anti-Russian ABM system, which, he felt, would only encourage Moscow, and at far less cost, to make a compensatory increase in Soviet offense.

Although the Joint Chiefs offered a solid front, only the Army cared much about missile defense; no other path to a strategic role was available to the Army. Not surprisingly, the Army wanted the heaviest possible deployment: in effect, national coverage, with the full panoply of huge and small radars, long and short-range interceptor missiles, and the exquisitely refined computer and data-processing hardware upon which the structure would rely.

In 1955, the Army had asked the Bell Laboratories to make an ABM-feasibility study. Could you shoot a bullet with another bullet? Ever since, the Army has largely controlled the design of ABM, which has assured that the emphasis, as well as most of the money, was devoted to defending cities, instead of Air Force Minuteman sites. A few systems analysts fretted, aware that the cost of defending cities is exceeded only by its difficulty. Defending ICBM fields is a simpler matter. For one thing, in defending ICBM's, there is psychologically less pressure to respond, and, hence, more reaction time available before firing ABM's; the radars thus have more time to discriminate between warheads and decoys. For another, the required level of performance is far lower; a single warhead, if it penetrates, can destroy a city, or most of it, but the loss of a certain number of Minuteman would not necessarily be critical. Finally, the hardware for defending Minuteman sites is far less elaborate and costly than the more exotic systems needed for urban defense. The radars would be less vulnerable to attacking missiles, the computer and data-processing equipment simpler, more reliable, and easier to develop.

No such sensible considerations were to deflect the course of the ABM-deployment decision. The Air Force interest in the issue was limited to discouraging hard-site defense of its Minuteman force. To defend Minuteman, after all, might narrow chances of gaining approval for cherished new systems, especially for larger offensive missiles. So the Air Force, for purely internal reasons, supported the concept of city defense. The Navy, too, treated the issue as a function of its own interest, in this case gaining approval for a sea-based ABM. Such a system, the Navy argued, would have the political advantage of permitting us to defend our NATO allies and Japan from enemy missiles. Of the Navy, Morton Halperin writes that it

> wished to proceed with ABM in a way which kept open the possibility that later additions to this system would include a Navy-controlled sea-based system. In return for Army support of the Navy system, the Navy was prepared to support an Army land-based system. Moreover, the Navy was concerned, as was the Air Force, with maintaining the system of unanimous Joint Chiefs of Staff support for Service procurement programs.[11]

Not that it would matter, but the State Department and ACDA strongly opposed ABM deployment. Both agencies feared the instabilities that might follow. The State Department also worried that once the United States deployed ABM, its NATO allies would ask for similar protection. Defending European cities against the 700-odd Soviet missiles targeted against them, if feasible at all, would pose a technical problem of staggering complexity.

In any case, the State Department was excluded from the decision-making process. Not even Rusk was consulted, or even informed, at the various stages. Under Johnson, the forum for focusing high-level attention on major security issues was the famous "Tuesday lunch" at the White House. Besides the President, the regular participants were Rusk, McNamara, Richard Helms (Director of the CIA), Walt W. Rostow (Johnson's Special Assistant for National Security), plus a note-taker. The agenda was arranged a day or so before, and each man arrived briefed and equipped with a working paper prepared by his staff. Discussion was lively, the notes later summarized and distributed for policy guidance to a limited group of officials spread around the government.

The ABM issue never reached the Tuesday lunch agenda. The question of deployment, as well as the political pressures animating it, would remain a private matter between Johnson and McNamara. Though not consulted, Rusk did have views. He recalls having "always disliked ABM's in principle," and he says "I always felt that it was a system unlikely to work and potentially destabalizing."

Across the Potomac, McNamara and Systems Analysis were, in 1965, developing an attitude toward ABM best described as ambivalent. They were closest to the issue, knew most about it, and faced directly the pressure from the Joint Chiefs and from the growing congressional bias in favor of ABM.

Rather tentatively, McNamara and Systems Analysis began to review steps to block the thick anti-Russian ABM, head off the congressional problem before it became serious, and do something about ABM that would do no violence to stability, strategy, or cost effectiveness. His closest civilian advisers of the time now say that McNamara was from the start unimpressed by the argument for the modest hard-site option of defending Minuteman. He felt, they say, that anything of the kind could be easily overcome by Soviet offense. Moreover, the potential SS-9 threat to Minuteman had not clearly emerged, and he was unwilling to deploy hard-site ABM's against a Greater-Than-Expected-Threat in this form.

McNamara's aversion to other alternatives squarely posed the option of deploying a thin-area ABM designed to protect cities against Chinese missiles and accidental launches. At least initially, the idea made a certain amount of sense to some systems analysts and to several outside consultants. It also made some sense to McNamara. Which of the arguments impressed him most is not clear.

Even in Washington, most people think that McNamara saw an anti-China ABM simply as a hedge against the thick coverage he feared. Still, he must have recognized, as others did, that to build a system that was unambiguously anti-China was just not possible. One has only to look at the globe to see that attacking missiles from Russia or China would travel an almost identical trajectory.

Could Moscow then be expected to regard Washngton's anti-China ABM deployment as other than a start toward a large anti-Russian system? The hardware, whether called anti-China or anti-Russia, would be the same.

His former colleagues cite two other considerations that influenced McNamara. First, he, like everyone else, read Lin Piao, and he may have taken seriously the prospect of eventual Chinese lunacy. Second, they suggest, there was continuing pressure on the Office of the Secretary of Defense to keep some faith with America's other strategy—damage limitation. "The Chiefs," recalls one analyst, "kept coming at him with damage limiting proposals involving new offensive weapons. It's hard to say no all the time. He would knock down most of these proposals with the argument that they were asking him to spend ten dollars for something the Russians could offset by spending one dollar. Yet he didn't reject the damage limiting options, *per se,* insisting only that they meet his test of cost effetciveness."

This position left McNamara vulnerable on the issue of an anti-China, anti-accident ABM deployment. The thin system, it appeared, would at modest cost buy a good deal of insurance against an irrational Chinese act. Never mind that the Chinese threat was at least a decade away; or that Chinese planners might even design a means of penetrating a first-generation American ABM.

The best clues to the path of McNamara's thought on ABM were contained in a bureaucratic innovation of his, the Draft Presidential Memorandum (DPM). DPM's were highly classified studies, usually of a weapon, prepared by Systems Analysis. Most DPM's went through several versions; they were actually intended less for the President than as guidance for involved agencies. On ABM (and other sensitive issues), McNamara occasionally communicated directly to the President through "out-of-cycle" memoranda; these were ultrasensitive documents and seen by only a small handful of people.

In the summer of 1965, a DPM on the anti-China system was written at McNamara's direction. But, according to one former systems analyst, "McNamara took a holding position, and the DPM was never sent to the White House." Apparently, his thinking on the issue shifted back and forth. A year later, in the summer of 1966, just as Systems Analysis itself was becoming leery of the anti-China ABM, McNamara sent an out-of-cycle memorandum to the President. In it, he identified three roles for ABM: anti-China, anti-accident, defense of Minuteman. The memorandum expressed a bias in favor of deploying a thin anti-China and anti-accident ABM. It may be no coincidence that in May, shortly before this out-of-cycle memorandum was sent to the President, China exploded its first thermonuclear device.

Just at this moment—the late spring and summer of 1966—congressional pressure abruptly became critical. First the House, then the Senate, approved funds ($167.9 million) for procurement of ABM hardware. McNamara had not, of course, requested the money, and he telephoned one committee chairman to protest angrily against the action, making clear in the bluntest possible language that he had no intention of spending one dime of the appropriated funds.

Round him raged the arguments, old and new, for deployment. ABM, even if it couldn't prevent Soviet penetration, would at least "deny the enemy a free ride"—that is, force Moscow to invest heavily in penetration aids. Failure to deploy would deny the United States operating knowledge of a vital weapons technology, leaving the field to the Russians. The Army, DDR&E, and other parts of the Pentagon feared that only by deploying could they sustain ABM research and development. The laboratory groups must be kept intact and busy.

Vietnam aside, ABM deployment had become the consuming problem within the Pentagon. As the tempo of maneuvering and debate rose, McNamara's doubts deepened. His apparent ambivalence, even on anti-China deployment, had shifted to the tough, negative line for which he is best remembered. Still, however hard his position, he could not control the ABM issue. He might have contained antagonistic forces within the Pentagon, but the deployment decision lay ultimately with Lyndon Johnson.

The President shared McNamara's bias for restraint and for capping the arms race, but not his aversion to the ABM. Johnson, after all, had to deal at the political level with such congressional powers as Richard Russell (then chairman of the Senate Armed Services Committee) and John Stennis in the Senate and George H. Mahon in the House. What's more, after long association with these men, Johnson respected their judgment. Some idea of the situation can be had from Russell's oft-repeated statement regarding ABM, that if only two human beings were to survive a nuclear war, he wanted them to be Americans.[12]

Morton Halperin, who was there, wrote later:

> Johnson does not appear to have seen any major national security stakes in the decision whether or not to deploy the ABM. It was an issue that generated intense passion in others and hence one of importance to him, but he does not appear to have seen any intrinsic importance in terms of . . . American security. He was, apparently, concerned about possible Chinese irrationality, having recently received a number of reports that the Soviets believed that the Chinese were dangerous. Thus an ABM against China, while not imperative, made sense to him.[13]

Although never in the picture, Dean Rusk feels that the "China issue was dragged in by the heels and became a makeweight for the decision." Nobody, not Rusk, not McNamara, nor anyone else, knows how Johnson weighed the various pressures to deploy something against the argument not to deploy. Clearly, he was impressed by the dramatic gesture of his old congressional colleagues in appropriating funds for ABM that his Administration had not sought. Everyone knew that Johnson had frequent telephone conversations with Russell, Mahon, and others. But, inevitably, Johnson was also looking ahead to the 1968 elections. Having helped mightily to foster the notion of a missile gap in the late 1950s—an issue used to advantage against Nixon in the 1960 election—he obviously wished to avoid facing a Republican charge of an ABM gap. Like McNamara, he had decided that the moment for *serious* talks with Moscow about arms limitations had come. Unlike McNamara, he was not convinced that an American ABM would discourage prospects for such talks.

A decision of some kind could be put off no longer. Autumn in Washington is a time for thrashing out the budget for the next fiscal year. The autumn of 1966 seemed to be the moment for deciding whether to request funds for ABM deployment. McNamara was to do all he could to avoid, or delay, deployment; at the same time, he began the process that would lead to talks with the Russians.

McNamara's first move was to hold long private talks with key Pentagon civilians, trying to bring them round to his viewpoint. For a time, at least, even Johnny Foster acquiesced in the no-deployment position.

McNamara was to have three meetings with the President in Texas, chiefly to discuss the budget and Vietnam. The meetings were scheduled for November 3, November 10, and December 6. Shortly before the decisive meeting of December 6, he called in the chief executive officers of AT&T, Bell Laboratories, and Western Electric—the contractors for the Nike-X ABM America was deploying. He asked what they thought about deployment, after assuring them that anything said would remain strictly confidential. He knew, he said, that a leak casting doubt on the reliability or readiness of Nike-X would rebound to the disadvantage of their stockholders. According to the one recorded version of the meeting, he "asked for their private judgment. Don't deploy, they said reluctantly, it's not ready. McNamara regarded the self-denying recommendation as a historic act of industrial statesmanship."[14]

This account squares with McNamara's recollection. Another participant in the meeting remembers it in somewhat different terms, saying: "Fred Kappell, then the head of AT&T, observed that nobody would get rich from the contract, and he took no direct position on deployment." McNamara, he recalls, said: "We may decide to go ahead. If so, I'll want you to be in charge. Don't let them [the Pentagon] impose an IOC* on you. Don't worry about an arbitrary date." McNamara, by this account, was trying to relieve the contractors from any pressure to force the pace of their work, while they in turn listened carefully, but declined to take a position on the deployment issue itself.

His first two meetings with Johnson at the ranch in Texas were inconclusive. The second session, on November 10, was followed by a press conference at which McNamara was asked a number of questions about ABM deployment. He used the occasion to reveal the Soviet deployment of the Galosh ABM system around Moscow. He also called attention to the China threat, and said: "We concluded that it's much too early to take a decision against

---

* Initial Operating Capability; this signifies the date set for a weapons system to come into service.

the Chinese threat and we haven't arrived at a decision on any other deployment. We'll continue our discussions on this subject in the weeks to come."

For initiates, the Texas press conference disclosed a McNamara ploy in trying to head off ABM. He asserted the Administration's intention of procuring a new missile, Poseidon, though without describing its novel MIRV quality. Clearly, he was trying to go public with the argument he was making in private to the President: that the best way to hedge against a Soviet ABM was to improve U.S. offense instead of matching the Russian folly.

The die was cast in the form of a tenuous and perishable compromise worked out by McNamara and Vance in the meeting with Johnson in Austin on December 6. All the Joint Chiefs were also present, and they unanimously urged on the President an anti-Russian ABM defense of American cities, a system larger than the anti-China alternative and one with sturdy growth potential. The ground on which McNamara's hard position rested was crumbling. He had already cut from the next year's budget funds for initial ABM procurement that had been requested by the Joint Chiefs. At this meeting, it was decided to restore the money, about $375 million. McNamara then offered the President his compromise, a suggestion that the Administration hold off spending the money, or making a firm decision on what type of ABM system to deploy, until the State Department had explored with Moscow the idea of talks on limiting strategic arms, especially ABM's. Johnson bought the compromise, but the Joint Chiefs and other ABM adherents now felt reasonably secure that the path to deployment had been cleared.

On returning to the Pentagon, McNamara immediately called the State Department. Rusk was out of town, so he talked to Nicholas de B. Katzenbach, then Under Secretary of State, and Llewellyn E. "Tommy" Thompson, who was returning to Moscow in January for a second tour as Ambassador. McNamara told Thompson he was authorized to contact the Russians and, if possible, to get negotiations started. The three then called Johnson in Texas just to be "doubly sure," as one of them put it, that "L. B. J. was fully on board." He was.

For closely involved figures, like Garthoff and the late Tommy Thompson, the days and weeks that followed marked the precise beginning of SALT. It was an intensely focused, remarkably eventful period. Though not due to arrive in Moscow until January 11, Thompson, almost immediately after his meeting with McNamara and Katzenbach in December, contacted Soviet Ambassador Dobrynin to explore informally the possibility of talks. When they met, Thompson put the stress on ABM's while Dobrynin, by this time instructed, noted the need to discuss offensive weapons as well.

On arriving in Moscow, Thompson proposed to the Soviet leadership that talks be carried on secretly in the two capitals. His initiative was followed up by Johnson in a letter along similar lines that was sent to Kosygin on January 27.

While Thompson was making contact with the Russians, Garthoff and a few colleagues from State and Defense began working up a U.S. position for the talks the Administration was pressing so vigorously. For a few days in January, they worked almost around the clock, dealing with all the issues—ABM limitations, a MIRV ban, Tallinn upgrade, and mobile missiles, as well as others. Among other things, the work of Garthoff's group showed sensitivity to the Soviet requirement that talks, if they should develop, would have to cover offensive, as well as defensive, weapons.

One who remembers the paper that flowed from this enterprise says it was "a good job," but that "a caveat was attached at a high level in the form of an option to deploy an anti-China ABM system."

Most of this activity, especially the work of Garthoff's group, was very closely held. Whole agencies, like ACDA, were kept entirely in the dark. So, initially, were the Joint Chiefs. McNamara, according to one of his very senior colleagues, "feared that something like this would trigger a lot of conflict with the Chiefs, so he insisted that it be kept small and private." Probably no more than a dozen or so people in the State and Defense Departments were fully aware of what was happening.

On January 24, in his budget message to Congress, Johnson said he would continue intensive development of the Nike-X system, but would "take no action now" on deployment. The following day, McNamara and General Earle G. Wheeler, Chairman of the Joint Chiefs, testified before the Senate Subcommittee on Appropriations. McNamara presented his posture statement, and even now remembers precisely what he said about ABM deployment; he can almost recall appropriate page numbers of the hearings. "The language," he says in a rather understated way, "was very carefully chosen. I wanted to leave open the loophole that even a failure to start negotiations would not necessarily mean that a decision to deploy would be taken."

The language was actually composed by McNamara and Vance. The relevant passage reads:

> We propose: (1) To pursue with undiminished vigor the development, test and evaluation of the Nike-X system . . . but to take no action now to deploy the system. (2) To initiate negotiations with the Soviet Union designed, through formal or informal agreement, to limit the deployment of antiballistic missile systems. (3) To reconsider the deployment decision in the event these discussions prove unsuccessful; approximately $375 million has been included in the fiscal year 1968 budget to provide for such actions as may be required at that time. . . .[15]

His posture statement showed McNamara continuing to extol the virtue of better offense. "We must," he said, "for the time being, plan our forces on the assumption that [the Soviets] will have deployed some sort of an ABM system around their major cities by the early 1970s."[16] Deploying Poseidon and Minuteman III, plus developing improved penetration aids—MIRV's—would be the best way "to overwhelm" Soviet ABM complexes.

The subcommittee found his aversion to city defense against Russian missiles to be complete and unshakable. The split between McNamara and the Joint Chiefs on this point also emerged and entered the public record. When the subcommittee chairman, the late Senator Richard Russell, asked specifically for the views of the Joint Chiefs, General Wheeler replied:

> We believe, sir, that we should go ahead now and start to deploy a light defense as a first step. . . . You will recall that last year the Joint Chiefs of Staff recommended deployment [of] an area defense of much of the country, with defense also of [deleted] of the highest density populated areas. We made this recommendation for two reasons. First, we had con-

tinued to watch the growing Soviet ability to destroy our population and our industry, and second, the research and development program on Nike-X had reached a point where we felt that the Nike-X was ready for deployment.[17]

Meanwhile, McNamara continued maneuvering against the anti-Russian system. In late January, he sent to the President a DPM restating his position, but noting the possible utility of ABM defense against China. This, too, was the line he took with the subcommittee, suggesting that "this austere defense could probably preclude damage in the 1970s [from China] almost entirely."[18] He reckoned the cost of such a system at about $3.5 billion, much less than the estimated costs of anti-Soviet deployment.

To counter the Joint Chiefs and their congressional allies, McNamara tried to confront Johnson with other viewpoints compatible with his own. During this tumultuous January, he arranged a confrontation in the Cabinet Room of the White House between the President and all past and current special assistants to the President for Science and Technology (James R. Killian, Jr., George B. Kistiakowski, Jerome B. Wiesner, and Donald F. Hornig), plus the past and current directors of DDR&E (Herbert F. York, Harold Brown, and Johnny Foster). The Joint Chiefs were also present, but McNamara controlled the meeting. He put short, uncomplicated questions to the scientists. Should the government protect the American people against a Soviet missile attack with the kind of ABM hardware then being developed? Everyone, except Foster, was asked to speak and the replies were unanimously negative. (Foster's silence was interpreted as concurrence.) To the question whether an anti-China system should be deployed, opinions differed, but the majority said no.

The pace of activity in February, both between Washington and Moscow and within the executive branch, continued unabated. The Russians announced they were, in fact, deploying an ABM system around Moscow, and boasted of the ease with which incoming American missiles would be knocked down. On February 9, at a news conference in London, Kosygin was asked whether he considered an ABM moratorium possible. He replied that "maybe a defensive system is more expensive than an offensive system, but it is not a cause of the arms race but designed instead to prevent the death of people." The best course, he said, was to "seek renunciation of nuclear armament and the destruction of nuclear weapons." Five days later, *Pravda* issued a kind of clarification, saying that "the Soviet Government was ready to discuss the problem of averting a new arms race, both in offensive and defensive weapons."[19] Nonetheless, inhibiting offense, not defense, was to be a hard Russian position for the next two and one-half years.

Rusk answered Kosygin immediately. On February 10, in a televised statement, he said that ABM deployment by both great powers, followed as it would undoubtedly be by increases in offensive missiles to saturate the ABM's, could lead to "new plateaus of expenditures . . . with no great change in the . . . strategic situation."

So far, Washington's position on linking offense to defense had been studiously vague. But on February 18, Thompson saw Kosygin and communicated willingness by the United States to discuss limits on offensive systems. Kosygin's response, as transmitted by Thompson, was "vaguely positive," according to one of the very few Americans who read it. At this point, neither ACDA nor the Joint Chiefs had as yet been "cut in on the action," as one who was deeply involved puts it, and McNamara and Rusk were personally clearing the messages to Thompson.

The White House meeting with the scientists had impressed the President. It bought some time, but not a great deal. Everything now depended on arranging talks with the Russians, and the message from Moscow fostered some optimism. Preparations continued, and by March most of the U.S. delegation had been selected. Thompson was to be chairman (a role for which he would have been admirably suited in 1969, when SALT began, had his declining health permitted). The late John McNaughton, a close associate of McNamara's, was to represent the civilian side of the Pentagon; at the time an as yet unnamed general would have represented the Joint Chiefs; and Harold Brown, then the Secretary of the Air Force, almost certainly would have represented the scientific community, just as he does now. The State Department delegate was to have been Garthoff, who had done so much of the preparatory work and who served as executive secretary of the delegation, during Phase I of SALT.

By March, of course, ACDA and the Joint Chiefs of Staff were involved, though not closely. The United States proposed holding the talks in Moscow, as this seemed the best way for the McNamara/Rusk group, working through Thompson, to maintain tight control. Put differently, various senior officials sought to minimize ACDA's role. Although its Deputy Director, Adrian Fisher, was widely admired, ACDA itself was held in low repute by General Wheeler and others upon whose good will and cooperation a great deal might depend. Thompson, however, had the confidence of every key personality and the Russians as well.

On March 2, Johnson announced that Kosygin had answered his letter of January 27, and agreed to bilateral talks on "means of limiting the arms race in offensive and defensive nuclear missiles." Washington immediately put forward a more formal offer to the Russians, suggesting that, besides ABM's, the talks might set limits on offensive systems, specifically land-based missiles (ICBM's) and submarine-launched missiles (SLBM's).

The day before Thompson delivered this proposal to the Soviet Government, its content was disclosed to other NATO governments. It was during this consultation in Brussels that America's allies first heard of the MIRV program. It fell to Herbert (Pete) Scoville, then running ACDA's Science and Technology Bureau, and the versatile Garthoff to describe this exotic multiplier of U.S. strength.

The momentum apparently gathering behind the talks was deceptive; it was generated in Washington, not Moscow. Kosygin's responses committed the Soviet Union to nothing specific, and Washington's optimism was self-induced. McNamara and those allied with him needed the talks. Less-involved skeptics in the Pentagon and State Department saw that the pressure to deploy an ABM would be hard to sidetrack, talks or no talks. They also believed that even if the Russians *were* ready for self-limiting steps, the timing was poor; certainly, the Soviets would find it hard at that moment to bargain with a government that was not only at war with their ally, North Vietnam, but worse, was systematically trying to bomb the country into submission.

Washington exaggerated the appeal its formal willingness to limit U.S. forces would have to Moscow. McNamara, after all, had been scattering the public record with declarations of unilateral restraint; Congress had repeatedly been told that America's ICBM and nuclear submarine forces would not be increased; also, that America would not procure a new strategic bomber. Perhaps unfortunately, the Russians knew nothing then of MIRV. Briefly, with the United States holding a rough strategic advantage of three to one, the Russians had little incentive to join the United States in self-limiting steps. Let Washington exercise restraint, they must have concluded, while the Soviet Union narrows the gap. And that is just about what happened. Until the gap was closed, a Soviet ABM program doubtless seemed a useful hedge against superior U.S. forces and, more important, the potential threat from China. Almost certainly, the Soviet military, especially the Strategic Rocket Forces and the Air Defense Command, strenuously opposed talks with the United States about limiting offensive and defensive missiles. (Even now, the Soviet military dislikes SALT.)

With talks far from assured, the deployment issue remained foremost. And it would be misleading to suggest that the support for ABM was confined to the Joint Chiefs and the Congress. What may be said is that the military and congressional partisans of ABM wanted a big anti-Russian system; the Joint Chiefs, as noted, urged a system with the greatest possible growth potential. Their views coincided with the curious preference of many congressional figures who wanted to defend American cities against Russian (not Chinese) missiles, simply because Galosh might defend Russian cities against American missiles. "Monkey see, monkey do," recalls a former senior official at ACDA.

The argument swirled around McNamara, reaching into various parts of the Pentagon's civilian bureaucracy—Systems Analysis, ISA, and DDR&E. Points of view varied sharply. McNamara had converted some people, partially converted others, failed to influence still others. A few prominent civilian figures supported thick anti-Russian deployment; more of them favored the thin anti-China system. Then, too, support had finally begun to grow, especially in ISA, for the hard-site option of defending Minuteman fields.

A letter to McNamara dated February 21 drew considerable attention within the Pentagon. The writer was Albert Wohlstetter, a pioneer strategist of the nuclear age and certainly among the most rigorous and far-sighted. Wohlstetter, who had met with McNamara frequently in the past, was writing at the suggestion of Alain Enthoven, director of Systems Analysis. Wohlstetter had for long been an advocate of both hard-site ABM and light-area defense against China and accidental launchings. In five and a half closely reasoned pages, he presented the case for a thin anti-China deployment. If his personal preference was to start with a hard-site system, he knew that the design, to say nothing of the hardware, for such a system was not far enough advanced. His language was blunt, occasionally critical of the arguments being used against modest ABM deployment.

The effect of the letter obviously cannot be measured. Added to McNamara's deep respect for Wohlstetter was the force of an admirably presented argument from a man who held no official position and had no ax to grind. Moreover, the argument was one to which McNamara, as noted, had occasionally been drawn.

Just beyond the vortex of all this were assorted bureaucrats urging either no ABM deployment or hard-site deployment. Some apparently pushed for hard site as a means of heading off an area ABM and its destabilizing effects. Others found real virtue in hard site. They had been impressed by the views of people like Wohlstetter, who argued that the best check against the improving Soviet forces would be "to protect the hard fixed elements of [America's] strategic force. . . . Simply adding more vehicles [offensive weapons] is costly and more destabilizing than active defense of these hard points, since increasing vehicles also increases the capacity to strike first."[20]

Hard site fell between two major factions, with one which included the Joint Chiefs, maneuvering for area defense and the other, which included McNamara, arguing that improved offense was the only rational hedge against a Greater-Than-Expected-Threat. Hard site was never clearly rejected. It always turned up as one of the options in McNamara's annual posture statements; but it was never pushed. Hard site, unlike the other options, never in those days had a major bureaucratic constituency (it belatedly does now). Its brightest moment came in the spring of 1967 when one version of a DPM then in preparation argued for Minuteman defense as the best option. A few people in ACDA and the State Department, upon hearing of this document (most of them never saw DPM's), tried to mobilize support for it; but there was no time. A few days later, a new version of the same DPM shot down the hard-site option and restored the bias in favor of anti-China deployment.

In April, Soviet Ambassador Dobrynin sent word to McNamara through an intermediary suggesting a talk. McNamara responded to this singular initiative by offering to meet in his office or home. Dobrynin came alone to McNamara's home and they talked for three hours. Dobrynin then flew to Moscow for consultation. McNamara and the few who knew of this meeting could be excused for hoping that the Soviet leadership, especially Kosygin, who seemed to be handling the matter, were becoming serious about talks and more rigorous about the issues.

The meeting, as it turned out, proved nothing of the sort. There was no follow-up. The Thompson talks in Moscow continued on a desultory, inconclusive course. Indeed, when Thompson returned to the United States in June for the Kosygin visit and the famous Glassboro, New Jersey, summit, he conceded in a news conference that Moscow had not yet set a time and place for talks.

Glassboro was anticlimactic. Kosygin's unyielding attitude reversed the hope, by then guarded, that talks on limiting arms could be arranged in the near term, if at all. One week before Glassboro, China tested another thermonuclear device, a considerably more disturbing event to the Russians than to the Americans.

Dean Rusk recalls that the Americans tackled Kosygin at Glassboro "in a go for broke fashion. There was lots of staff work," he says, and "L.B.J. approved it all before the talks. He was saying, in effect, to Kosygin: 'Just set a day and I'll have McNamara there in Moscow.' Kosygin's problem," Rusk continues, "was that he didn't have a negotiating position. He clearly had no authority to discuss limiting arms, least of all ABM's. He replied, in effect: 'How can you expect me to tell the Russian people they can't defend themselves against your rockets?'"

Johnson had raised the ABM question immediately after lunch on the first day and asked McNamara to take over. In the words of one observer, McNamara "made a long, detailed and impassioned presentation." Russian ABM's, he warned repeatedly, would simply oblige the United States to increase its offense. Kosygin did show interest; he was apparently impressed, if not surprised, by the intensity of the Americans. And he did ask for another meeting, one that had not been on his schedule. The Glassboro experience may have moved Kosygin and some of his colleagues to do what Washington thought they had already been doing—looking hard at the problems of stable deterrence. Glassboro, as Rusk suggests, may have been the start of SALT for the Russians.

Closer to home, Glassboro dissolved any lingering hope of starting talks before the next budget message to Congress. The deployment decision could be put off no longer. In July, a heated debate on the issue erupted in Congress. A few days before, Mc-Namara had called in a small group to discuss a speech announcing ABM deployment. He has never told *anyone* that Johnson instructed him to make such a decision. Yet that is what many of those who were then closest to him believe. Some, in fact, say that certain members of Johnson's staff told *them* that McNamara had been so ordered by the President.

The group with whom McNamara first consulted on the speech included Paul Nitze, Deputy Secretary; the late John McNaughton, then Assistant Secretary for ISA, and Morton Halperin, then a deputy to McNaughton. Halperin was asked to draw up a draft outline of the speech, and McNamara said that he, too, would do one. He and Halperin met the following week. Other drafts were prepared, including one that came down against deployment, and then McNamara put his private speech-writer to work on the final version. At that point, the enterprise disappeared from view; McNamara discussed it with no one, except presumably the President. One of his former colleagues remembers lively betting both ways, "even in the building," about what the speech would finally say. To some, the announcement to deploy an anti-China ABM system came as a genuine surprise, even though the ineluctable path of the issue should by then have been apparent. The opponents of ABM deployment had been routed, although very few of them knew it at the time.

About two weeks before the speech surfaced again, Under Secretary of State Katzenbach called the Pentagon to ask for guidance. The State Department, he said, understood there was to be an ABM announcement. Either give us a copy, he suggested, or make the speech conform to what we tell our allies it will say. As it happened, the European NATO governments had no more than two or three days' notice. McNamara had given a copy of his speech to Rusk, but he showed it to no one else at State.

The speech, when delivered in San Francisco on September 18, kept its audience, the editors of United Press International, on the edge of their chairs until the very end. Right up to the concluding passage, it presented a forcible case for restraint, for stability, and for avoiding pernicious agents of instability, especially ABM's. Indeed, as they listened, the editors must have been silently anticipating headlines the next day proclaiming the Johnson Administration's refusal to bow to pressure to deploy an ABM system. They heard warnings from McNamara about the "mad momentum intrinsic to . . . all new nuclear weaponry"; they heard that uncertainties had mislead us into developing larger forces than we needed, which in turn had inspired the Soviet Union to follow suit. "It is precisely this action-reaction phenomenon that fuels an arms race," McNamara said.

Then, suddenly, the other shoe fell. Although anti-Russian ABM's would be costly, futile, and even dangerous, a light deployment against the future China threat would be "prudent" and "relatively inexpensive."

"We have," he concluded, "decided to go forward with this Chinese-oriented ABM deployment, and we will begin actual production of such a system at the end of this year." The stress was on China, but he noted some "concurrent benefit: a further defense of our Minuteman sites against Soviet attack [and] protection of our population against . . . accidental launch of an intercontinental missile by any of the nuclear powers."

Since neither the public, nor the press, nor the NATO allies (nor even most of the government) were familiar with any of the background—the high-level skirmishing on the ABM issue, the Thompson talks, the standoff at Glassboro—McNamara's speech aroused strong but incoherent reactions. The press and public had trouble distinguishing between threats from Russia and China; the distinction seemed confusing and vague, as indeed it was. Within the government, those who wanted large ABM deployment swiftly claimed the so-called anti-China system as just the beginning—not even a bad beginning. General Wheeler assured Congress that the thin anti-China system also had anti-Russian potential and could grow into a thick system.

McNamara tried to blunt the effect of this predictable thrust in a long interview printed in *Life* magazine and timed to follow the San Francisco speech by a few days. He said:

> There will not be any misunderstanding by the Russians because they are sophisticated enough to see, in the deployment plans that will be made public, the distinction between Chinese-oriented and Soviet-oriented population protection systems. It is very important that our own people do not misunderstand that point.[21]

Almost certainly, the Russians either would misunderstand or would remain highly suspicious of our ABM program. McNamara's was only one voice, and one of declining influence. Other voices had been taking the other line and would continue to do so. As Senator Russell commented: "The Chinese are not completely crazy. They are not going to attack us with four or five missiles when they know we have the capability of virtually destroying the entire country . . . I don't like people to think that I am being kidded by this talk of defense against a Chinese nuclear attack."[22]

The Russians knew as well as the Washington bureaucracy that a thin-area ABM defense system, whether called anti-China or anti-Russia, would look essentially the same and would have large growth potential. The popular reaction, shaped by the press, was that McNamara had reversed himself in deciding to deploy any kind of ABM.

Curiously enough, McNamara might have been able to reconcile the apparent need to deploy something with a plausible disavowal of intent to defend American cities against Russian missiles. A decision to put ABM's around Minuteman sites need not have aroused Russian fears of a large-area ABM system. But the obvious weakness of this alternative lay in its virtue: Its lack of potential growth into the thick urban ABM network for which the Joint Chiefs and congressional leadership were pressing. Nor did McNamara himself harbor sympathy for defending Minuteman sites. One of his senior colleagues—one who had been deeply involved in all of this—now says: "McNamara believed in the anti-China rationale. In fact, he would have liked the system to be named in such a way as to make that [rationale] clear."

Naming the system was a problem already distracting various high-level figures in the Pentagon at the time of the speech. For a while, it appeared that all the appropriate names had been adopted either for other weapon systems or for male contraceptives; and the latter, of course, would not do. Ironically, it was the dovish wife of one official—a woman strongly opposed to the war in Vietnam, ABM's, and most things military—who hit upon the name Sentinel at a dinner party in Washington where the problem was being aired conversationally. She is not, it appears, at all proud of her role in the ABM saga.

Both the San Francisco speech and *Life* interview provoked difficulties with other NATO governments. The major allies were highly irritated about being neither consulted nor informed in the normal way before so major a decision by the United States. One NATO unit, the Nuclear Planning Group (NPG), had been working on an ABM study and had scheduled a meeting in Ankara for late September. For the European NPG members not to be consulted on McNamara's September speech was adding insult to injury, and the tone of the Ankara meeting, at which McNamara represented the United States, was one of undisguised hostility.

The *Life* interview created a different kind of problem. For weeks prior to his announcement of September 18, McNamara had been "peppered with memos," in the words of a former colleague, urging him to come down in favor of hard-site defense of Minuteman sites instead of the anti-China option. Curiously, the language used by McNamara in the *Life* interview tended to put Minuteman defense on more of an equal footing with anti-China defense. After noting the dual purpose of Sentinel (at the time, as yet unnamed), he said:

> We considered . . . adding more missiles, a new manned bomber, or even a new strategic missile system. We reached the conclusion that one of the most effective steps we could take, and the one least likely to force the Soviets into a counter-

reaction, was the deployment of an ABM system which would protect our Minuteman sites, so that our own deterrent is not diminished.[23]

To deploy an anti-China ABM, it could be argued, was really none of NATO's business. But to talk about defense against Soviet missiles seemed to the Europeans very much their affair. The distinction between defending cities and defending Minuteman sites was lost on them, just as it was on the American public and press. In European eyes, any kind of American defense against Russian ICBM's raised all kinds of disturbing questions. Was there to be an American-Russian ABM race? Would Europe have similar protection? Would Moscow react by building more missiles, some of them targeted against Western European cities?

McNamara, taken aback by the Ankara meeting, immediately began to deemphasize Minuteman defense upon his return. He did not want the ABM decision ensnarled in NATO problems. A *New York Times* report of the Ankara meeting said: "Although no communique was issued after the session, McNamara was known to have emphasized anew that the deployment of a limited ABM system in the U.S. was aimed at the Chinese Communists and not at the Soviet Union, and that its establishment would not upset the balance of power between the two nations."[24]

There remained only to appropriate the necessary funds for Sentinal and to remind Moscow of the surpassing interest in starting talks. On October 6, a close associate of McNamara's, Assistant Secretary of Defense Paul Warnke, gave a speech in which he said that the United States still hoped the Soviet Union would agree to limit strategic forces, either by parallel action or formal agreement. And, promised Warnke, if talks could be started, the United States would avoid getting bogged down on the intractable inspection issue. Instead, he suggested, a parallel action or agreement might be verified by "our own unilateral capability."

In January, the Administration asked $1.2 billion for production and deployment of Sentinel, whose estimated eventual cost was by then about $5.5 billion. Ironically, the threat from Russia and China was beginning to look rather different than it had the year before. The combined Galosh-Tallinn threat, against which our MIRV program was supposedly directed, seemed to be declining. McNamara, in his January, 1968, posture statement, told Congress that "although construction of the Galosh ABM system around Moscow is proceeding at a moderate pace, no effort has been made during the last year to expand that system or extend it to other cities."[25]

In fact, the Russians were slowing down Galosh deployment, and it was to take them several years even to fill the holes with interceptor missiles. In this same posture statement, McNamara also said that "the majority of our intelligence community no longer believes that this so-called 'Tallinn' system (which is being deployed across the northwestern approaches to the Soviet Union and in several other places) has any significant ABM capability."[26]

In the spring of 1968, Secretary of the Air Force Harold Brown told another congressional committee that Tallinn, in his opinion, "has almost no ABM capability."[27]

The intelligence community was also reporting in early 1968 that the Chinese strategic-weapons program had slipped and was still slipping. Even McNamara, the public sponsor of an anti-China ABM, told the Congress—again in his posture statement in January, 1968—"it is now clear that [the Chinese] failed to conduct either a space or a long-range ballistic-missile launching before the end of 1967, as we thought possible last year." In the same hearings, Johnny Foster said that Washington did not expect China to launch its first ICBM as soon as had been previously predicted. Inexplicably, the Chinese dismantled their ICBM test stand between 1968 and 1969. Three years later, in the spring of 1971, Foster told a congressional committee that the Nixon Administration, upon taking office and reviewing the strategic situation, learned that "Chinese progress toward testing an ICBM had slowed down."[28]

Still, the issue never really turned on the rhythm of the Chinese ICBM program. One day China will have such a capability. The issue is whether Washington should have based an ABM-deployment decision on the China contingency. Even at the time, the logic of the decision was lost on the larger part of the bureaucracy and arms-control community, although many individuals had originally been attracted to the idea. Now, of course, the anti-China option has lost all standing. The truth is that the

United States launched its ABM program because Washington felt pressed to do something, sensible or not. Ballistic-missile defense, especially defending ICBM sites, was an option well worth exploring. It was not, however, explored systematically and dispassionately in 1966 and 1967. Washington instead found itself caught up in a wave of ABM hysteria, and the decision, like so many others, was not measured. It was driven by essentially tangential concerns, among them: the failure to start immediate talks with the Russians; the pressure to appease members of Congress who insisted on emulating the Russian example; the understandable White House fear of ABM becoming a solid Republican issue in 1968.

Few, if any, competent China experts thought it wise or prudent to deploy Sentinel against the inchoate Chinese program. The prevailing view among Sinologists was that a Chinese nuclear capability posed no special danger to anyone, and would probably serve as a politically restraining influence, just as possession of nuclear weapons constrains other nuclear powers, especially in their relations with one another and the allies of one another.

By 1968, it was becoming clear—certainly clearer—that MIRV and Sentinel were responses to threats that either had not materialized, would not materialize, or were not even threats at all. Bureaucracy's worst-case notion, the Greater-Than-Expected-Threat, should not have inspired, or helped to inspire, these deployment decisions. Both MIRV and ABM should have been held within the level of research and development. Neither bore much relation to the really significant buildup of enemy strength.

In the winter of 1967 and 1968, Washington learned from intelligence reports that the Soviet Union was nearing parity with the United States in land-based ICBM's, and was believed to be deploying its first solid-fueled missiles. McNamara, in his January, 1968, posture statement, told Congress that the Russians had more than doubled their ICBM force—from 340 to 720—in the space of a year. On December 13, Johnny Foster announced that the United States had a weapon to counter the Soviet ICBM buildup. The weapon was MIRV, which, as Foster revealed for the first time, could send multiple, separately targeted warheads against the enemy. Quite possibly, this was the first hard information Moscow had been able to receive about the true character and capability of Poseidon and Minuteman III.

One can only speculate about the reaction of Soviet leaders. Their small, primitive Galosh system must have seemed to have earned them an American deployment of both ABM and MIRV. The Americans, then as now, hold a commanding lead in both technologies. The Soviet military bureaucracy was becoming noisily assertive, demanding larger and more-balanced forces. Almost certainly, the Glassboro affair had a sobering influence on Soviet political leaders, though not enough to spare them—and America—the effects of two deployment decisions that were to complicate enormously the problem of stable deterrence.

Soviet diplomats can always be relied upon to take a tough line on U.S. defense programs. The American people, they argue, are victimized by a military-industrial complex that obliges Washington to plunge ahead in an endless arms race. One of their diplomatic SALT experts takes this conventional line, but once added solemnly: "It's too bad we waited so long. If only we had gone ahead with talks when McNamara was pressing for them. Don't think we weren't studying the problem. It was just too soon. We didn't think we were ready."

These words convey a great deal. They imply that in building up their forces, the Soviet Union was replicating the American experience. As the forces grow, so do the competing claims of the different parts of the military bureaucracy. The Soviet Government in 1968 must have begun to sense that the "mad momentum," of which McNamara spoke, flows impartially from either the "action-reaction phenomenon," of which he also spoke, or the skirmishing of competing parts of the military establishment, itself spurred by the impulse of technology.

The elegaic words of the Russian diplomat also imply that in 1967 a great chance was missed to contain both the ABM and the MIRV technologies. Doubtless, he was also thinking of 1968, when a second chance was missed. By then, the Soviet leadership apparently felt obliged to do something about inhibiting the arms race. In May, Moscow took a deep breath and signaled to Washington a willingness to begin talks. Washington, no less anxious, set busily to work. The term SALT abruptly surfaced within the government. Talks would have started in the autumn had not the Soviet government also felt obliged, in August, to invade Czechoslovakia.

3   Face-Off

Dean Rusk now spends most of his time in a modest office on the third floor of the law school at the University of Georgia in Athens, a community in which he leads a quiet, equally modest existence, which is the style he managed to preserve even while Secretary of State. Rusk is still among the most discreet and careful of men, but he does talk freely and persuasively about arms control and the origins of SALT,

"Johnson," he recalls, "wanted to present the Russians with a simple clear proposal for the opening of the talks. He knew that SALT would become lengthy and very complicated. But he didn't want it to get bogged down in a lot of detail at the start." Rusk took the same view.

Rusk himself, with a fondness for colloquial metaphor, told colleagues that SALT, of which he was a strenuous advocate, would probably become "history's longest permanent floating crap game." He meant that the great powers were launching a process that, like trade and tariff negotiations, would go on indefinitely.

The signal that the Russians had completed their post-Glassboro exegesis and wanted to talk came on May 20, 1968, in New York, when First Deputy Foreign Minister V. V. Kuznetsov, in a speech at the United Nations, announced that his government was "ready to reach an agreement on practical steps for the limitation and consequent reduction of the strategic means for delivering nuclear weaponry."

Informal diplomatic contacts nailed down the impression that the Soviets had come a long way since the Thompson talks in Moscow a year earlier. Absolute confirmation arrived on June 27 when Foreign Minister Gromyko announced to the Supreme Soviet that the Kremlin was ready to discuss the "mutual limitation and subsequent reduction of strategic means of delivery of nuclear weapons, both offensive and defensive, including antiballistic missiles."

Johnson responded swiftly. Three days later, on July 1, he used the occasion of the signing of the Nonproliferation Treaty to announce that the two governments were agreed to "enter in the nearest future into discussions on the limitation and the reduction" of offensive and defensive strategic weapons.

All this was heartening. Although each of the great powers was embroiled in profoundly unsettling external crises—the war in Vietnam, the gallant Springtime of Prague—both could, it appeared, still move themselves and the world some distance toward sanity and stability. The Nonproliferation Treaty, after years of hard bargaining and over the objections of some Western European governments (shared, in part, by the State Department), had been signed. Of greater importance, SALT, it seemed, was at last on the track.

The appearances were deceiving. The Nonproliferation Treaty was hardly a milestone on the path to arms control; Moscow wanted it badly, though. The disavowal by signatories of any intent to procure or develop nuclear weapons amounted, from the Soviet point of view, to yet another self-denying ordinance from West Germany. That Germans must never have access of any sort to nuclear weapons was basic to the Moscow litany, recited by every Soviet negotiator and spokesman, from Kosygin down. Butch Fisher, who was still Deputy Director of ACDA and America's most experienced arms-control negotiator, now says: "I think that for the Russians the Nonproliferation Treaty was a precondition. They didn't spell it out formally. But there was tacit understanding that we had to stand shoulder-to-shoulder with them on the treaty before going on to SALT."

As a practical matter, neither Moscow nor Washington was well positioned or organized to start SALT, as would be shown by the tumultuous six-week drama that followed Johnson's statement. Both capitals were beset by internal conflict and doubt. And each was virtually consumed by its external dilemmas.

Gromyko's statement, however historic, offered a strong whiff of Moscow's troubles, especially with its military bureaucracy: "To the good-for-nothing theoreticians who try to tell us . . . that disarmament is an illusion, we reply: 'By taking such a stand you fall into step with the most dyed-in-the-wool imperialist reaction [and] weaken the front of struggle against it.' "[1]

The "theoreticians," to a man, were military officers, active or retired. The buildup of Soviet forces had not been accompanied by a formal strategic doctrine. There had been no Soviet equivalent of assured destruction, as such, even though Malenkov, as early as 1954, had observed that possession by both sides of nuclear weapons and the means of delivering them would create a kind of mutual deterrence.[2] Khrushchev, after attacking Malenkov's moderate tendencies, emulated his example and sought, with no great success, to refrom and trim some parts of his military establishment, notably the surface navy and the army. Probably the Soviet military leaders played no direct role in Khrushchev's removal, but almost certainly the Central Committee got prior assurance that the military would not oppose the action. Almost certainly, too, the Central Committee would not have moved against Khrushchev without this assurance.

The Brezhnev-Kosygin leadership sustained Khrushchev's avowed policy of preventing nuclear war through deterrence, but, again, nothing like a rigorous strategic doctrine was laid down. Then, as Soviet military strength began to build up all along the line, a split took place; the group identified with Kosygin took a moderate line on nuclear strategy—agreeing on SALT talks, for example—while the military leadership, or part of it, spoke in bolder terms.

In the Soviet system, the Central Committee insists on full political control; the military, in turn, assert full authority to perform their professional tasks according to their own best judgment. As nuclear parity developed, the line between policy and arms became blurred. On some issues, of which SALT is a notable example, the interests of the Central Committee and those of the military began to clash. As early as 1965, Soviet military strategists were saying that nuclear war could not be ruled out; thus, deterrence alone was not adequate security for the Soviet Union, which must be prepared to wage war at every level. Preparation for nuclear war would require weapons and delivery systems in adequate quantity and quality. Phrases like "favorable relationship of forces" crept into Soviet military journals, along with assertions that defense is a matter best left to military experts. An American observer of Soviet military attitudes writes:

> Those who have opposed SALT have . . . taken a pessimistic view of the danger of war . . . imperialism is unalterably hos-

tile to socialism [and] has actually become more aggressive
. . . the danger of war has become even greater. . . . The military opposition to arms control negotiations . . . has pointed
out the significance of the military-technological revolution;
just because the pace of scientific development has accelerated,
opportunities must not be lost which might alter the balance of
power even more favorably to socialism. Officers with this view
have stressed the relative importance of military "hardware"
over economic or moral factors in determining the strength of
the socialist countries. In its most radical form, this position has
asserted the relatively greater competence of the military to
make decisions affecting the strategic posture of the Soviet Union
and has almost appeared to call for a rearrangement of the traditional role of the military in the Soviet decision-making
system.[3]

Perhaps inevitably, the Russians were repeating an American
experience. For their phrase "favorable relationship of forces" substitute American notions of damage limitation, to which a large
part of Congress and the Washington bureaucracy, especially the
military, remained faithful in 1968. Hearings before the influential
Senate Preparedness Subcommittee in the spring of 1968 seemed
designed to force from the Pentagon assurances that America
would not be content with parity, would not forego some margin
of superiority. Harold Brown, then Secretary of the Air Force,
told the subcommittee:

> . . . in addition to the basic deterrent capability, our measure
> ment of deterrence should include two other criteria, less cen
> tral but still important: (1) ratios of surviving population and
> industry must not be badly adverse to the United States, and
> (2) the surviving military balance should remain in our favor
> . . . if deterrence should fail, a favorable surviving military
> balance could make it easier for us to negotiate an end to the
> war and limit further damage to the United States.[4]

In the same hearings, General Wheeler said that planned improvements in U.S. forces—mainly MIRV's—"will give us a very
substantial margin of superiority."[5] And Alain Enthoven, then running Systems Analysis, assured the subcommittee that: "We do
not intend to allow our policy of basing the size of our forces on

assured destruction to result in the Soviets overtaking us or even matching our strategic nuclear capability."[6]

Obviously, the Soviet leadership, both political and military, paid close attention to these hearings and drew who knows what conclusions. Almost certainly, the military bureaucracy fueled its arguments for larger and better forces with these and other statements from American counterparts testifying before Congress. Washington's policy of restraint, in a sense, was obscured by exaggerated claims and assertions.

Each side was using the other's internal debate and actions to fortify, if not vindicate, its own policies. Enthoven said in these same hearings: "[Russia's] traditional interest in active air defenses, their deployment of an ABM system around Moscow, and their rather extravagant investment in Tallin-type anti-bomber defenses imply some concern for a damage limiting capability, particularly against the imagined threat of a U.S. first strike on their weapons and their cities."[7]

Neither in 1968, nor again in 1969, did Washington really know why Moscow had opted for SALT. Perhaps the Kremlin leaders thought that talks aimed at a formal agreement would be a check on this disturbingly freewheeling military attitude. The other side of the coin, a better grip on defense spending, may also have been a consideration. American analysis showed then that the Russians traditionally had spent much more money on defense than offense. The ratio was about three to one, compared to America's one to one. Their abrupt, yet enormous, boost in offensive missile forces may have aroused serious concern about costs. Soviet rubles buy more manpower than U.S. dollars, because American manpower costs are much higher. But U.S. dollars buy more-sophisticated hardware than Soviet rubles. Thus, Soviet leadership may have started to look with real apprehension at the implications of an endless competition for strategic advantage. America's MIRV and ABM programs were doubtless both unsettling, if only because the U.S. lead in the vital computer technology must have seemed irretrievably broad. Moscow's attitude on limiting ABM's had probably started to shift in the McNamara direction. And in Lyndon Johnson, the Russians saw a President who would be leaving office in January, succeeded possibly by someone less committed to arms control and more impressed by conventional sentiment favoring

U.S. superiority. Thus, in the summer of 1968 Moscow saw little to be risked and perhaps something to be gained by pushing SALT into play while Johnson was still on the scene.

Although some similar thoughts had much earlier propelled Johnson toward SALT, internal stresses similar to some that had restrained Moscow might, it appeared, frustrate his ambition to get the talks safely under way before he left the White House. Johnson's problem would be to maneuver the "simple, clear proposal" through a government that would still be there when he left. Agreement on talks was one thing. Agreement on what, if any, truly self-limiting steps could be taken was quite another. The military bureaucracy, most notably the Joint Chiefs, would have to "sign off" on the American proposal, since the Senate would never ratify an agreement they opposed. Nothing less than a unanimously agreed-upon position was required. For the State Department, ACDA, and their allies in the Office of the Secretary of Defense to pursue a course more daring than the Joint Chiefs were likely to accept would have been quixotic, even risky. The Chiefs would have blocked them, if only by offering a scaled-down substitute proposal; a stalemate might have followed, the talks delayed, the momentum lost. As always, Washington would have to negotiate among its parts before negotiating with Moscow. But this internal negotiation was to be unlike any other.

Unanimity on SALT really meant reaching agreement within the Pentagon. If competing interests within the building could somehow be reconciled on a single piece of paper, there would be no great problem in securing the endorsements of the other key agencies—the State Department, ACDA, and the CIA. The White House was not directly involved in the process. Neither Johnson nor his staff would take part in bureaucracy's epic struggle to produce not just a "simple, clear proposal," but one that would actually make a serious matter of SALT. In Johnson's day there was no Henry Kissinger to hold the bureaucracy in line and to force up Presidential options, as distinct from the preferences of the various parts of the government. Unlike Nixon, Johnson—as everyone in government knew—wanted *agreement*, not options. This meant that the Joint Chiefs *had* to be on board.

Maneuvering them on board would have been easier the year before, around the time of Glassboro. Johnson was not then a lame duck, a sitting President so diminished by excessive commitment to a war he didn't start that he felt obliged, in March, 1968, to announce he would not run again. McNamara, the apostle of SALT and, more important, the man with the best record of managing the Chiefs, had left in February; he, too, was used up, another casualty of Vietnam. John McNaughton, McNamara's surrogate on SALT and related matters, had been killed in a plane crash after Glassboro. With Vietnam consuming the government's attention, the loss of McNaughton's grasp and commitment seemed a severe blow. McNamara was replaced by Clark Clifford, whose views on deterrence and SALT were unclear, but who was suspected, perhaps unfairly, of entertaining only mild interest in the subject. In any case, he lacked experience with this range of issues and in grappling with the Joint Chiefs. More important, he would be fully occupied with helping first to arrest, then to reduce, the commitment in Vietnam.

McNaughton's successor as Assistant Secretary of Defense for International Security Affairs was the Pentagon's General Counsel, Paul C. Warnke. Warnke, who now practices law in Washington with Clifford, was known to share the McNamara-McNaughton bias for restraint and arms limitation, but he, too, would have his hands full in helping Clifford find his way on Vietnam.

Moderating the war not only absorbed the attention of the senior figures in the government, but also tended to obscure other issues, like SALT. And that was probably a good thing. Shifting direction on Vietnam inevitably set off conflict with the uniformed military, who, if they were by and large never happy about fighting a major war in Southeast Asia, wanted to win it as swiftly and decisively as possible. Open skirmishing on SALT would have sharpened existing tensions within the Pentagon and deepened the anxieties of the Joint Chiefs about a proposal to limit strategic arms. Thus, the ABM program was a related and potentially troublesome factor. Whereas, up through the middle of 1967, the deployment decision hung in the air, Washington was by this point committed to Sentinel, which the Chiefs and others insisted on treating as the start of a large anti-Russian ABM system.

Everything pointed to playing SALT, an issue of surpassing importance, in a minor key. Open disagreement at the highest level might well have derailed the project. The critical influences were

Johnson and Wheeler, neither of whom were to take part directly. They were off-stage powers whose different interests and responsibilities would interact and shape the actions of the more directly involved lesser figures. Each was obliged to respect—even to bend —to the other's preferences.

Johnson was the President, and he was insisting on a reasonable —hopefully negotiable—SALT position. Wheeler, serving at Johnson's pleasure and under his direction, could not ignore that. He had to cooperate. Neither could Johnson ignore his senior military adviser, whose office gave him direct access to Congress and enabled him to sink bureaucratic initiatives before they reached the Oval Office. Butch Fisher, recalling his experience, says: "The State Department and ACDA would, on the theory of completed staff work, often make a proposal and refer it to the Chiefs, who just as often would append a stinging critique; their recorded opposition would undercut the President before he could take a position. Such action by the Chiefs threatened eventual congressional opposition before the issue had really emerged." Briefly, Wheeler and the other Chiefs, if pushed too hard, could have denied Johnson and blocked SALT.

The Joint Chiefs of Staff operate both as military heads of their services and as an institution. In the latter role, they normally speak with one voice, an achievement that requires a good deal of internal compromise. The process of compromise often denies the President a clear impression of the real position of each service on an issue. But their solid front is useful, if not essential, to the Joint Chiefs in dealing with other agencies.

Although it made complete sense to handle SALT with the lowest possible visibility, nobody knew how to do it. Much less-important issues were normally managed by senior people operating through their staffs. A Committee of Principals had been created to handle arms-control matters, and it had supervised the work on the Nonproliferation Treaty. Rusk chaired the committee, which also included the Director of ACDA, William Foster; the Secretary of Defense; General Wheeler; and the President's Special Assistant for National Security, Walt Rostow. Just beneath this group was the Committee of Deputies, chaired by Butch Fisher, ACDA's

Deputy Director. In grinding out the SALT proposal, however, neither group was to play its presumed role. Too much was at stake. By this point, Rusk had more influence with Johnson on security issues than anyone, but he could not have managed the Joint Chiefs; he had always relied on McNamara to do that in matters where State Department interests were involved. Obviously, Rusk had not yet established with Clifford anything like the warm, intimate relationship that he and McNamara had achieved. On most important issues, those two had been allies. Sidestepping the Committee of Principals made sense if only because ACDA served as its staff, and ACDA long before had aroused the suspicions of the Joint Chiefs, who looked upon it as a collection of ritual disarmers. For the same reason, ACDA's Butch Fisher, for all his skill and experience, could not have achieved much by using the Committee of Deputies as the "action" group on SALT.

Who, then, or what was going to handle SALT? A bureaucratic void had developed, and nobody at the senior level seemed to have an idea on how to fill it. "People were throwing messages about SALT over the wall, but nobody was doing anything," recalls one of the closely involved personalities. Down at the third and fourth echelons it was recognized that the normal procedure must be avoided. Instead of giving the Joint Chiefs something to shoot at, prudence suggested devising a procedure that would contain their doubts and exclude their direct participation until something generally acceptable had been worked out. But again, how to do it?

Someone had to take an initiative, and someone did: Morton H. Halperin. He had come to the Pentagon from Harvard to serve as Special Assistant to John McNaughton for the academic year 1966–67, despite the admonishments of Cambridge colleagues that his primary interest, arms control, would find little scope in Washington. He thought differently, decided to stay on, and proved himself right.

Had he arrived sooner in the Pentagon, Halperin would have been labeled one of McNamara's "whiz kids"; he had, in fact, just turned thirty in the summer of 1968. Halperin was, par excellence, a defense intellectual, one of a number summoned from academia and the "think tanks" to work either in Systems Analysis or ISA. Most such people quickly acquire a taste for government and prefer staying on; some move back and forth and think of themselves as "in-and-outers." Halperin is no exception. As a breed, the defense intellectuals have been regarded with great suspicion by the larger part of the uniformed Pentagon bureaucracy; again, Halperin is no exception. His open aversion to ABM's in all forms and his sturdy arms-control bias had already made him controversial within the building. His major attribute, an intuitive sense of how to maneuver an idea through the Washington labyrinth, became a critical force behind the first U.S. SALT proposal and left Halperin an established and much-discussed personality throughout the government.

Most of the action began right after Johnson's July 1 statement. Over the July 4 weekend, the Committee of Deputies was reactivated and procedures worked out; for the most part, these would be bypassed. Halperin, who then held the title of Deputy Assistant Secretary of Defense for Policy Planning and Arms Control, drafted a memorandum to Clark Clifford for the signature of his own boss, Paul Warnke. It proposed using Warnke's bureau, ISA, as the action group on SALT, which also meant that Halperin himself would coordinate the enterprise. Warnke, who had swiftly gained the confidence of Clifford, sent the memorandum on, and Clifford approved it. In effect, it licensed Halperin to handle SALT within the Pentagon. Any group within the building seeking to oppose ISA's maneuverings would have to appeal directly to Clifford.

Halperin had earlier persuaded an old friend from Harvard faculty days, Richard H. Ullman, to leave his teaching job at Princeton's Woodrow Wilson School for the academic year 1967–68 and work with him in ISA. Ullman, he decided, would be his alter ego, confidant, and collaborator on SALT. Determined to keep the enterprise small and private, Halperin ignored the staff of uniformed and civilian arms-control specialists already assigned to him. They were cut out of the picture, neither consulted nor allowed to see most of the paper that began to flow. As the work burden grew, Halperin borrowed from ACDA a gifted young technician named Jerome Kahan, now one of his colleagues at the Brookings Institute. Led by Halperin, the trio filled the bureau-

cratic void and somehow managed to nudge a SALT proposal all
the way up to the desk of Lyndon Johnson.

Shortly after taking office, people around Nixon began reviewing
the SALT experience. They were appalled and thoroughly dis-
approving of the way in which the 1968 proposal had been
handled. They had reason to be. It was preposterous that a wholly
irregular tiny *ad hoc* group of middle-level bureaucrats, *faute de
mieux*, should have been handed the major responsibility for preparing this country's position for what might be its most important
negotiation. Such issues as whether to limit the number of ABM's
and ICBM's, whether the United States should propose a ban on
MIRV testing, or on MIRV itself, and whether such a self-limiting
step could be safely verified were left largely in the hands of
bureaucrats. However complicated, these were first and foremost
political questions on which the bureaucracy was divided and
which should have been resolved one way or the other by the
highest political authority, the President, acting on the advice of
his senior advisers. Nixon was to insist on deciding such questions
himself. In 1968, however, they never reached the attention of a
President who insisted only on a proposal that the various competing groups could agree on. And that is what he got.

Halperin, quite obviously, did not do it alone. He needed the
sympathetic help and even indulgence of persons in many parts
of the government. The point is that he got this help, partly
through persuasion and wile, partly through the goodwill of others,
partly through chance.

General Wheeler, a reasonable man who was also aware of his
duty to meet the President at least halfway, took an initiative of
his own that greatly simplified matters. Just as Halperin ignored the
arms-control specialists assigned to him, so Wheeler dispensed with
a group attached to his Joint Staff that was supposed to protect
the interests of the Joint Chiefs on arms-control matters. These
people, as described by one who dealt with them at close range,
"were normally headed by some fifth wheel, generally close to
retirement—usually a two-star general or admiral who could be
relied upon to take the line least likely to upset any of the Chiefs."
In bypassing this group, Wheeler recalled from Hawaii Royal B.
Allison, a two-star Air Force General, who had earlier served as

Deputy Chairman of the Special Studies Group of the Joint Chiefs of Staff. Allison had a solid background on the weapon systems to be covered by SALT, plus the reputation of being a uniformed diplomat. His striking good looks and impeccable tailoring inspired comparisons elsewhere in the bureaucracy with Steve Canyon, or Gregory Peck in *Twelve O'clock High*. Others, who looked more closely, saw Allison as something of an operator. His assignment to represent Wheeler on SALT seemed, rightly enough, to suggest that Wheeler, too, hoped to satisfy the need for a workable proposal. Allison, of course, is now a member of the U.S. SALT delegation, a role he largely earned in the summer of 1968 when he functioned as a broker between the interests of the Joint Chiefs and those of Halperin and his allies. Allison and Halperin swiftly built a smooth-working relationship.

The work itself was done swiftly—hastily, in fact. The typical bureaucrat, once his project becomes operational, tries to generate great impulsion, but in this case, another reason added subtly to the need for haste, although the bureaucracy was unaware of it. Unbeknownst to Halperin or his immediate superiors, or indeed to most of the Administration, Johnson wanted to launch SALT formally at a summit meeting in Russia well before the 1968 elections. That meant September. It also meant that Johnson would need to see a proposal sometime in mid-August. The haste, combined with the irregular procedure, adds retrospectively to the impression of a patchwork operation propelled along in a dizzying rush of activity, all of it hidden from the Congress, press, and most of the government.

That is one way of looking at it. It was also seen "as an absolutely fabulous piece of bureacracy" by a former Pentagon bureaucrat who watched the Halperin group at close range. The strategy Halperin's group decided on was to avoid an "agenda-based" ACDA proposal, to which the Pentagon would say no, thus repeating a dreary pattern. The Joint Chiefs, with some pain, had acquiesced in the partial test-ban treaty as well as the Nonproliferation Treaty, which had not really bothered them. SALT was something else; it foreshadowed actual limitations, possibly even reductions, of major weapons.

Strategy aside, the initial draft memorandum *had* to come in a formal sense from the building in Foggy Bottom that houses both

ACDA and the State Department. ACDA was nominally the action agency, and what was needed was an ACDA paper, agreed to by State, that would not be shot down immediately; the Pentagon ISA group could not appear to take the first step. Halperin not only needed a useful initiative from the normally responsible agencies, he also needed technical back-up on verification issues from the CIA, the agency best equipped to provide it. In short, his job was to respond, not to initiate or even appear to be initiating. Yet Halperin and his colleagues knew best what the Joint Chiefs would be willing to consider and what would immediately put their backs up. The only course then was for Halperin, operating clandestinely, to establish—virtually to dictate—an ACDA–State Department position. He had set about doing precisely that even before the Gromyko statement of June 27.

Butch Fisher has qualities rarely found in combination along the Potomac. Ever the skilled negotiator and technician, he is also philosophical and irreverant, untroubled by vanity, and admirably incautious in speech though never indiscreet; he has an eye for the human comedy ignored by most but there to be seen in Washington's endless internal battles. Fisher, who is now Dean of the Georgetown University Law School, understood the strategy: the need to yield the initiative to Halperin, a junior figure, and to keep his own agency in low profile. "ACDA," he says succinctly, "always faced the problem of not raising too much hell so as to avoid being crowded out of the act." It was also generally known that General Wheeler and William Foster, then ACDA's Director, had clashed on the Seabed Treaty. As is so often the case, personalities as well as issues had to be reckoned with. So did language. Fisher recalls that "certain words, like 'parity,' had to be avoided. They made too many people mad."

Halperin's group had drafted a working paper. It became the substance of the ACDA–State Department position. A round of strictly private meetings between Halperin and appropriate people in ACDA and State was swiftly arranged. Among Halperin's larger tasks was persuading colleagues on the other side of the Potomac to exclude from ACDA's memorandum a numerical limit on ABM's and a ban on MIRV. Having tested the Pentagon waters, Halperin was convinced that neither proposition would long survive. Fisher's help was critical in nailing down this point, at least within ACDA. The State Department posed a different problem. Its small group of bureaucrats involved in SALT were divided, some supporting ACDA's full-blown approach, others leery and far from persuaded that SALT could amount to anything much. In the end, though, they also went along.

ACDA's paper would normally have gone directly to the Joint Chiefs for comment. This time a finesse was tried. Agreement would be reached at lower levels of the Pentagon before involving the seniors. The tactic had merit. It meant that, as the deadline for sending a proposal to the White House drew near, the pressure on the Joint Chiefs to concur would grow. More important, by the time the Joint Chiefs saw it, the proposal would have been worked over and tailored to remove their major anxieties. The dominant goal was not an ideal proposal, but a U.S. SALT position that all sides could live with.

Wheeler, to his credit, accepted the procedure and seemed content to rely on Allison to monitor the Halperin operation. It could also be argued that since Rusk and other senior members of the Committee of Principals were standing aside, Wheeler could do no less. In any case, the question was whether this novel procedure really could work. Success depended largely on avoiding a split between the Office of the Secretary of Defense, where Halperin had the "action," and the three services.

Seen as a game or piece of theater, it was even more complicated. The image of ISA and the Joint Chiefs monopolizing the stage is too simple. It was a multiparty drama, if only because the Pentagon is a hodgepodge of bureaus and offices and offices within offices, each with its own interests. One way or another, SALT could affect many of these interests, and each office sought reflexively to acquire some leverage on the process. On the military side, besides the Joint Chiefs and their staffs, there were the sprawling Army, Navy, and Air Force intelligence services, whose combined budgetary resources dwarf the CIA's. On the civilian side, apart from ISA, the key groups were Systems Analysis, DDR&E, and the DIA.

Each of the services would cling to its share of the strategic responsibility, which meant clinging to the weapons it deployed and those it hoped to deploy or modernize. The services were also deeply concerned with verification. Would Soviet cheating be detected, and, if so, at what stage? Since some amount of cheating could always go undetected, was there an unacceptable risk of massive violations in a SALT agreement?

Verification was the leitmotiv, the point of reference where issues were joined and major interests diverged. The Navy and Air Force cared little about ABM's; the Army did. The Army and Navy cared little about a limitation on bombers or the future vulnerability of Minuteman; the Air Force did. A MIRV ban was unacceptable to the Air Force and Navy, but of little concern to the Army. It was verification that drew them together, as it drew DDR&E and the DIA together. DDR&E shared, and perhaps fortified, many of the reservations of the services, and it wanted to influence estimates on verification. The same was true of DIA, the smallest of the intelligence groups but no less competitive than the rest. It, too, wanted the largest possible piece of the "action" on verification estimates, and it instinctively sided with the Joint Chiefs on many issues, the better to strengthen its competitive position.

All of the Pentagon intelligence groups either collect or coordinate information on Soviet weapons developments. But, as Butch Fisher says, "the CIA was set up to evaluate intelligence with no axe to grind. Service-related intelligence units," he continues, "tend to fit assessments to the interests of the respective services, a tendency deeply disturbing to those who must live with it."

The services and their intelligence groups saw things differently. The CIA, they feared, was unreasonably sanguine about Soviet weapons programs and objectives. Experience did show that the CIA had underestimated the pace and scope of the Soviet missile buildup, but had proved reliable in forecasting the character and quality of the weapons themselves. The Halperin ISA group chose to rely on CIA estimates. They really had no other choice. Agreed estimates reconciling the views of the entire intelligence community were just not attainable (although the CIA and the DIA did sometimes take the same position on an issue).

As always, chance played a role. The drama was shaped in part by the personal styles of the various figures—Fisher, Warnke, Halperin, Johnny Foster, Allison, and Harold Brown. Clifford, for example, seemed to find Warnke and Brown more persuasive than some who took a more skeptical line on SALT. Indeed, ISA's most formidable and reliable ally was Harold Brown, who was to represent the Department of Defense at the talks. As Secretary of the Air Force, Brown did much to temper its attitude. Being named the SALT delegate from the Defense Department extended his writ in the building. This dual role, combined with Brown's scientific competence and long experience with strategic weapons, was used to sustain many of the Halperin group's positions on the jumble of technical issues.

Most often these dealt with detection and verification. A pattern developed. Once an issue surfaced, ISA would formally request an estimate from the CIA in a letter or memo signed by Warnke. The Halperin group learned to draft a query so that it would be referred to the most-congenial and quickly reacting CIA office. Since the CIA position on most of the verification issues was generally consistent with ISA's, the estimates usually supported the Halperin group. Contesting views within the Pentagon, often from different sources, would be asserted; these sometimes originated with or were backed by DDR&E or the DIA. At that point, Brown would be asked to arbitrate, and he was frequently able to silence or dilute the opposing viewpoint. Brown left day-to-day operations to Halperin and functioned as a higher-level partisan and troubleshooter on SALT. The CIA, as a practical matter, functioned as a technical wing of ISA on SALT. So, too, did Systems Analysis.

As if there weren't voices enough, ISA toyed with weakening some by adding others. It proposed the creation of service committees chaired by civilians. Halperin went to each service secretary and asked him to appoint some high-ranking figure to organize a committee and serve as a point of contact with his own group. The Army and Air Force named their respective Undersecretaries, David E. McGiffert and Townsend Hoopes, the Navy a slightly lesser-ranking figure.

Normally, the Service Secretaries would have had little to do with SALT preparations. Roping them in, it seemed, might help to restrain the Joint Chiefs and their allies, might even create splits between the civilian and military leadership of a given service. If, for example, one of the Joint Chiefs were to dissent from the proposal, or some part of it, he might then be speaking strictly for his own office and not necessarily for the entire Service. The idea seems to have been of some use, but, in fairness, it is equally true that certain military members of this web of committees, especially a brace of Air Force colonels, took a wholly constructive line on SALT preparations.

SALT was complicated enough without the internal drama in which it was embedded. The issues were and would remain plentiful and varied. Some were inherently complex and hard to handle, while others were made unnecessarily burdensome by fertile brains determined to identify and hedge against every diabolical scheme the Russians might invent.

To the outsider, as well as some insiders, nuclear deterrence is a fantasy world, having nothing to do with the real issues dividing the blocs. If each side has enough power to maim the other beyond repair, of what importance are modest disparities in numbers of missiles, bombers, ABM's, radars, and nuclear submarines? The one who strikes first, after all, stands to lose about as much as his putative victim. If, then, deterrence cannot be allowed to fail, why treat the issues of SALT with such elaborate punctilio?

However reasonable, this tempting overview ignores the pressures on politicians to hedge against the prospect, probably remote, that deterrence *could* fail. It also ignores the internal politics that would collapse any regime that allowed the other side to establish, or reestablish, a convincing superiority. Parity is as much a political as a military value. Neither great power can concede other than marginal strategic advantage to the other. Deterrence is fragile; it relies on the credibility of each side's confidence in its strategic power. It even relies on the world's confidence that neither side can be intimidated by the other. At stake is the balance of power, a crude and imperfect equilibrium upon which stability rests. SALT preparations were borne along by such considerations. Some may think of them as the abstractions or fantasies of bureaucrats unable to see the wood for the trees; bureaucracy sees them as the realities of power in the nuclear age.

The task was first to reach agreement on the issues without doing violence to any one of numerous attitudes toward deterrence; second, to wedge all this into the "simple, clear proposal." The issues divided along the line of defensive and offensive weapons.

The hardest to handle would be a limitation on ABM's. With

Sentinel approved, the pro-ABM lobby within the government and Congress was enjoying a strong favorable wind. Nothing really restrictive on ABM's seemed feasible. Sentinel, much larger than Russia's Galosh, was planned as a twelve-site system (with options for three more sites) and something like 1000 launchers in all.

Johnson was known to be sensitive to the strong sentiment of Senator Russell and others, including the Joint Chiefs, in favor of a big anti-Russian ABM system. ISA's nominal ally on SALT, Systems Analysis, harbored a mild bias in favor of defending Minuteman sites with ABM's. Congressional opposition to ABM's had not yet crystallized; in any case, Congress was not being consulted on SALT preparations.

Restricting ABM's would also have meant restricting certain types of radar, a move to which the Joint Chiefs would have been hostile and the Russians no less so. Just as important, the old issue of Russia's Tallinn air-defense system was still fuzzing perspective on ABM's. Converting Tallinn into an ABM system, however unlikely, would give the Soviet Union an apparent advantage. Briefly, in the summer of 1968 (unlike the summer of 1969), there was little effective support for limiting ABM's to a small number, let alone banning them.

Sentiment on offensive weapons ran just a little less high. Here there were two groups of issues, the first turning on which weapons to limit, the second on whether various refinements, like MIRV, should be restricted.

The tiny ISA Halperin unit became the nucleus of a Pentagon committee that controlled the SALT process. The group never had a name, although the services called it the SALT Committee. Halperin chaired it; the other participants included Allison, of course, Ivan Selin of Systems Analysis, the service undersecretaries, a flag officer designated by each service chief, and a member of DDR&E (representing Johnny Foster). This little *ad hoc* band identified the issues, analyzed them, and solicited estimates, often independently, from various parts of the intelligence community.

Halperin established his strategy and set the tone in the first meeting of the group, in which he unveiled the ACDA–State Department paper that he had largely written himself. The job, he said in effect, was to respond to that proposal, not to offer another. The group could modify the proposal and add caveats;

failing agreement, the group might even reject the proposal, but Halperin stressed its clear duty to send something to the President within a reasonable period of time. This, as one of his colleagues recalls, "was putting their feet to the fire. The others knew he was right—that they had to come up with something for Johnson." Halperin also made clear his own role as the action officer of the Department of Defense, his authority flowing straight down from Clifford, who would be kept informed by Warnke and would take full responsibility.

It was then that the whirl of activity began. Issues were not taken up methodically one by one, but in groups. The pace was so intense that at times it was unclear whether agreement on a given issue had or had not been achieved. Everyone was meeting with everyone else, and everyone was both writing assessments and soliciting them. A torrent of paper flew about, threatening to swamp filing systems. Ullman wrote seventeen issue papers in two days; according to a colleague, it was probably the record. The papers were sent out to the services, which would respond with comments and then submit their own campanion papers. All the papers represented instant analyses of complex, sensitive problems, and all were prepared by people working twelve- and fourteen-hour days under terrific pressure. So swiftly did the work move, according to one of Halperin's colleagues, that "at some moments nobody knew where it was. Some issues simply dropped off in the blur of activity only to pop up later."

The Halperin ISA group did not even have its own conference room in which to meet with the SALT Committee; it relied on borrowed space from the service secretaries. As the pace developed, Halperin stopped attending interagency meetings on the Vietnam peace talks in Paris. One of his colleagues, Leslie Gelb, editor and project manager of the Pentagon papers, took on most of ISA's heavy responsibilities for Vietnam.

It bears repeating that while much of the work was apparently very good, the hurried and seemingly illogical shape of the operation sharpened the incoming Nixon Administration's doubts about the quality of its predecessor's analytical work on SALT. Halperin himself shared misgivings about the lack of Presidential involvement and became a partisan of the White House–centered national-security system. Indeed, ironically enough, he was in a few months to assist Henry Kissinger in devising the Nixon system.

The strategy on ABM was to avoid trying for a specific limitation. The Joint Chiefs, as ISA knew, might reject the whole package if it contained a low or even a reasonably high ABM number. The Navy no longer cared about ABM's and left to itself would have taken any kind of limit. The Air Force would have cheerfully accepted a low ABM number. Both services, however, were counting on the Army's support on other issues of importance to them. So they backed the Army and elected to present their united front on ABM's.

The united front also owed something to the Tallinn issue—as always, troublesome. Tallinn, in the summer of 1968, posed two continuing questions: Was it really an ABM system in disguise? Could it be upgraded to have an ABM capability? By 1968, only a few voices were arguing that Tallinn was designed as an ABM system. But the Joint Chiefs refused to go on record as saying that it could not become an ABM system. CIA estimates doubted Tallinn's potential, but people read into these what they wanted to see, while the DIA sided half-heartedly with the Joint Chiefs and argued that Tallinn had some minimal upgrade potential.

Tallinn was the intractable issue. More than 200 pages of analysis failed to bridge the differing viewpoints. On the military side, some argued that Tallinn would have to be counted as part of the Soviet ABM capability, or be policed by on-site inspection. Eventually, ISA had to refer the problem to the Committee of Principals. It was the only issue that did require high-level intervention, and even then agreement eluded the government.

Rusk, who chaired the Committee of Principals, did manage to blunt the issue. To the argument that, for negotiating purposes, Tallinn should be treated as part of Russia's overall ABM network, he demurred, saying prophetically that surely the eventual goal must be the lowest possible number of ABM's on both sides. He and others squashed the on-site inspection issue, and everyone finally decided simply to disagree on Tallinn's possibilities. In the Nixon Administration, the question would have been resolved, one way or another, in the White House. In Johnson's day, Tallinn never reached the attention of the White House.

The ABM language eventually agreed upon by the Halperin SALT Committee could scarcely have been less daring. It proposed an equivalent number of launchers on either side within a range of 100 to 1000. Since the Sentinel system was unlikely to have more than 1000 launchers, this approach seemed to risk nothing. Moreover, the Russians showed no sign of expanding their Galosh ABM system beyond the 64 silos clustered in the Moscow area.

Other issues were excluded altogether, either because internal agreement was unlikely or because raising them was just too dangerous. Bomber limitations fell into the first category, MIRV restrictions into the second. Bombers were bypassed, mainly because distinguishing between strategic and tactical aircraft is horrendously difficult. Also, the Joint Chiefs argued that a bomber limitation was irrelevant since both sides were reducing their strategic bomber forces.

The MIRV issue, if anything, was more explosive than the ABM. The first flight tests of the two MIRV'd missiles, Poseidon and Minuteman III, were scheduled for mid-August, about a month before SALT was supposed to begin.

As seen by ISA, the State Department, and ACDA, there were two questions: Should the United States cancel the MIRV tests? Should it include a MIRV testing ban in the proposal? From the start, it was clear that any effort to squeeze a MIRV ban into the proposal ran the risk of losing the Joint Chiefs altogether. Some thought that such an initiative, if pushed hard, might even provoke resignations, a horrifying prospect. Canceling the upcoming tests was considered briefly, but not seriously. It, too, was risky.

Dean Rusk, reflecting on the MIRV problem, seems to harbor second thoughts. He says: "At that time, we could have taken the step [a MIRV testing ban] more easily than now, because the Soviet MIRV program was not really underway. Now we need to worry about inspecting such a ban."

Rusk also recalls that he did not oppose America's MIRV tests on the eve of the talks. "It was," he felt, "something that could be worked out during the negotiations." He says he was not pushing a "negotiation-through-strength argument, but would simply have preferred to work it out at the talks."

ACDA followed Rusk's line. As a former senior official puts it: "ACDA did not oppose the scheduled tests, but put the other agencies on notice that it would do so later if our MIRV testing program became a stumbling block in the negotiations. ACDA," he adds, "was not buying the negotiation-through-strength argument, but relying on the negotiations to head off MIRV."

Within ISA, a modest effort to cancel the tests was mounted, then dropped when it appeared unlikely that Rusk and Clifford would press the issue. Here again, a question that should have been decided by the President—or, at the very least, should have involved him—didn't reach his attention.

Another issue that could have unhinged the affair but on which ISA would stand firm concerned the nuclear submarine. The Joint Chiefs were known to be against trying to limit SLBM's on the grounds that reliable verification was doubtful. Also, Admiral Thomas H. Moorer, then the Chief of Naval Operations and now Wheeler's sucessor as Chairman of the Joint Chiefs, was regarded within the government as the most hard-nosed of the skeptics on SALT. The Navy dug in its heels on more issues than either of the other two services, and while nothing suggested that the Navy wanted to expand its fleet of forty-one nuclear submarines, it was feared that Moorer would rebel against a formal limit. But CIA estimates showed convincingly that any Soviet violation of an agreement on SLBM's in excess of half-dozen or so boats would be detected. For Moscow to cheat for so small a gain seemed unlikely, so the military flip-flopped. SLBM's were folded into the proposal, and the Navy chose to make its case on other grounds.

Nothing about the preparation for the SALT talks in 1968 was so remarkable or unprecedented, really, as the willingness of the Joint Chiefs to accept restrictions that could not be verified with full reliability. Up to that point, the Joint Chiefs and others had rejected any proposed limitation or ban that conceded the possibility of some cheating by the other side. Had they clung to that position in 1968, Johnson would have had little to negotiate about. Moscow rejects on-site inspection, and American surveillance techniques are fool-proof only in the case of large, fixed ICBM and ABM installations.

Another case in point was the issue of mobile missiles. These could be destabilizing because of the obvious difficulty in counting them. Although Washington itself had no plans to shift Minuteman missiles from silos to railroad cars or trucks, the bureaucracy worried, as it does today, that Moscow might do just that, if only to protect Russian ICBM's from American missiles. Once again, the argument that verification would be difficult was silenced by estimates conceding that clandestine deployment of mobile missiles was quite feasible, but not on a scale large enough to risk upsetting a formal SALT agreement. Again, the Joint Chiefs acquiesced.

Little of the preparation for SALT had much reference to Moscow's attitudes; Washington didn't know what these were. The concern was, not what might be negotiable with Moscow, but what could be negotiated within the Pentagon. Kosygin had revealed little at Glassboro, and the Administration had no indication of what, if anything, Moscow might be specifically contemplating. A "Red Team" group was organized to try to anticipate what the Russians might put forward or accept, but it was groping with unknowns and ambiguities. Washington knew only that they were ready to talk.

Precisely because SALT was a novel and major departure in great power relations, it was misted in uncertainty. Nothing in America's experience with the Soviet Union on lesser matters suggested other than that the talks would be long, arduous, and quite possibly useless. On any issue, the Soviet interest could be defined in two ways. Take parity for example. Since it hadn't really been achieved, the Russians had a presumed incentive to use SALT as an extended talkathon during which they could catch up. On the other hand, a formal halt or slow down of the arms race might deter a new administration, very possibly Republican, from recapturing a more visible U.S. lead.

On more specific issues, the phrase "frozen into a position of inferiority" began to bob up. A MIRV testing ban would halt the Poseidon and Minuteman III programs, a presumed gain for Moscow. On the other hand, would the Soviet political and military leaders agree to remain innocent of the technology of multiple re-entry vehicles? By coincidence, Moscow had, in fact, scheduled the first test of the so-called SS-9 triplet—three re-entry vehicles borne aloft by the world's largest missile—the week after America's MIRV tests were to begin.

SLBM's posed an even broader conflict of interest. A freeze or limit on nuclear submarines would carry a lot of advantages from Washington's point of view, but none from Moscow's. The sea, as noted, is the most secure strategic environment, and the SLBM, as everyone agrees, is the one weapon likely to survive an uncertain future. Could the Russians be expected to accept a permanent American advantage in the number and quality of nuclear submarines and the missiles they carry?

A ban on mobile missiles also seemed doubtful. Logically, such a step would promote stability and confidence, but the Russians were unlikely to bar the door on a weapon that could best enable them to exploit their only geographic advantage—immense, sparsely populated territories. Finally, if words meant anything, the Russians were even less sympathetic to an ABM limitation than the Pentagon. They did, after all, trail in all categories except warhead size. If for no other reason, Moscow's internal debate was almost certainly as arduous as Washington's, the attitude of the Soviet military bureaucracy more hostile to SALT than the Pentagon's.

The proposal was due to reach the Committee of Principals on Wednesday, August 14; Fisher had arranged the deadline. The Committee would review both the proposal and a memorandum from Clifford to the President explaining the proposal and a memorandum of instructions to the SALT delegation. This package of documents, with a covering note from Rusk, would be sent to Johnson.

Halperin was the chief author of the proposal and of the draft memorandum from Clifford to Johnson. He had gone over both documents carefully with Allison and showed them to others from the three services. He was determined to keep both the proposal and the crucial interpretive memorandum as simple and short as possible. The proposal was just three and one-half pages—the outline of a treaty, really. The Clifford-to-Johnson memorandum was held to four pages, and was frankly designed to reassure the Joint Chiefs, with caveats and comments expressed in language that they might have written themselves. In fact, the memorandum specified that the views of the Joint Chiefs should have special weight. Even then, few, if any, were willing to wager much that the Joint Chiefs would actually approve the substance of the proposal. Indeed, there was real concern that Admiral Moorer might dissent categorically.

One week before the Wednesday deadline, Clifford formally transmitted the proposal and the Clifford-to-Johnson memorandum to Wheeler. This was the signal for the Chiefs to go into "the tank," as the secure conference room of the Joint Chiefs is called. There they meet, often for extended periods, without interruption. But first a meeting of the Committee of Principals was called on the same day, August 7, chiefly for the purpose of allowing Rusk to remind his colleagues that the President was not interested in their disagreements, but in having a proposal he could offer the Soviet leadership. This admonition, as everyone understood, was addressed to Wheeler for transmission to the other Chiefs. The pressure was on.

The Joint Chiefs met part of Wednesday and all day Thursday and Friday; they resumed early Saturday morning. Apart from the broadly permissive language on ABM's, the essence of the proposal was a freeze on long-range missiles—both ICBM's and SLBM's—at existing levels. Mobile missiles were banned. In order that MIRV testing and deployment could proceed unthreatened, the proposal excluded so-called qualitative limitations, with a single exception: the external configuration of missile silos could not be altered. Then as now, Washington worried that such a restraint was needed to prevent the Russians from replacing older and smaller ICBM's with the giant SS-9, the most destructive weapon in anyone's arsenal. Such a step would vastly increase Soviet offensive power and also threaten U.S. Minuteman missiles if and when the SS-9 force was multiplied by the miracle of MIRV.

The only other major restriction was on "freedom to mix." Like the ban on silo modification, the idea was to discourage a constant process of change and modernization. Freedom to mix would allow the parties to replace old missiles with new and bigger ones, or to replace old, diesel-fueled submarines with improved nuclear-powered boats. And so forth.

Washington was prepared to argue that freedom to mix would not only encourage surprise innovations but mightily complicate verification. How could American intelligence (barring on-site inspection) verify that the older weapons—a diesel-fueled submarine, for instance—had actually been destroyed? Or that silos containing the older, replaceable missiles had been fully dismantled. Satellite photography might have revealed only that the hole was covered. Who could say that it wasn't covered with three inches of dirt concealing a still-functional ICBM underneath?

The freedom-to-mix constraint would not have bothered the United States, which has no diesel-fueled missile-firing submarines and very few obsolete missiles. Washington planned no modernization other than the MIRV program, which the proposal did not affect. But it was most unlikely that the Russians, whose weapons were inferior, would have swallowed so bold an effort to "freeze" their inferiority. Again, America's proposal, understandably enough, was directed not to their anxieties, but to its own.

As expected, the Joint Chiefs emerged from the tank on Saturday morning. Halperin and others from ISA and Systems Analysis sat around in sports shirts, chatting with each other and even the children whom a few of them had brought along for the occasion; everyone nervously awaited the result. At last it arrived in the form of a Joint Chiefs of Staff memorandum with the reassuring red stripe that solemnly signals concurrence. The Joint Chiefs were on board.

Their memorandum amounted to a mild revision, but it did approve the basic elements of the position. It suggested only one change in the proposal, striking a reference to limiting ABM radars. It contained one dissent—from Admiral Moorer—on the freedom-to-mix provision; the Navy, possibly looking ahead to the vulnerability of the Minuteman force, wanted to keep open the option of shifting missiles from land to sea. But the package also contained a memorandum from Wheeler sharply critical of Moorer's dissent. Finally, the Joint Chiefs proposed a number of changes in the Clifford-to-Johnson interpretive memorandum, most of which were of minor importance. The language on limiting ABM's to a number between 100 and 1000 was changed to some "set and equivalent number" taking into account the threat from third countries, that is, China.

Only one of their suggestions came as a surprise. The Clifford memorandum had pointed out that, since both sides would remain free to deploy MIRV's, the Soviet SS-9 might one day menace the Minuteman force. A number of hedges against this danger had been noted: making Minuteman mobile; superhardening the silos; protecting Minuteman with ABM's; moving them, or some equivalent weapon, out to sea. In their memorandum, the Joint Chiefs excluded the language on Minuteman vulnerability. Nobody knew why, although ISA guessed that Wheeler took this decision; he may have felt that calling attention to a still-hypothetical threat would provoke interservice rivalry on how to deal with it. The Navy would have pressed for putting the missiles out to sea, the Army for defending them with ABM's, the Air Force for super-hardening the silos.

The ISA group, after digesting the JCS memorandum, swiftly decided to accept all of it. A new Clifford-to-Johnson memorandum absorbing all of the Joint Chiefs' alterations was prepared. It and the proposal, along with Admiral Moorer's appended dissent, were put before the Committee of Principals on the appointed Wednesday.

Some of those involved could scarcely believe that the Joint Chiefs had really acquiesced in a serious proposal to limit strategic arms. There was a tendency to look for an explanation. A few took the gesture at face value, believing that the Joint Chiefs recognized their duty to oblige the President. Other, more-skeptical souls found that thinking implausibly simple and felt that Johnson must at some point have taken a hand himself, possibly in a private telephone call to Wheeler. That, say the skeptics, might account for Wheeler's decision to dispense with his own arms-control unit and bring Allison back from Hawaii to manage SALT for him. All this is conjecture, since neither Johnson nor Wheeler has said anything.

What seems reasonably clear is that the Joint Chiefs bought the package at the price of excluding both a MIRV testing ban and an ABM limit. They may have felt that the proposal carried little risk of moving the talks toward agreement. The first sentence of the proposal was directed not to the Russians but to reassuring the Joint Chiefs. It said: "This proposal should be viewed as an entity, since that is the basis on which it has been evaluated." Narrowly interpreted, this language meant that any alteration of the proposal during negotiations might nullify the whole. It showed the degree to which the Americans were obliged to negotiate with themselves. It probably encouraged the Joint Chiefs to take comfort in the thought that some combination of Soviet intransigence and counterproposals would return the project to square one and dictate an internal renegotiation of America's SALT position under a new administration. The presidential elections lay just ahead, and some Republicans were already pronouncing a decline in the U.S. strategic position.

The big tumblers had clicked into place. Both the Russians and the Joint Chiefs had agreed to talks. Accumulated years of anxiety about the arms race and earlier efforts to inhibit it had at last conspired to maneuver the issue to the conference table. Or so it seemed. In fact, a moment of rare anticlimax lay just a few days ahead.

The proposal and various memoranda were sent by the Committee of Principals to the White House; there, Johnson approved in principle the entire package. Washington and Moscow settled on a date, September 30, to start the talks. A joint announcement was prepared for release on August 21. There remained only to pick the site, either Moscow or Leningrad; the United States was leaning toward Leningrad and the Russians almost certainly would agree. Johnson had also been pressing for a summit conference to start the proceedings, and, on August 19, Ambassador Dobrynin informed Washington that his government had agreed to the Johnson-Kosygin meeting on September 30.

At this point, only a handful of senior officials were informed of what was going to happen. It didn't matter, though. On August 20, units of the Soviet, Polish, Hungarian, Bulgarian, and East German armies invaded Czechoslovakia.

Preparations for the summit conference were abruptly halted. Rusk telephoned Dobrynin on the night of August 20 and informed him of the need to kill the joint announcement, scheduled for the following day. Everything was off. In explaining this decision, Rusk says: "The Russians, so far as we knew, were still prepared to go ahead. We felt we could not. Public opinion in the United States and in the West would not have comprehended a summit meeting and the start of talks right after the invasion of Czechoslovakia."

A senior U.S. official asked Dobrynin a few days later what Moscow had been thinking about in planning to invade Czechoslovakia on the eve of a joint statement announcing the start of SALT. Dobrynin replied that the two things had doubtless been on different tracks and had never connected in the minds of the leadership. Each, he said, had its own internal dynamic.

This was a diplomatic way of saying that SALT was again the victim of unfortunate timing. A year earlier, Moscow had not been ready, and talks could not begin. In August, 1968, after being formally scheduled, the event was swept aside by a matter far more immediate and urgent—Moscow's need to crush what seemed otherwise uncontrollable liberalizing forces in a satellite state of the first importance.

The emotional effect on most of those directly involved can be left to imagination. For some, it appeared that SALT had not been merely put off, but indefinitely shelved. With the Democratic party in severe disrepair, the signs pointed to a Nixon White House and, with it, a reassertion of the U.S. strategic advantage and diminished concern with limiting arms.

The ABM and MIRV programs, launched by Johnson and McNamara, would promote this purpose. The first flight tests of both Poseidon and Minuteman III were conducted on August 16, just five days before the joint announcement was to have been made. Russia's SS-9 triplet was tested on August 28. Also in August, the Senate rejected a move to cut $277 million from the Sentinal ABM program. All this suggested that a race for qualitative advantage was on, that time was running out on SALT.

A few reflective minds took a more balanced view. While not shrugging off this blow to their hopes, they felt SALT had an inner logic to which any President would have to respond. Putting a lid of some sort on strategic arms was a perceived need, whether it was to be done in the interest of stable relations between the great powers or in the long-run interest of stabilizing defense spending. This more-balanced view also took encouragement from the events of the summer, notably the precedent of JCS concurrence in a SALT proposal. Now that the Joint Chiefs had gotten their feet wet, dealing with them next time would hopefully be easier, especially for a Nixon Administration unburdened by past quarrels with the brass and the heavy residue of mutual suspicion and mistrust.

It was a curiously transitional moment, and not only because a change in administrations lay a few months off. Opinion was changing more rapidly than anyone could see. In August, 1968, a used-up President would probably have lost public and congressional support had he tried to override the Joint Chiefs on SALT. One year later, the Nixon Administration came within an eyelash of losing Senate approval of its ABM program. The outcry against the Vietnam War was crescendo. Other irritants, like the celebrated cost overruns on various weapon systems, combined to feed a broadening if not very articulate concern about military spending and overseas commitments.

The incoming Administration was greeted by a rare degree of public and congressional skepticism of much that passed for conventional wisdom. Still, the Nixon team began with serious misgivings about SALT. Its attitude was, of course, influenced by the bizarre nature of the preparations in the summer of 1968. Orderly minds were affronted by what seemed to them a cabalistic, almost conspiratorial, enterprise. And just before quitting office, Lyndon Johnson was to reinforce the suspicions of his successor by making an eleventh-hour, wholly quixotic effort to do precisely what events had not allowed him to do on September 30.

Skirmishing

"Too frightened to fight each other, too stupid to agree," said Talleyrand of his illustrious colleagues early in the Congress of Vienna.

By strong-arming the Czechs, the Soviet Union risked collapsing a finely tuned policy of lowering tensions with the West. For eighteen months, the Soviets had been having their own internal debates on SALT, and the drama in Czechoslovakia now left advocates of the talks perched on a badly torn limb.

Meanwhile, the luckless efforts to inaugurate SALT had inspired unilateral restraint on neither side. Inevitably, the Soviet offensive buildup had developed a momentum of its own. (The same was true of the ABM and MIRV programs in the United States.) To complement its exuberant ICBM expansion, Moscow had put to sea Russia's first nuclear submarines. America's forces apparently served as both model and catalyst for the Russians. The United States, after all, had been first to deploy large numbers of ICBM's in hardened silos. And it had invented both the nuclear submarine and the SLBM. The Sentinel ABM program, far more ambitious and advanced than Russia's Galosh, may well have encouraged the rapid buildup of a giant Soviet missile, the SS-9; such a weapon, it was doubtless argued in Moscow, would be needed to overcome the ABM defenses of U.S. cities; even were only one SS-9 to penetrate the ABM defense, it could level a large city. Another American innovation—multiple warheads—became still another technological hurdle for the Russians.

Such is the action-reaction cycle as perceived by many scientists and bureaucrats. Others among them demur, arguing that all of these weapons and each of the refinements have long been known to *both* sides and were always within the grasp of each. Thus, their argument continues, it is the impulse of technology, not an action-reaction cycle, that drives the arms race.

Wherever the truth may lie, in 1968, candidate Nixon seemed unimpressed by America's qualitative advantages. On October 24,

he accused Democrats of "creating a security gap for America."
The ICBM lead, he said, had "become only marginal" and would
"soon be gone." He characterized parity as a "peculiar, unprecedented doctrine," and promised "to restore our objective of clear-
cut military superiority."[1]

The lame-duck Johnson Administration would present Republicans with the smallest possible target on this issue. In a news conference on October 25, the day after Nixon's blast, Clifford said:
"I was comforted when I came into the Department to find the
extent of the superiority which we have over the Soviets. I have
continued in that direction. We have today a substantial military
superiority over the Soviet Union, and I shall certainly do all in
my power to continue to maintain that superiority as long as I
hold this position." Clifford gave precision to the claim by specifying a nearly four-to-one U.S. advantage over the Soviet Union
in deliverable nuclear weapons. A question about SALT drew a
reply best described as skeptical. After observing that "we must
proceed with caution," Clifford went on to recount the parable
of the hunter and the bear. The hunter, about to shoot, was asked
by the bear what he wanted. "A fur coat" was the reply. "The
bear," Clifford continued, "said, 'Well that is reasonable. What I
want is a full stomach. Let's sit down and negotiate.' So they sat
down and they negotiated. After a while, the bear left alone. He
had a full stomach and the hunter had his fur coat."

The assembled reporters, and possibly Clifford, too, would have
been surprised had they known that Johnson would try to revive
SALT and a summit conference before leaving office. Yet, SALT,
too, had a momentum of its own. The agreement to combine
talks with a summit that had been reached before August 20
hadn't expired; only the date had passed. Fortune had conspired
against the September 30 meeting, but both sides were reluctant
to abandon a project that had absorbed so much internal effort
and high-level commitment. Such things die hard in government.
On August 24, four days *after* the invasion of Czechoslovakia,
Washington put together its formal SALT presentation for the
September 30 meeting that had already been canceled.

A few closely involved bureaucrats hoped to start talks, but at
a more-subdued level than a summit conference. They felt that
the Czech affair and the upcoming presidential elections argued

for nudging SALT into play with the least possible fuss and visibility, and they thought that the proposal Johnson would have taken to Russia could be put to the service of private talks between the American and Russian delegates to the Geneva disarmament conference. They had no idea what the Administration might be planning. Neither did anyone else.

SALT was being kept alive rhetorically. On October 26, the day after Clifford's news conference, Under Secretary of State Katzenbach told an interparliamentary meeting in Paris that the dialogue with the Soviet Union must continue in spite of Czechoslovakia. Rusk had also mentioned SALT in guarded language ten days earlier.

Both sides were waiting watchfully, each recording the comments and signals, however understated, of the other. It was tacitly understood that not until the shock of Czechoslovakia had begun to subside and the presidential campaign run its course could SALT again become a serious matter. November and December would be the critical months, or so it seemed to those in the two capitals who harbored the notion—the illusion, as it turned out—that Mr. Nixon would arrive at the White House saddled with a solemn negotiation he would be obliged either to sustain or to squash.

Rusk recalls that he and Gromyko did not discuss SALT at all when they met at the opening of the U.N. General Assembly in September. The idea, he says, "was reopened in November, and we took the initiative." America had to take the initiative, because it was America that had cancelled the September 30 affair.

Strictly speaking, Washington did take the initiative, although Moscow, for its own reasons, was most eager to play the game. The collective leadership, after all, had opted for SALT. There was now the fresh incentive to soften the reviving image of the Soviet Union as heavy-handed oppressor of the weak; promoting elevated projects like arms control could serve this purpose.

In typically Soviet fashion, Kosygin strayed outside normal channels by choosing to talk with Robert McNamara, the American who, eighteen months earlier at Glassboro, had openly pleaded with him to start talks. McNamara, accompanied by his wife, was en route to Kabul on business for the World Bank, of which he had become president after leaving the Defense Department. He had scheduled a short stopover in Moscow so that he and his wife could look around a city they had never seen. Kosygin sent word that he would like to chat. The subject was SALT. That was November 11. The following day, Moscow's U.N. Ambassador announced that his government was ready "without delay to undertake a serious exchange of views on this question."

The initiative, as Rusk suggests, lay with Lyndon Johnson. One can only speculate on his thinking. He may have wanted to strike a blow for *détente* and stability—a valedictory *beau geste;* or to show that his tragic commitment to a war he had begun to moderate concealed the soul of a negotiator and peacemaker. One of his former associates argues that many presidents have been tempted to do something major in their lame-duck phase. It is just as true that one president cannot commit another.

The little drama that followed was played out in Washington and New York—more specifically in the White House and the Pierre Hotel, where President-elect Nixon and his staff were installed. Contact was opened with the Soviet Embassy in Washington, and the early signals from Moscow were positive. At this point, Johnson decided he might need some congressional backup, and he elected to involve Senator J. W. Fulbright, Chairman of the Committee on Foreign Relations. Fulbright recalls that, sometime after the election, Johnson asked him to the White House for a private talk; he thinks it was around the first of December. The call came as a surprise. Johnson, he says, had not invited him to the White House for other than ceremonial occasions in over three years; Vietnam and related issues had transformed their once-warm relationship into a celebrated feud.

At their meeting, Johnson informed Fulbright of his plan to launch SALT at a summit conference and asked for his support. Fulbright was aware, he says, that this was "not an orthodox action for a man leaving office"; but he had no objection and wished Johnson well with the project.

The meeting had been confidential; Fulbright did not even note it on his appointments calendar. And this was understandable. Circumstances required that the affair be closely held, because it involved not only the Soviet Government, but the President-elect as well. Johnson needed both a firm date from the

Russians and a blessing from Nixon. The two things were linked. However well disposed, the Russians could hardly oblige Johnson over the objections of the President-elect with whom they would be dealing directly in a few weeks.

Emissaries from both the White House and the Soviet Embassy made contact with the small Kissinger staff working with Nixon at the Pierre Hotel. The answer on SALT was flatly negative. Each high-level emissary was told that Nixon would not be responsible for anything that Johnson might do. A senior Soviet diplomat recalls that the language used at the Pierre Hotel was blunt, amounting "to something stronger than just saying 'we won't be bound.'" Nixon, says one American who was also involved, threatened to "repudiate" any last-minute agreement that Johnson might reach. Here, then, was a veto: Moscow had no choice but to deny Johnson a date for the cherished meeting.

As late as December 15, Clifford limned the stalemate by publicly criticizing the foot-dragging on SALT and urging that talks begin as soon as possible on whatever level the two sides could agree to. His remark was aimed both at Nixon and at the Russians. But it was already too late for what, in any case, was a misguided and futile enterprise.

Although nothing more could be done—not, at least, with the Russians—some parts of the bureaucracy were curiously unwilling to concede Nixon an entirely free hand on SALT. NATO, it seemed, might be the forum for keeping SALT alive and imparting some measure of international authority. Nixon was correctly assumed to be pro-NATO, and, as such, unlikely to do much about SALT without the concurrence of America's major allies. Folding NATO in, then, might prove to be the tie that binds. This notion found its way to the highest reaches of the Administration and was swiftly approved. Just before Johnson's departure, the NATO member countries would be presented with *A Catalogue of Objectives and Principles* on controlling strategic arms.

The language of the catalogue had an interesting background. Earlier in the autumn, Johnson instructed W. W. Rostow, his special assistant, to give Soviet Ambassador Dobrynin a memorandum containing the objectives and principles of SALT that had been cleared for the September 30 summit conference. In November, Dobrynin submitted an undated three-page response from his government. With a few mild revisions, Moscow was accepting the American statement. A memorandum from Clifford to Rusk, commenting on the reply, noted that it was "consistent with the U.S. proposal developed for presentation to the U.S.S.R." The catalogue, transmitted on January 13 to America's NATO Mission in Brussels, blended the language of the U.S. text with elements of the Russian reply.

On January 15, just five days before Nixon's inauguration, Johnson's NATO Ambassador, Harlan Cleveland, offered the catalogue in a "private meeting" with his colleagues held in the conference room of the then Secretary-General, Italy's Manlio Brosio. Private meetings are rather infrequent at NATO. They are limited to ambassadors, who are summoned by telephone, without being informed of the subject, and who appear unaccompanied by their interpretors and note-takers. No official record of such meetings is kept. Their purpose is to allow people to speak more frankly on topics of special sensitivity, which, as often as not, fall outside NATO's writ.

Cleveland's catalogue contained four objectives and two principles. Although the entire package aroused considerable unease, one of the objectives was especially disturbing. It read: "To improve U.S.–Soviet understanding by establishing a continuing process of discussion of issues arising from the strategic situation." This bland and seemingly blameless language genuinely disturbed European diplomats. To them, it hinted that Washington might deal over their heads directly with Moscow on issues of as much concern to Europe as to America. Suspicions of an emerging great-power condominium come naturally to America's European allies. They worry that the United States and the U.S.S.R. will jointly decide how to deal with threats to peace and stability; in turn, this might mean that, in the event Moscow were suddenly to revive the cold-war tactic of pressure and intimidation, Washington would look the other way. Western Europe's sense of security relies heavily on a constant process of reassurance from the United States.

A British diplomat found the catalogue initiative "quite remarkable. . . . The Johnson people were tipping their hats as they went through the door." He recalls that "the European reaction was not good. Condominium anxieties were aroused." And Italy's

Brosio felt much the same way. On January 23, he recorded the members' reaction in a single sentence: "The Council supported the general lines proposed by the U.S., noting the importance of bearing in-mind the interests of the Alliance as a whole." This euphemistic language only barely concealed NATO's aversion to the catalogue. A number of Europeans privately communicated their unhappiness to American colleagues.

Not surprisingly, the new Administration reacted more bearishly. The catalogue was seen as just one of a series of irritants, part of a pattern that included Johnson's remarkable try for a last hurrah at the summit. The effect was to reinforce, if not exaggerate, the suspicions held by Nixon, Kissinger, and others close to them that Johnson's people had hoped to close off the strategic options available to the new Administration before it had taken power. Of special annoyance were the catalogue's two principles. One said that "the limitation and reduction in strategic armaments should be carried out as a complex including both offensive and defensive weapons systems." This was taken to mean that Nixon, instead of continuing the ABM program, should seek to hobble it. The second principle said: "The limitation and reduction in strategic armaments should be so balanced that neither side could obtain any military advantage and that security should be assured equally for both sides." This was taken to mean that Nixon should embrace parity, a concept he had rejected during the campaign and about which he and his advisers had genuine misgivings. One of Nixon's advisers was harshly critical, describing the Johnson initiatives as "an end run which achieved nothing other than to give the Europeans condominium shudders," and he still feels that the paperwork on arms control prepared for the incoming Administration "was written so as to try to befuddle us." The outgoing group, he says, "tried to show that the ABM issue was all but settled within the bureaucracy."

It is certainly true that the Johnson people, having made the ABM decision, were moving in the other direction. The position of Rusk, who had always regarded the ABM as a menace, was, toward the end, ascendent; about to be shorn of power, Johnson no longer had cause to bend to the Joint Chiefs and the ABM lobby in Congress.

Nixon was determined to find out for himself and to make

his own decisions based on a broad range of choice. He arrived at the White House to find the Soviet Union simultaneously pursuing a tough line and a soft line. The tough line showed up in the declared intention to intervene in the affairs of any wayward satellite state, like Dubcek's Czechoslovakia, plus a venturesome diplomacy along the southern Mediterranean littoral and deeper into the Middle East and South Asia. Moscow's attitude toward China was also hardening. The soft line showed up in efforts to improve relations with the Western bloc. It was high-risk diplomacy. If the hard line could foster trouble, if not conflict, wherever applied and further complicate relations with Washington, the soft line bore the risk of encouraging Eastern European dissidence, if not open protest. Moscow finds it hard to cultivate better relations with the West without allowing its client states some movement in the same direction. Moreover, a high-risk Soviet diplomacy argues for large Soviet military forces of all kinds, including strategic. It strengthens the hand of the military bureaucracy, which for some time has been asserting a stronger claim to influence in its area of special competence. If the political leaders elect to take risks, goes the military thinking, let them give the military the responsibility for buying whatever forces may be needed to back Soviet policies and commitments.

Nixon and Kissinger were in no hurry to get on with SALT. Among other things, Soviet eagerness was disconcerting. On January 20, the day of Nixon's inaugural, a Soviet Foreign Ministry spokesman announced that Moscow was ready to "start a serious exchange of views" with the United States on a "mutual limitation and subsequent reduction of strategic nuclear vehicles, including defensive systems." He added that "when the Nixon Administration is ready to sit down at the negotiating table, we are ready to do so, too."[2]

Nixon replied a week later. On January 27, he told a news conference that he favored strategic talks with the Soviet Union, but he stressed that the timing and context of the talks were vitally important. Talks, he said, should promote progress on "outstanding political problems," like the Middle East. He wanted to be certain that the United States had "sufficient military power." It was at this news conference that he identified the term "sufficiency" as more useful than "parity."

The new President was saying, in effect, that if Soviet leaders were so keen on SALT, they should pay for it. The term "linkages" cropped up: Progress on SALT would be linked to political progress on matters of immediate concern—Vietnam, as well as the Middle East. Arms control, then, would be treated as one of a number of interrelated issues, not as an end in itself.

Ambassador Dobrynin called on the new Secretary of State, William P. Rogers, on February 13 and reported Moscow's readiness to "resume" or "start" the talks, subject to agreement on dates. He wasn't certain, he said, which of the two verbs was appropriate Rogers answered jokingly: "We could start to resume."

Four days later, on February 17, Dobrynin called on Nixon. His government, he said, also wanted to move toward the era of negotiation to which Nixon had called attention in his inaugural speech. The Soviet leadership would be prepared to move forward on a number of issues, notably the missile problem and the Middle East.

Nixon's reply was noncommittal. With regard to SALT, he said, the U.S. position was being reviewed by the government and decisions would have to await completion of this review, as well as consultation with America's allies. He added that the world political atmosphere would be important to progress on arms control matters.

Nixon had clearly expressed his Administration's hesitancy about SALT at this early stage. It recognized the opportunity that talks might offer, but the new President and his uniquely powerful adviser, Dr. Kissinger, were mistrustful both of Soviet motives and of what seemed to them the erratic and single-minded tactics of their predecessors in pursuing talks. They worried that nobody —not the bureaucracy, not the people around Johnson—had sought analytically to see how SALT meshed with Soviet purposes. The negotiations, they felt, would be tougher than the outgoing Administration had been willing to concede. A Khrushchev might have been more certain of his authority than the collective leadership, hence possibly easier to deal with. Since the Soviet military had presumably helped, if indirectly, to install the new leaders, its influence would be correspondingly larger. (This judgment was borne out later, after talks began, by the lamentable

ignorance of Soviet civilian negotiators about the numbers, locations, and characteristics of their own weapons. The military, as
noted, kept them in the dark.)

To the new Administration, it seemed essential to know more
about the motives of the Soviet military, especially whether and
to what degree these diverged from the thinking of the political
leaders. Why, for example, might both groups favor parity and
a letup in strategic arms development? How valid was the assumption that Soviet leaders feared the harsh economic penalties that
another major round of strategic spending would impose? Did
Soviet political leaders reckon that parity would allow them to
mount a more aggressive diplomacy with reduced risks of confrontation with the United States?

Henry Kissinger had arrived with one of academia's glossiest
reputations as a thinker and writer. He had served as a consultant
and troubleshooter to Democratic administrations, and was no
stranger to the habits of bureaucracy. His writing and his advice
to presidents often deplored bureaucracy's insensitivity to the
effect of domestic politics on foreign policy. In the Soviet Union,
domestic politics means the interplay between powerful interest
groups. For Kissinger, then, America's SALT position would have
to take these into account. Perhaps the Soviet Army and Navy had
decided that nuclear parity would free resources for building up
troop and surface-ship strength. Kissinger and his staff also wondered about other military interest groups, notably the Soviet
Strategic Rocket Forces and the Air Defense Command. Would
they accept a limit on their offensive and defensive missiles without trying to work around the agreement? Could they cheat undetected on a large scale? Might they make common cause with
the Kremlin and use SALT as a means of pressuring Nixon,
through the American public and Congress, to hold back on ABM
and MIRV deployment?

Nixon and Kissinger felt a need to know much more about Soviet
purposes before commiting themselves to a negotiation that might
serve to promote these purposes. The first step, then, was to "get
the attention of the bureaucracy," as some in Washington put it.
A blizzard of questions from Kissinger's office descended on the
intelligence agencies and the blue-ribbon White House staff he
was assembling. Some people may have looked upon SALT as an

answer to such problems as slowing the arms race, but for the new group, SALT begged many questions and answered none. Not until the questions were answered would the Administration rest easy about SALT. The novel White House-centered system for which Nixon had opted seemed the ideal vehicle for setting bureaucracy to work on tough questions instead of rehearsing old positions.

Henry Kissinger seems to have had more of a chance meeting than a rendezvous with history. He could have expected to occupy center stage in a Rockefeller presidency, but, to the casual eye, his close association with Nelson Rockefeller was not likely to commend him for the loftiest foreign-policy job that Mr. Nixon, or any other President, has conferred on any individual.

Friends in government and academia expected to see Kissinger appointed to some interesting job in either a Nixon or a Humphrey Administration. Assistant Secretary of Defense for International Security Affairs was thought to be a lively possibility. The job had been held successively in the two preceding Administrations by Paul H. Nitze, William P. Bundy, the late John McNaughton, and Paul C. Warnke. It had accumulated a good deal of authority and scope. Kissinger might well have taken it.

Nixon clearly knew enough about him and had read enough of his published work to see that Kissinger shared much of his thinking about world problems, the virtues of a strong chief executive, and, perhaps more important, the pernicious drag of bureaucracy on presidential power. On this point, their's would be Shakespeare's "marriage of true minds," to which few if any impediments would be admitted.

George Reedy, who toiled many long years for Lyndon Johnson, both in the Senate and the White House, has written as revealingly about the high office as anyone: Presidents, he notes, have remarkable discretion in the use of their time:

> Despite the widespread belief to the contrary . . . there is far less to the Presidency, in terms of essential activity, than meets the eye. The psychological burdens are heavy, even crushing, but no President ever died of overwork, and it is doubtful whether any ever will. The chief executive can, of course, fill

his working hours with as much motion as he desires. . . . But in terms of actual administrative work, the Presidency is pretty much what the President wants to make of it.[3]

Nixon's preoccupation is foreign policy. In a sense, the same was true of his immediate predecessors, Kennedy and Johnson, upon whose attention the cold war and then Vietnam did make heavy demands. Obviously, Nixon, too, was obliged to cope with Vietnam and the whole established range of security issues. But from the outset, he seems to have had a special sense of commitment—even a vocation—to foreign affairs, dating probably to his days as Vice President, when he travelled widely, spoke a great deal about security problems, developed views, but could do little to affect decisions.

He arrived in power determined not to endorse decisions largely shaped by bureaucracy's talent for narrowing choice; instead, he sought to extend the range of choice and to make independent decisions. He would not be, like some presidents, one of a number of players, albeit the key player. Instead, working through Kissinger, he would make of the White House the fountainhead of initiative and the solitary instrument for decision. Bureaucracy would march —and briskly at that—to a tune written, orchestrated, and played in the West Wing. No less an authority than France's President, Georges Pompidou, has said, "it is American Gaullism in action."

The Nixon-Kissinger relationship is a source of endless, though futile, conjecture. The precise nature of their respective roles is known only to them. We know that Kissinger's power dwarfs that of any preceding White House adviser; that his influence probably exceeds that disposed by such powerful Secretaries of State as Acheson and Dulles. We know that he shapes Nixon's options by defining the questions to which bureaucracy must respond. He says—and there is no reason to doubt him—that the options are impartially presented to the President, who decides. Much less-clear is the degree to which Nixon, in deciding, relies on advice from Kissinger. Nor is it clear whether various major initiatives and departures are the invention of the President, or of his confidential adviser. Kissinger, we also know, executes such initiatives through private negotiations with other governments carried on with a secrecy so remarkable that they are often hidden from members of his own staff and senior officials of the Administration.

In style and background, they are different men, though not entirely. Nixon is a private person, and so, basically, is Kissinger. Neither the publicity that streams round him nor the endless analysis of his role reveals the essential Kissinger, who remains as private as the essential Nixon. One wonders which, if any, other President would have tolerated an adviser who, if anything, attracts even more attention than the country's senior politician. Nixon, so far, has seemed not to mind. Indeed, there is a fair presumption that he finds Kissinger's celebrity useful; he has, after all, both fostered and sustained it.

His instant eminence and unrivalled access to Nixon set Kissinger up as the new Administration's largest attraction for the star performers of the Washington press corps and the town's best addresses. He was an instant hit in these more public roles. Journalists and notables alike were—and are—taken by a disarmingly candid style; the press also profited from his lucid backgrounders on problems and policies. His gift for the *bon mot* and a somewhat self-mocking style didn't hurt either. Very early on he was heard to say: "We will make our own mistakes in our own way and they will be completely new mistakes." More recently, after his secret trip to Moscow, made in late April, 1972 to prepare the President's voyage a month later, he said of the Kremlin's lavish hospitality: "I'd do anything for caviar, and I probably did." The quips reflect the natural and spontaneous side of an otherwise intense, deep, and somewhat enigmatic personality.

There may be a tendency to exaggerate Kissinger's influence. His formidable expertise and his talent for holding bureaucracy in line are clearly a source of comfort—indeed, are probably essential—to Nixon. The question is whether he is the President's alter ego on security matters or more nearly the instrument of Nixon's will. The truth may vary from issue to issue, but it bears repeating that Richard Nixon was always determined to make his own decisions on questions falling within his favorite realm.

What seems clear is that Kissinger serves a constituency of one, much in the manner of his early hero Metternich, who was "not a man of strong passions and of bold measures; not a genius but a great talent; cool, calm, imperturbable and calculator *par excellence!*"[4] Kissinger, too, has these qualities. The passions and the instinct for bold measures may lie with his constituent and principal.

On January 20, there arrived on all the appropriate desks in all the appropriate agencies copies of National Security Decision Memorandums 1 and 2. The NSDM is along with the NSSM—the National Security Study Memorandum—a Kissinger innovation. The NSSM rigorously assigns bureaucracy a task, most often a study assessing various policy options. Once the study is completed and accepted, the President chooses; at this point, a NSDM is prepared. It formulizes his decision and tells the government what is to be done.

NSDM's 1 and 2 solemnly established nothing less than an entirely new national security system. The documents were based on a lengthy Kissinger memorandum to a President-elect who knew exactly what he wanted. The new system would restore to the twenty-four-year-old National Security Council the prestige and authority it had been losing since the Eisenhower days. Kennedy and Johnson had found the NSC too elaborate; they preferred a smaller, looser, more flexible system that would be responsive to immediate problems and crises, and they sought advice more informally, relying on those whose judgment they valued most on given issues at a given moment. Johnson's famous Tuesday lunch typified this preference for the informal style.

The Nixon-Kissinger design went far beyond merely restoring the statutory role of the NSC. Their system would be invincibly White House controlled. Other agencies and institutions—the Departments of State and Defense, the Joint Chiefs of Staff—would be held strictly subordinate to the President and his senior adviser. A number of new devices would clip bureaucracy's wings, not least the NSSM-NSDM innovation. Both are written in the White House and signed by the President, which means that only he (and his staff) can assign the issues to be studied and frame the questions to which bureaucracy must respond. Thus, the NSSM allows him to monopolize initiative, while the NSDM, the decision memorandum, becomes a kind of executive order. Bureaucrats may appeal a NSDM, but only with great difficulty can they undercut it or work around it.

The problem, as seen by Nixon and the immediate Kissinger

staff, was how to block bureaucracy's tendency to obscure or deny presidential options by presenting agreed positions that trouble no agency's special concerns. Blocking this tendency meant taking hold of the committees through which government does so much of its work. To do this, Kissinger would kill a few, add a few, and remodel others.

First to go was the most prominent, the Senior Interdepartmental Group (SIG), which was chaired by the Under Secretary of State. Since its creation in 1966, the SIG had been controlled largely by the State Department. Its decisions had to clear Rusk's office before going on to the White House. Kissinger replaced SIG with a Senior Review Group, which had much the same membership but which he would chair. He was, in fact, to chair all but one of the six new senior committees that were to follow. And the writ of these committees would cover the whole range of national security issues.

Rogers agreed to the new system before the inauguration, but his department was not happy with the abrupt decline of its initiative and responsibility. Much of its work was incorporated into the White House operation. Still, bureaucracy's reaction was by and large favorable; the changes seemed to make sense. In any case, the agencies were flooded with assignments from Kissinger and there was little time for complaint or for trying to outmaneuver the White House. And many bureaucrats felt that not only were the right questions being asked, but that they were being asked with refreshing precision and rigor.

A dozen NSSM's issued from the White House in the ten days following Nixon's inauguration. By April 30, the number was up to fifty-five. Out went the NSSM's and in flowed the studies, often graded barely passing and sometimes even unacceptable by Professor Kissinger.

It rapidly became clear that Kissinger and his staff had seized control of national security policy and that Kissinger dominated his staff. He alone dealt with the President. He assigned staff members their tasks, but told them no more than they needed to know. Questions began to pose themselves. The system had obvious merit: Presidents should have broad freedom of choice, since they normally bear the responsibility for decisions; yet, could one man, for all his gifts, establish presidential options by dominating the security system of the world's greatest power? Is the role of a modern Metternich or Talleyrand really available in an age when history is made overnight and some states deploy nuclear weapons? Any system, however solid its intellectual underpinnings, is only as good as the men, or man, running it.

In short, people wondered whether so concentrated a system was workable. The risk of overloading was self-evident. Some issues, it was feared, would be lost or buried owing to the limits on the time and endurance of a handful of people and, ultimately, on the one man with access to the President. There was also the risk that the normal function of the agencies in advising the President would be compromised, if not altogether lost. The system then might have the defect of its virtues: The White House must have the cooperation of the agencies in running foreign policy, and thus the need for a bureaucratic consensus remains. Nixon and Kissinger understood that; they had simply elected to acquire this consensus by other than the traditional means. There remained the question, Would they succeed? Would the system work?

SALT was an issue admirably suited to the new system. It raised endless questions, required exhaustive analysis, and offered considerable lead time, since the Administration had decided against proceeding with haste, and the pace of negotiations would necessarily be slow. SALT was to place heavier demands on the system than any other issue, excepting Vietnam. Indeed, SALT was to test both the system and its chief architect.

Kissinger and his staff did not seize control of SALT as swiftly as they did most other issues. Gerard C. Smith, named director of ACDA by Nixon, regarded the statute that had originally created the agency as giving his office the chief authority. Under Smith, a SALT interagency working group was created; although it was chaired by Smith's deputy, Philip Farley, much of its work was done by Johnson Administration holdovers who had not yet been replaced and by bureaucrats who had been over the ground before. Many of these felt a sense of commitment to the August, 1968 proposal and to the analytical work that produced it. Hence, to nobody's great surprise, Smith was to find himself at odds with his own Administration.

The new Administration obviously felt no attachment to the

past. Still less did it admire the method and the work that had shaped the 1968 enterprise. Tailoring a SALT proposal to suit Joint Chiefs of Staff attitudes seemed, understandably, something to be avoided in the future. The system would see to that. And Kissinger would demand a more methodical and rigorous approach to verification and related issues. Rightly or wrongly, he found much of the earlier work lacking in rigor, and he, along with a few associates, placed the blame in large part on the CIA. For some time, this agency would operate well out of the new Administration's favor, partly—perhaps mainly—because its work on SALT was thought to have lacked detachment, to have reflected an uncritical support for arms control.

ACDA and its allies throughout the bureaucracy wanted to move faster on SALT than the Administration. They were blocked by Kissinger's system. Not until the White House issued a NSSM on SALT could anything serious begin to happen. The two sides were at cross purposes, with Smith's people arguing that SALT was urgent business: How else to halt the race for improved and potentially destabilizing weapons? MIRV tests were proceeding briskly, and the Soviet Union was continuing to test its SS-9 triplet. Moreover, Nixon had made no decision on Johnson's Sentinel program. The sooner talks began, the easier it would be, the SALT advocates argued, to navigate a proposed ABM ban through the government. ACDA began circulating memos warning that time was working against SALT, that options like a MIRV testing ban might be foreclosed by the activities of both great powers.

In the Defense Department, the new leadership opposed this thinking, and the White House concurred. Before taking a stand on SALT, the Administration would require an exhaustive study of its military and strategic position. Before contemplating self-limiting steps, the White House would decide for itself how much strategic hardware would be enough. The operative term was to be "sufficiency," and the Administration would lay down its own "sufficiency criteria."

On January 21, the day after Nixon's inauguration, seven NSSM's were issued. Number 3, titled "Military Posture," grappled with the sufficiency question. ACDA and its allies could hardly dispute a White House decision to explore this terrain. Any new

Administration had the right, if not the duty, to make its own measurements of security needs. But a large part of the burau-cracy's SALT lobby—and it amounted to that—did think that such an exercise should proceed in tandem with SALT prepara-tions. These, they argued, need not await completion of the NSSM 3 exercise, or even limp along behind.

Meanwhile, the political climate was changing more rapidly than most Washington institutions recognized. Congressional attitudes had begun to shift, partly to keep up with public opinion, and the internal debate on SALT was to be affected—to some degree shaped—by the shift. SALT was no longer an acronym available only to bureaucrats, foreign governments, various specialists, and some journalists. The term was becoming known to a more general audience, which was also becoming even more aware of related terms, like ABM and MIRV, and the ABM was hitting close to home: In the cities where sites were to be built, the Sentinel pro-gram was breeding hostility. Congress began to respond. The public neither understood nor cared much about the rationale for Sentinel, but metropolitan ABM sites were feared as potential light-ning rods by people living next door to the sites. A kind of political action-reaction cycle began, with aroused voters in cities like Boston and Chicago chivvying those they had elected to office in November. In turn, those members of Congress who already dis-liked ABM's fueled the popular concern by rehearsing the argu-ments of scientists and other academics hostile to Sentinel. And a large part of the academic community, including some who served as government consultants, was strenuously opposed to ABM de-fense of cities.

People who had served Lyndon Johnson might well have been pinching themselves. Who among them in the summer of 1968 could have predicted so wild and rapid a swing in congressional thinking? Or that a new President would confront a tough bipar-tisan coalition of ABM adversaries, instead of the formidable con-gressional lobby that had helped push Johnson toward the Sentinel deployment decision?

In February, the pseudogothic figure of Mendel Rivers, the since-deceased autocrat and chairman of the House Armed Services Committee, frowned upon Sentinel; his committee, he judged, would not approve the Chicago and Washington ABM sites.

In the Senate, rising protest foreshadowed the hard sledding that ABM would henceforth have there. Some members, including Edward M. Kennedy, urged the new Secretary of Defense, Melvin R. Laird, to freeze deployment, if only temporarily. Laird had already endorsed Sentinel as a means of strengthening the U.S. negotiating position whenever SALT got under way. The so-called bargaining-chip argument, a legacy from the Johnson days, was to remain a basic and perhaps the most convincing part of the ABM rationale. But now a new Administration decided to back off for a moment. On February 6, Laird ordered a temporary halt in Sentinel deployment pending a one-month review.

With Sentinel in deep trouble, the Administration had a number of alternatives to consider. It could halt Sentinel and continue ABM research and development; it could scrap Sentinel's discredited anti-China rationale and opt for a thick, expensive, and frankly anti-Russion ABM defense of cities; it could discard city defense altogether and choose to defend only Minuteman sites with simpler and more inexpensive hardware; finally, it could strike a compromise by shifting the hardware already being developed for Sentinel away from cities to Minuteman sites.

The Administration chose to compromise. It changed the name of the system from Sentinel to Safeguard. In its first phase, Safeguard would defend Minuteman sites; but neither city defense nor the anti-China rationale was scrapped. In its second phase, Safeguard, like Sentinel, would defend cities. In short, the Nixon team sought to have it both ways. Critics of city defense would be disarmed by the initial shift of hardware to Minuteman sites, while adherents of city defense in the Pentagon and Congress would be mollified by the promise of the second phase. Finally, budget-cutters would be pleased because in its first year or so Safeguard could be made to cost less than Sentinel.

Nixon had arrived in the White House determined to save money. At the very start, a brief memorandum was prepared listing major items in the defense budget and the sums requested for them by the outgoing Administration. The figure for Sentinel, about $1.8 billion, seemed ripe for pruning, especially since the public outcry in affected cities was gathering force. A cheaper, less city-oriented system would, it seemed, be easier to sell to Congress. In addition to the advantages of economy and the public-relations value of moving the sites away from cities, the move seemed consistent with a changing strategic situation. The National Intelligence Estimates continued to downgrade the Chinese threat, but the Soviet Union was rapidly expanding its SS-9 force, testing MRV's, and, presumably, heading toward a MIRV capability. Here, then, was a threat that frankly alarmed the new Administration and seemed to give ABM the plausibility it had lacked. A MIRV'd SS-9 force of a certain size, warned Laird, could all but wipe out American ICBM's. Minuteman, then, would have to be defended.

On March 14, Nixon announced his decision in language as carefully worded and alert to the hazards of misguided ABM deployment as McNamara's San Francisco speech of September, 1967. Sentinel, said the President, would be changed. The first objective was "protection of our land-based retaliatory forces against a direct attack by the Soviet Union." Nixon went on to say that, while he would have liked to "provide the American people with complete protection against a major nuclear attack, it is not now within our power to do so. The heaviest defense . . . still could not prevent a catastrophic level of U.S. fatalities. . . ." In a passage reminiscent of McNamara, he added: "And it might look to an opponent like the prelude to an offensive strategy threatening the Soviet deterrent." The modified system, he said, "has been designed so that its defensive intent is unmistakable." Finally, Nixon reckoned that the total cost of the new system would run between $6 and $7 billion, but, he pointed out, holding deployment to a "deliberate pace" would halve the funding that Johnson had asked for Sentinel.

The moderate tone of the statement somewhat reassured the arms-control bureaucracy, who saw the switch in priorities from city to Minuteman defense as a step toward stability. Additionally, the more deliberate pace might rule out any ABM deployment if SALT got underway. The statement suggested as much.

Unhappily, it also left some questions open and injected others. The anti-China rationale was not discarded, only toned down. Nixon himself was known to be impressed by the China argument, even if some around him were not. Besides defending Minuteman, his new system would, he said, protect "against an accidental attack . . . and against the kind of attack which the Chinese Communists may be capable of launching throughout the 1970's." Because of what he also said about hardware, this passage could not be construed as unserious rhetoric aimed at placating the city-defense lobby. "The system," Nixon revealed, "will use components previously developed for the Sentinel system." And it is this decision that has most bedeviled Safeguard's troubled history. City and missile defense, in the eyes of most experts, are as different as apples and oranges. Using Sentinel's components to defend missiles, they were soon to argue, would produce a system incapable of reliably defending anything.

If ABM technology doesn't defy comprehension, it does require a leap of the imagination. How to intercept an attacking missile traveling at four miles per second with another one traveling at about one mile per second? Something called a phased-array radar tracks incoming missiles by electronic scanning and guides interceptors. It relies on huge data-processing centers, which consume and disgorge vast amounts of information on objects whirling and flying in the sky. The center is a mélange of computer processors, memory banks, displays, tapes, and discs. It is the brain and heart of a city- or area-ABM defense. It is also very expensive and infinitely complex, and it required more lead time in research and development than any part of the ABM system. This radar center is also an Achilles heel, being vulnerable to almost any kind of attacking missile.

A Safeguard system seems to require two of these monuments to advanced technology. One is known as the PAR, not because it is a phased-array radar, which it is, but because it has been functionally designated the Perimeter Acquisition Radar. The other one is called the MSR, which stands for Missile Site Radar. It, too, is a phased-array radar, which, because its beams are steered electronically, can track innumerable objects simultaneously. The PAR is supposed to identify objects at ranges up to 1500 miles, while the MSR has the same task somewhat closer in. Were the PAR to detect an incoming warhead, its computers would define the ballistic trajectory and relay this information to the MSR, which in turn would prepare interceptors for launch and then guide them. In theory, the PAR's range would allow some ten minutes to launch the interceptor missiles.

The first PAR, located near Grand Forks, North Dakota, is

housed in a concrete structure about 200 feet square at the base and 130 feet tall. It has its own underground power plant and assorted administrative buildings. The MSR, about 40 miles away, is wedged into an underground building about 230 feet square, with a 75-foot-tall turret above the ground showing four radar "faces." Nearby are the 150 Minuteman deployed at Grand Forks Air Force base, which are to be defended by the combination of PAR, MSR, and two kinds of interceptor missiles.

One of those interceptors is called the Spartan. It is a 55-foot, three-stage missile launched from an underground silo and capable of flying many hundreds of miles. Spartan's third stage is supposed to destroy or disable attacking vehicles far beyond the atmosphere. For this, it carries a warhead in the astonishing range of four to five megatons. None of the U.S. offensive missiles has a fraction of this destructive power. Systems Analysis fought this warhead and proposed something smaller and cheaper. The fight was lost "spectacularly," according to one participant.

The other, less-controversial, interceptor is a 27-foot, two-stage missile, called the Sprint. It is launched from underground cells and operates at shorter ranges. The Sprint has a thermonuclear warhead in the kiloton range, and is designed for what is known as "terminal" defense, which means it can defend places—missiles sites, command and control centers, or even a single city.

Spartan, on the other hand, is designed for defending large areas. Spartan and PAR in combination could provide some defense of regional population centers, while Sprint and the MSR in combination might provide some protection for Minuteman sites. By scrambling them all together—both the radars and both the interceptors—the Administration risked confusing, if not compromising, Safeguard's purpose.

The length and intensity of the debate that followed Nixon's ABM policy statement surprised both the Administration and the bureaucracy. Vietnam aside, Safeguard probably inspired more debate and more testimony on Capitol Hill in 1969 and 1970 than any other security issue. Closely involved bureaucrats and officials doubted that subtle distinctions between city and missile defense would be made in the debate or hearings. They were wrong, as it turned out.

Neither the debate nor the expert testimony was always logical, objective, or even relevant. Extravagant claims and assertions were made by people on both sides of the issue. Administration witnesses exaggerated the imminence of the SS-9 threat to Minuteman, while some scientists and academics who should have known better tended to write off the threat and to load the case against Safeguard. The Administration, in turn, conceded none of Safeguard's obvious weaknesses and applied the hard sell. Some Senators and Congressmen heard only what they chose to hear and took hard positions; others were frankly confused by the exquisitely complex argument.

A few of Safeguard's Senate critics were led so far astray as to flirt with such radical solutions to the SS-9 threat as "launch on warning." This piece of folly suggests that the only sure way to prevent the destruction of one's missiles is to launch them on electronic warning of an attack. If the warning turned out to be a false alarm of some kind, the missiles would be disarmed en route to their targets. The dangers and uncertainties packed into this simple notion are staggering, obvious, and too numerous to mention. It is worth noting only to illustrate the extreme thinking to which the Safeguard debate seems to have driven some otherwise serious people.

Nobody could rank the arguments which, in the summer of 1969, caused half the Senate to vote against the Safeguard authorization, and just miss defeating it. Still, out of the hundreds of thousands of words of testimony there emerged a reasonably strong case against the system; and it stuck. One among the expert witnesses whose testimony stood out and who probably established the case most convincingly was Dr. Wolfgang K. H. Panofsky, the Director of Stanford University's Linear Accelerator. Panofsky, a high-energy physicist and former member of the President's Science Advisory Committee, has the respect of all sides, including the Pentagon. He is neither a ritual disarmer nor a knee-jerk enemy of the ABM. To the contrary, Panofsky advocated building an ABM defense of Minuteman, but only *if* SALT failed to limit offensive missiles and the SS-9 threat *did* emerge. His argument with the Administration turned on hardware. Panofsky urged developing the so-called hard-site option for missile defense and opposed the Sentinel-Safeguard components. The hard-site components, as he explained, would be simpler, much cheaper, more reliable; the radars would be less vulnerable. The entire system, he maintained, was exactly tailored to the role of defending Minuteman sites.

On March 28, 1969, just two weeks after the President's statement, Panofsky told a Senate Foreign Relations subcommittee why he thought that using city-defense components "for a very different purpose is necessarily a very poor engineering decision."[5] His unassailable point was that a defense installation should be as blast resistant as the hardened missiles it is supposed to protect. Safeguard's "eye," the MSR radars, can withstand less than one-tenth of the blast effect of the missiles they are to help defend. The Russians, if they chose, could attack Safeguard with some portion of their 950-odd SS-11's, thus blinding the system and probably exhausting its supply of defensive missiles, at which point the much larger SS-9's, trailing behind, could attack Minuteman fields with impunity.

Panofsky pointed up other weaknesses and anomolies of Safeguard, most of which were privately conceded by a good many of those who were obliged to defend the system. Indeed, with time, the rationale for Safeguard became even shakier, the ring of supporting rhetoric distinctly hollow.

Yet there remained one argument beyond the reach of critics, even if some never did accept it. For all its weaknesses, Safeguard could be a bargaining chip at SALT. One way to discourage Soviet ABM's, or, better, to negotiate an ABM limitation, would be to deploy an American system. Hardpoint might make sense, but it didn't exist. Thanks to the ardor of the city-defense lobby, hardpoint had barely entered the design stage, whereas the contractors could begin pouring concrete for the first two Safeguard sites once Congress approved the money, as it finally did late in 1969.

Nobody knows, but Sentinel and Safeguard may well have been critical in turning Moscow from a pro- to an anti-ABM bias. Russia's experts knew as well as America's that neither Sentinel nor Safeguard would have reliably protected much of anything. But they also knew that each system had a lot of growth potential; either might eventually offer heavy protection of American cities. For Washington to go down that road might in turn reduce or deny Moscow's capability of striking these cities. Planners on both sides tend toward gloomy calculation; they reckon with all contingencies, including the most remote, and they become the victims of an internal rhetoric, now exaggerating the qualities of the opponent's forces, now doubting the performance of their own. As Lord Salisbury put it: "If you believe the doctors, nothing is wholesome; if you believe the theologians, nothing is innocent; if you believe the soldiers, nothing is safe." To the Russians, the Sentinel-Safeguard components—radars and missiles alike—were not only far more sophisticated than their own, but a base on which the Americans might build something that would actually work.

Congress was less impressed. Added to all the other objections, many members saw little reason to deploy a system whose components cost a lot more than the missiles they might, or might not, be able to protect. On August 6, the Senate came within one vote of denying Safeguard the breath of life. The Administration barely won the battle for the first two sites, and it actually lost the larger doctrinal struggle, for a corner had been turned in the ABM saga. The intensity of the debate and the scope of the protest plunged Safeguard's future as a multibillion dollar dual-purpose ABM system into grave doubt.

Hindsight shows that the angry Safeguard debate cleared the air. The setback to the Administration contained in its narrow victory enfeebled the ABM advocates. All the highly theoretical and abstruse argument about whether ABM's would work and, if so, what kind of ABM's, deployed at what strength, and at what cost would not again appear so formidable. The ABM was simply sliding into disrepute.

If for rather different reasons, both Washington and Moscow would seek a limitation, perhaps even a ban, on ABM's. The bargaining would be tough and erratic, but the goal was roughly the same, because neither side could be sure of the other's intentions on ABM deployment, and each was sensitive to its own limitations. The Russians knew that the Americans could build better ABM's at less cost; they were especially laggard in the critical computer technology. And the White House was now alerted to the declining public and congressional tolerance of ABM's, even though it would continue pressing Congress for more Safeguard sites while negotiating with Moscow.

In the early spring of 1969, a number of things were coming together. As the interaction between ABM and MIRV became more apparent, the anxiety about the former was broadened to include the latter. MIRV, too, might be destabilizing, said prominent critics of the ABM, including a number of Senators. MIRV's could breed ABM's, and vice versa. It seemed both to the arms-control bureaucracy and to congressional skeptics that America's MIRV program, by then coming along nicely, might discourage Moscow's incentive to limit offensive missiles and, at the same time, add momentum to the Soviet weapons buildup, also coming along nicely.

Within the government, the split over how fast to proceed with SALT preparation was spreading to include two closely linked issues, MIRV and verification. The conflict on verification would remain a closed internal affair, but disagreement on MIRV occasionally surfaced, because the issue was public. ACDA was predictably anxious to slow down MIRV, and parts of the State Department, including the new leadership, seemed to take the same view, if somewhat cryptically. It was nothing openly said at the State Department; rather, it was the subdued tone of Rogers's comments, which differed sharply from the uncluttered and strenuous advocacy of MIRV coming from Mr. Laird's side of the Potomac.

Notions of a MIRV moratorium and of putting MIRV in escrow developed lively support on Capitol Hill and within the bureaucracy. The President said, in a news conference on June 19, that he was "considering the possibility of a moratorium on [MIRV] tests as part of any arms control agreement." A few weeks later, Gerard Smith, replying to a letter from Republican Senator Edward Brooke of Massachusetts, stated his personal opinion that a MIRV testing ban should be a priority item at SALT. Under Secretary of State Elliot Richardson took the same line.

Laird himself sharpened the MIRV debate by repeatedly warning of the SS-9's potential as a first-strike weapon against the Minuteman force. Others then wondered whether Moscow might look upon America's MIRV in the same light, especially when, in April, Laird sought funds to "significantly improve the accuracy of Poseidon missiles." Indeed, the request was quietly withdrawn later in the year precisely to head off accusations that the United States might be headed for a first-strike MIRV.

As with Safeguard, the bargaining-chip argument was put to the service of MIRV, though less plausibly. It was never likely that the Soviet Union would agree to freeze an impressive American lead in the exotic technology of multiple re-entry vehicles. Although this was understood by many critics, they felt that a strenuous effort to shelve MIRV, however slim its chances, had to be made. The internal debate on MIRV lasted well over a year; it has never been fully shut off. It probably aroused deeper passion and livelier skirmishing than any security issue of the time.

Splits were developing on other issues, but these became part of the stakes in an overarching struggle for control of SALT. The day before Nixon's March 14 Safeguard announcement, the bureaucracy got a green light in the form of NSSM 28, which asked for a SALT study. Kissinger and his staff saw the study as an extension of the NSSM 3 review of U.S. military posture; most of that work was judged to be done. NSSM 3, in theory, had set out the criteria against which U.S. military needs were to be measured; NSSM 28 would show what limitations the United States could accept or propose that did not intrude upon those needs. Metaphorically, NSSM 3 was the root, NSSM 28 the stem.

More by accident than design, the White House seized control of SALT by giving inherited procedures their chance to fail. NSSM 28 licensed ACDA to launch preparations for the most momentous and elaborate negotiation of the nuclear age. Typically, though, the sense of occasion was swiftly blurred by internal conflict. ACDA had the initiative and it also had stout support from the State Department and the CIA. ACDA set up the working groups and chaired them all. But in three months, all that would change because the White House had strong doubts about the quality and reliability of the work, and the Pentagon, in the words of a closely involved former Kissinger aide, "did not deliver."

Bureaucratically, SALT was a mess. ACDA needed cooperation and concurrence from the principal interest groups inside the Pentagon. These are the Joint Chiefs of Staff and the Office of the Secretary of Defense (OSD). The Joint Chiefs were openly dragging their feet on NSSM 28. And OSD was for the time being all but paralyzed by its own internal competition; DDR&E, Systems Analysis, and ISA were all maneuvering for the major Pentagon share of authority for SALT preparation. As one official recalls the moment, "ACDA tried hard but didn't have the clout to shake loose the necessary paper from the Pentagon." Briefly, there was no central direction, because ACDA was unable to provide it.

White House doubts were fed by a suspicion that ACDA and its allies would rig the SALT options emerging from NSSM 28 in favor of the August, 1968 proposal; many of the same people were still closely involved. They in turn were aware of the White House suspicions, which they resented and rejected but could do nothing to affect. Not surprisingly, one of NSSM 28's five options did resemble the 1968 proposal on which so much work had been done.

Even then, ACDA might have sustained the brightest moment of its institutional career had it not been for the two issues that most troubled its antagonists. These were the old issue of verification and the new issue of the Soviet SS-9 as a potential threat to America's force of 1000 Minuteman missiles. In tackling both issues, ACDA relied heavily on CIA estimates, just as the Halperin ISA group had done nine months earlier. But the new White House, like the Pentagon, was leery of the CIA's eternally optimistic bias on verification and frankly disturbed by what seemed its equally sanguine view of the SS-9's so-called triplet.

An enigmatic and virtually unanswerable question lay at the heart of the issue. Once deployed, what could the triplet do? By stacking three large warheads aboard an SS-9 missile, were the Soviets reaching for a simple MRV capability or a real honest-to-goodness MIRV? The distinction is terribly important. Multiple re-entry vehicles, known as MRV's, offer better assurance of hitting a single target—a city, for example—but, unlike MIRV's, they cannot be individually aimed at widely dispersed targets—Minuteman installations, for example. MRV's are not really worrisome; MIRV's are.

Nobody in government doubted Moscow's intention to develop a MIRV, but the technological journey from MRV to MIRV is long and arduous. Opinions clashed over how long it would take and just what stage of the journey the SS-9 triplet represented.

Another of Kissinger's former associates, also deeply involved in SALT, recalls the CIA taking "a strong position that the SS-9 triplet was no more than a MRV, not a potential MIRV." He says that the CIA "defended this position in general terms," and that DDR&E took the lead in "strenuously attacking" this kind of generality.

Early in April, a DDR&E official had a late-evening conversation at the White House with a member of Kissinger's staff; in the course of it, he made a strong and highly specific case against the

CIA position. The triplet, he argued, was, for practical purposes, already a MIRV. His case was partly based on a test of the triplet that, according to U.S. intelligence, showed the three warheads landing in a pattern that roughly conformed to the layout of Minuteman fields. This pattern is called a "footprint," a technical term the President would use in a news conference two months later:

> . . . in recommending Safeguard, I did so based on intelligence information at the time. Since that time new intelligence information with regard to the Soviet success in testing multiple re-entry vehicles . . . has convinced me that Safeguard is even more important. However we may argue about that intelligence, as to whether it [the triplet] has an independent guidance system as ours will have, there isn't any question but that it is a multiple weapon and its footprints indicate that it just happens to fall in somewhat the precise area in which our Minuteman silos are located.[6]

Curiously enough, the late-evening White House tête-à-tête marked the start of a process that ended with ACDA yielding control of SALT to Henry Kissinger. DDR&E's man had made an impressive case, or so it seemed to his interlocutor, who reported the conversation to Kissinger. It was immediately decided to set up a MIRV panel, which Kissinger would chair. In turn, the panel would supervise an interagency working group on MIRV. This group was to produce a stream of intensely focused studies, most of which went through several drafts, with the authors rigorously challenged along the way by Kissinger himself.

By July, Kissinger's MIRV panel had produced a report perfectly suited to the White House taste. It reached no conclusions, but exhaustively laid out data and identified areas of disagreement, including the reliability of a ban on MIRV testing. Very quickly, the style of the MIRV panel convinced Kissinger and his staff that they had hit on the right device for handling SALT. It reinforced their feeling that bureaucracy, left to itself, would throw up set agency positions instead of dispassionate analysis. Panels controlled by the White House and backed by working groups seemed the ideal means of dealing with the analytical problems of SALT. There remained the problem of how to relieve ACDA of its burden of initiative. ACDA itself quickly provided the solution.

The occasion was the formal presentation of NSSM 28, the SALT study, to the National Security Council on June 25, 1969. The work was finished, the results in circulation. Predictably, the verification issue swiftly became the focus of discussion, with General Wheeler, Chairman of the Joint Chiefs, making an unusually harsh statement in which he expressed "serious doubt" about the quality of the study's treatment of verification problems.

Nobody, including Kissinger, could ignore so hostile a line on a central issue from the President's senior military adviser. Everyone realized that something had to be done. Gerard Smith was clearly disturbed by this attack on NSSM 28, and he took the initiative. On June 30, Smith sent a note to Henry Kissinger suggesting that, in light of General Wheeler's position, there be created "a higher level verification review panel." The verification issue, in effect, would have special treatment.

The White House lost no time in exploiting this golden opportunity. Laurence E. Lynn, then the senior White House staff member on SALT, sent Kissinger a memo urging that Smith's idea be adopted; specifically, he urged the creation of a Verification Panel, which Kissinger would chair, and a Working Group, which Lynn himself would chair. These new groups would establish the central White House control of SALT that had been lacking. Lynn's proposal was approved. The Verification Panel was formally established on July 21, and held its first meeting the following day. Not long after, Kissinger directed the Verification Panel Working Group to begin reviewing all the strategic implications of SALT. The new group immediately took charge of all analytical work on SALT, a function it has never relinquished.

By June, it seemed that SALT was on the track it had jumped ten months earlier, when the Soviet army had crushed the Czechs' liberal experiment. After six months of internal debate and preparation, the President declared his Administration ready. He guessed, on June 19, that talks could begin "sometime between July 31 and August 15."[7]

In fact, SALT was not to begin in the summer, as the President had suggested and as his Secretary of State had been predicting as early as April. Both sides wanted talks, but neither would be pushed. The Nixon Administration began by feeling pushed and would not be rushed. Now Moscow, having been cast in the role of *demandeur* by Washington, would not be hurried. The great powers still resembled figures in a stately dance, occasionally drawing toward each other, sometimes passing, but never meeting. SALT had not yielded its elusive quality.

It was three weeks before Moscow answered Nixon. On July 10, Foreign Minister Gromyko delivered a guarded address to the Supreme Soviet; it was aimed as much at those opposing SALT on his own side as at Washington. He described the arms race as folly. Governments, he said in effect, unless they can control these complex high-speed instruments of destruction, risk becoming victimized by them and by events. The Soviet Union was prepared for SALT, a matter of "paramount importance." President Nixon's statements on the subject, he added, had "not, of course, gone unnoticed" by his government.

The next day, Rogers applauded Gromyko's speech for its "positive" tone. The United States, he said, considered SALT "a significant step forward in our relations with the Soviet Union" and awaited a reply on the time and place of the talks. The ball was back in Moscow's court.

The Russians now had some other things to think about, as they had had the summer before. One was linkages, the term adopted by the press for the Nixon Administration's original view that Soviet cooperation on other issues was a condition of SALT. Just two weeks before his June 19 forecast of a summer debut for SALT, Nixon told graduates of the Air Force Academy that "we are prepared for new initiatives in the control of arms in the context of other specific moves to reduce tensions around the world."[8]

Diplomatic circles recorded Soviet unhappiness with linkages, and an even stronger aversion to other SALT-related Washington rhetoric crept into the press. Thus, in August, the *Washington Post* reported Soviet sources as saying that boastful American claims in the ABM debate about the superiority of U.S. missiles were causing the Kremlin to re-examine its position.[9]

A lot of this amounted to sparring before the main event. To a degree, Moscow was signaling its own critics of SALT, along with Washington, that American notions of ABM and MIRV as bargaining chips would carry no weight. These programs were cited in and of themselves as a source of Soviet anxiety. Nixon's decision to sustain them, according to press reports, showed Moscow that Washington, alas, had no interest in serious talks.

Quite clearly, Soviet leaders were disturbed by ABM and MIRV, but equally clearly, they would have been very surprised, however agreeably, had Nixon discontinued either one. Complaining was a way to fish troubled waters. By midsummer, if not before, the split inside the Administration on a MIRV testing ban was in the open. The State Department and ACDA wanted to propose a ban or a moratorium, while the rest of the Administration was reluctant to do either. Moscow was later discovered to harbor the same reluctance on this issue, but took pleasure, and was not above encouraging, American disaffection with both MIRV and ABM.

A more genuine, and certainly a more-severe constraint on Moscow was a linkage problem all its own arising from the vagaries of Communist-bloc politics. Nixon gave point to these and annoyed the Russians by visiting Rumania in early August, a gesture showing, among other things, that two could play at fishing troubled waters. But far more important to Moscow than this unprecedented incursion by an American President into a satellite state—and a balky one at that—was the overriding problem of China.

Neither before nor since have things been quite so serious between China and the Soviet Union as they were in 1969. Moscow professed alarm about the radical excesses of China's cultural revolution, while Peking stepped up its anti-Soviet campaign partly to shift attention away from its own internal convulsion. Abruptly, Chinese and Russian military units clashed twice in March, 1969 on a disputed island in the Ussuri River along the common border. This was the first armed conflict between Communist powers and one that seemed to bear the risk of crossing the nuclear threshold. Numerous U.S. specialists feared a Soviet "surgical" strike against China's inchoate nuclear and missile installations. The Russians, in turn, have never discounted the possibility that China, fearing precisely that, might lob a nuclear device at Moscow. By 1969, there was general acceptance that the real purpose of the Soviet Galosh ABM was to protect Moscow from primitive Chinese nuclear weapons, as distinct from high-performance American missiles. Henry Kissinger somewhat obliquely made the point in a *Look* magazine interview on August 12, 1969, when he said: "I doubt if the Soviet Union will give up the Moscow [ABM] system, and I doubt I would urge with them to."

Over the summer and into early autumn, Moscow and Washington played rhetorical badminton with SALT, but not until the Russians could establish a parallel negotiation with China on the border issue could they sit down with the Americans. Soviet leaders had to show that they were no less concerned with the stability of the Communist bloc than with stable U.S.–U.S.S.R. relations. Not until they had opened communications with Peking could they adequately defend themselves against charges of selling out to Washington to solemnize a contemptible great-power nuclear monopoly. Not just the Communist bloc but the third world was looking on.

After March, Moscow alternately issued threats and offered compromises, while shifting large numbers of forces to the Far East. Fresh incidents touched off by the Russians on the Sinkiang border, plus the progressively more-plausible threat of a surgical nuclear strike, finally began to tell. China became less shrill and less obdurate. In September, Peking bowed to reality. Kosygin flew to Hanoi for the funeral of Ho Chi Minh, and went on from there to meet Premier Chou En-lai at the Peking airport on September 20. Chou agreed to open talks on the border issue on October 20.

It may or may not have been a coincidence that Nixon met secretly with Soviet Ambassador Dobrynin on that same day.[10] Five days later, on October 25, the world learned by joint announcement that SALT would begin on November 17 in Helsinki.

5   The Grand Negotiation

A sense of relief unalloyed with optimism greeted the news. With all sides wanting and expecting talks, there was general satisfaction that, on November 17, they were at last to begin. But Washington and Moscow took a wary view of the prospects. Both capitals were skeptical, perhaps even fearful, of the popular notion that SALT was not just the priority business between them but a vast enterprise that would begin by promoting stability and end by liquidating the arms race.

Meanwhile, both would continue what they were already doing, with each leading from strength. The Soviets were expanding their SS-9 force, testing the triplet, and stepping up production of nuclear submarines. The Americans had tested each of their MIRV'd missiles—the sub-launched Poseidon and the land-based Minuteman III—nine times; they would finish these tests in a matter of months and proceed briskly to deployment. They were also moving on the first two Safeguard ABM sites. Apparently, SALT and the process of refining weapons were disjunctive; the talks were to proceed *andante*, the arms build-up *allegro con brio*. Such was the concern of the arms-control community: that deployment of more and better arms would outstrip, perhaps frustrate, efforts to limit or reduce them.

A frank mistrust on either side of the other's motives would help to restrain the pace of the talks. Washington was troubled by the commonplace that SALT would formalize the parity principle. Parity, it was felt, would serve Soviet purposes, but not necessarily America's. Although parity may have seemed to lie in the cards, with or without SALT, the habit of strategic and political supremacy dies hard. Equality in strategic weapons would confer on the Soviet Union hefty political and psychological advantages. The concern was that Moscow would use SALT to nail down these advantages and then go on to exploit them. Washington also suspected that the Russians, while conceding nothing themselves, would maneuver SALT to sharpen public and congressional opposition in the United States to the Safeguard and MIRV programs. Finally, Washington worried (as it still does) that Moscow, if only for political purposes, would establish a first-strike threat to Minuteman, often called the backbone of the American deterrent.

Moscow's concerns were no less. Soviet leaders worried most about American ABM's. Safeguard, if and as it evolved toward city defense, would force them into yet another offensive-weapons cycle and perhaps even to develop a comparably sophisticated ABM system of their own.

The record of thirty months of negotiation doesn't reflect the collateral Soviet concern about the American MIRV; Moscow was determined to develop MIRV, not to talk about it. But tests of Poseidon and Minuteman III were unquestionably disturbing. With these due to end in 1970 and some Administration officials supporting proposals for a MIRV ban or moratorium, Moscow wondered whether Washington would seek by some such means to monopolize this technology after having mastered it. In short, the Russians suspected that Nixon might accept parity in gross numbers of weapons only if they agreed to accept—indeed, to legitimize— America's commanding qualitative lead in offensive missiles.

As November 17, 1969 drew near, each side was reliably certain only that the other was ready to talk. Neither knew precisely why. Neither, for example, knew what, if anything, the other might want to do about limiting ABM or MIRV, the companion technologies that most bothered the most people.

Hindsight shows that prospects for agreement were brighter than they appeared. SALT fitted the needs and purposes of the two countries more closely than their governments understood at the time. Soviet concern with stability was beginning to match America's. Better relations with the United States and Western Europe would permit Moscow to cope more effectively with China, then as now feared as Communism's church militant making doctrinal war on the established church and its leadership; then as now, this doctrinal struggle was really the visible overlay of a deeper conflict mocking ideology and pitting the new China— united, aggrieved, and tough—against a traditional antagonist, Russia.

Then as now, Moscow feared an understanding between Washington and China that would be put to work against Soviet interests. Somehow the China problem had to be held to manageable size so as to contain existing and latent heresies in Eastern Europe and to permit assigning more resources to the listless and somewhat retarded Soviet economy. Throughout the seven sessions of SALT that led to the May agreements, China was to be a silent off-stage presence, never mentioned by name—at least not by the Russians—but deeply affecting their position on a number of issues, most notably the ABM.

In time, stable relations with the capitalists would return such tangible dividends as increased trade and, more important, access to sophisticated Western technology in sectors unrelated to defense and essential to Soviet economic growth. In turn, diminished tensions and increasingly benign contacts would promote a supreme Soviet purpose, acceptance by the West of the status quo in Europe.

As the stronger of the two, America may have seemed to have less at stake. In fact, American interests could be seen to benefit at least as much from an agreement limiting offensive and defensive missiles. Above all, a limit or ban on ABM's would go far toward removing fears that either side harbored thoughts of a first-strike option. And then, the Safeguard debate alerted the Administration to the program's doubtful future; far better to work out an ABM limit with Moscow than to wait for Congress to starve Safeguard. As for offense, a ceiling on strategic missiles would constrain Soviet programs, but not American. Although embarked on MIRV, the United States was not building new ICBM's or Polaris submarines or bombers. The Soviets were building about 250 ICBM's per year and 128 SLBM's, which meant eight new submarines as well. At that rate, the United States would sooner rather than later find itself well behind in numbers of missiles and in "throw weight," or gross distructive power. Even more important, SALT would hopefully offer a means of achieving a limit on the single weapon system that most bothered Washington, the giant SS-9 ICBM. Indeed, negotiating a hold on the SS-9 program was not only basic to the U.S. position, but an excellent reason to press SALT vigorously.

In the autumn of 1969, it was too soon to measure the significance of SALT. The mere prospect of the superpowers talking nonpolemically about strategic arms was intriguing enough. Not before the talks were well underway would a full sense of occasion be borne in on the governments. Nixon had started by talking about an era of negotiation, but also, to Moscow's annoyance, by linking SALT to progress on other matters, especially the Middle East and Vietnam. By autumn, the linkage notion, if not entirely discarded, was in declining fashion. In May, 1972, the Moscow summit agreements would bury it once and for all, coming as they did on the heels of Nixon's decision to close off North Vietnam's ports to Soviet shipping.

Linkage of a different sort having nothing to do with Soviet good behavior does connect SALT with great-power politics. SALT is the centerpiece East-West negotiation helping to legitimize and bolster others. Quite possibly, the four power agreement on Berlin, for example, would have been concluded without SALT. Since history doesn't reveal alternatives, we really don't know. We do know that Moscow and Washington both wanted a SALT agreement, which suggests that a protracted stalemate might have troubled parallel negotiations as well as others that were to follow. Equally, it suggests that Soviet eagerness to nail down acceptance of Germany's frontiers and to promote *détente* in Europe may in turn have argued for reaching agreement with the Americans on SALT (as well as on Berlin).

With all kinds of East-West contacts popping up like crocuses, SALT became the single issue under exclusive great-power control. Unlike Berlin, the Middle East, or Vietnam, there are no other actors in SALT (even though Washington consults closely with the NATO allies). Thus, among other things, SALT reminds us that the world is not yet multipolar, as many suggest, but still bipolar. Neither Soviet phobias nor Nixon's foray into triangular politics can give China the modern attributes of a great power. Japan has a few of these, may yet acquire most of them, but is also several removes from the great-power game. Western Europe is still an assortment of small and middle powers, each ultimately dependent for its security on American commitments and guarantees; the dream of a tightly strung political community may become reality, but that day, if it dawns at all, lies well ahead.

With time, the Nixon people were to look upon SALT in much the same way as their predecessors had. Properly managed, the process would promote stability; it would show that even if still embroiled in Vietnam, the United States could carry on major transactions with the Soviet Union. And then, a SALT agreement, as in Johnson's day, would be good domestic politics; Nixon, like any president, had to think about congressional elections lying one year away.

All periods of history are transitional, but some, as the French political scientist Pierre Hassner says, are more transitional than others. SALT coincides with one of the more transitional moments, a time when the mass of cold-war tensions and differences is starting to shift; when the game of triangular politics in the form of contacts with China and improving relations with Moscow has become playable. It is still too soon to announce that the era of confrontation has been superseded by one of negotiation. The process by which the one may give way to the other is gradual; but the process is under way, and SALT is both its servant and its beneficiary.

In the autumn of 1969, the White House, if still tentative about SALT, took great comfort from the analytical preparations for round one. A gaggle of task forces had been organized: one dealt with verification, another with possible Soviet evasion schemes. Still others had broken down the weapons themselves into so-called central systems: land-based missiles, sea-based missiles, ABM's, and aircraft. The work of the task forces had been filtered and compressed into a report of some eighty pages designed to help the President make precise decisions. Nixon is believed to have read the report carefully.

In all, nine options were tossed up by the exhaustive studies on SALT that dated back to March. These were numbered I, II, III, IIIA, IV, V, VA, VI, and VII. Options IIIA and VA were mild variants of III and V. Option III was essentially the proposal ground out in the summer of 1968. Option V was known within the bureaucracy as SWA, or Stop Where We Are. It would have limited ABM's, frozen the missile and bomber forces on both sides, permitted MIRV, and banned mobile land-based missiles. Six of the nine options favored freezing both ICBM's and SLBM's at existing levels; five favored permitting MIRV, the other four banned it; all but one option banned mobile land-based missiles, which neither side has yet deployed. Seven of the nine proposed an unspecified limit on ABM systems, and one would have limited ABM's to something called NCA—National Command Authority —meaning that the ABM's of both sides would be confined to protecting Moscow and Washington. A great deal was to be heard about NCA, though not publicly. This deceptively simple idea became one of the two thorniest and most contentious issues of SALT's first four rounds and caused the White House lasting pain.

Pockets of support developed around various options, with some people pressing missile freezes, others a MIRV moratorium, still others a suspension of Safeguard. The White House shared none of these biases. Nixon and most of his staff wanted to avoid drawing battle lines either in Washington or in Moscow on the various alternatives. Round one, they felt, should be exploratory. The two sides should sort out major and minor issues and establish at least the outline of a working program for following rounds. None of the nine options would be presented to the Russians; rather, they would serve as guidance to the bureaucracy and to the U.S. delegation.

The White House regarded its options as "building blocks." The idea was that the elements of each could be shuffled into various combinations and packages, giving great flexibility to the U.S. negotiating position. If the Russians frowned on some parts of a proposal when it was offered, the other parts could be speedily mixed into some alternative without dictating a renegotiation within the U.S. defense establishment of the entire U.S. position. All agencies would have already concurred in all the options. The building blocks, in short, would permit swift reaction to the Soviets, while minimizing bureaucratic conflict in Washington. The building blocks were, moreover, yet another device by which White House control of SALT would be assured.

The delegation left with a brief stating merely the Administration's "willingness" to negotiate agreements on both offensive and defensive weapons. The delegation was authorized to discuss any Soviet proposals, with all decisions reserved to the President. But the Russians already knew from a secret White House message that Washington would not offer specific proposals. And Moscow apparently shared the White House reluctance to burden the preliminary round in Helsinki with actual negotiations. These would await the spring round in Vienna.

Both cities had been on the short list of sites acceptable to both sides, although the Soviets had a preference for Helsinki, the Americans for Vienna. The solution to this modest difference was simplicity itself. The short preliminary round would be held in Helsinki, the longer working round in Vienna, with the talks continuing to alternate afterward. The bargain satisfied all considerations, except creature comfort. It condemned the delegations— at least, in the early rounds—to spending the cold months in Helsinki and the warmer months in Vienna. By mid-1971, some recycling had been achieved and the pattern reversed.

The talks began with minimum fanfare and ceremony. The Finnish government welcomed the delegations with a reception at which the Foreign Minister hailed the "historic occasion." An opening statement by the chief Soviet delegate, Vladimir S. Semenov, was virtually unblemished by propaganda. His American colleague, Gerard C. Smith, read a message to his delegation from Nixon, which, while applauding the occasion, noted the "difficulty of their task" and the "suspicion and distrust that must be dispelled if you are to succeed in your assignment."[1]

The nearly 500 journalists dispatched to record the event learned only that the talks were "businesslike." They discovered that delegates on both sides met occasionally for dinner or lunch. The persistent handful of newsmen who remained were unable to capture even a few shreds of the substance of the biweekly meetings. Because these alternated between secure rooms in the American and Soviet Embassies, no other party, whether the host government or other embassy, had a chance to pry. Not even the American Embassy saw messages on SALT; separate communications were established between the delegation and Washington. The secrecy, faithfully observed by both delegations, was complete.

The opening round lasted thirty-five days, ending with a brief communiqué; its most consequential passage said that "an understanding was reached on the general range of questions which will be the subject of further U.S.–Soviet exchanges." Otherwise, the world learned only that SALT would resume in Vienna on April 16, 1970.

Some wrongly surmised that SALT I, as it was known inside the bureaucracy, was a kind of strategic seminar. In fact, the talks were closely focused, revealing, and consistently serious, as well as nonpolemical. In the formal meetings as well as during informal dinners and lunches, each side discovered a great deal about the other's attitudes. Each took some positions that would not be lightly abandoned and would heavily shape the actual negotiations that lay ahead.

The stress was on the central weapons systems, offensive and defensive. Among the early surprises was Moscow's concern about ABM's. Soviet thinking had reversed itself since the Glassboro meeting two and one-half years earlier. At Helsinki, a closely involved American recalls "both sides making McNamara-like noises about the destabilizing effects of ABM deployment; the Russians were surprisingly explicit on this point."

Moscow's delegation noted three possible ABM options: heavy deployment, limited deployment; and no ABM's at all. An American who was present says the Russians obviously felt that heavy deployment was undesirable and that the choice lay between zero and limited coverage. The United States position, he adds, was vague and noncommittal. Washington mistrusted the dovish Soviet overtures on ABM. People worried that Moscow, having remarked fifty Senate votes against Safeguard, would toy with an ABM ban in SALT so as to hasten congressional dismemberment of the American program.

Both sides were ready to talk about quantity—about numbers of weapons; they were much less willing to do so about quality— about MIRV's, improved support systems, and potential innovations. The Americans planned to raise some issues concerning quality, but in a tentative and exploratory way. They were not ready to ventilate any of these ultrasensitive problems. It didn't matter, though, because the Russians had clearly been instructed to avoid talking about them at all. They could discuss numbers of launchers, for example, but not the size of launchers, or the accuracies of warheads.

On November 11, a little more than a week before the talks began, the nine options were discussed at a meeting of the National Security Council. Afterward, Kissinger received a memorandum from a senior staff aide suggesting that instead of emphasizing options as such at this early stage, the Administration should focus on major issues, like ABM and MIRV, and on the links between them. This thinking prevailed. In Helsinki, the United States raised the MIRV problem, linking it to other innovations that might degrade one side's ability to retaliate. For Moscow to make an ABM network of its Tallinn air-defense system would be one such refinement. Improving warhead accuracies to the point where either side could contemplate a first strike against the other's forces would be another. In effect, the Americans, thoroughly aroused by the SS-9 and its triplet, wanted to back into a MIRV discussion by insinuating a list of qualitative issues onto the SALT agenda. But the Russians, who never mentioned MIRV themselves, refused to play this game. Even on ABM's, the issue to which they were most sensitive, they would discuss only numbers of interceptor missiles, but not their performance or that of the radars and other elements vital to the system; such matters, they said, were simply too complex for negotiation. Their attitude is better explained by technological lag; the United States was ahead in all or most qualitative aspects of offensive and defensive weapons, and the Soviet interest lay, not in discussing America's advantages, but in canceling them by some other means.

Nor did Moscow share Washington's abiding concern with verification. Any time the U.S. delegation raised the issue, the Soviet side would reply that any and all parts of a SALT agreement must be verified by "national means," as distinct from on-site inspection. At one moment in Helsinki, they relaxed slightly and seemed willing at least to entertain discussion of alternatives. But then, presumably acting on fresh instructions, they restated the national-means-only position, which the United States eventually swung round to.

If SALT I was less momentous than the following six rounds, it did establish a few continuities. One, the Soviet aversion to heavy ABM deployment, was mildly surprising. The other was both utterly unexpected and more than a little disturbing. As the delegates began discussing offense, the Soviets abruptly surfaced an issue that, like National Command Authority, was to agitate SALT and at an even earlier stage. Like NCA, it, too, became known for its three initials: FBS, which stands for the Forward-Based Systems, mostly aircraft, that the United States deploys in continental Europe and on carriers in the Mediterranean and the northeast

Pacific. Most of these aircraft are dual purpose, capable of carrying nuclear or nonnuclear bombs. They number well into the hundreds, about 600 in Europe alone. It never occurred to anyone in Washington at any time, whether then or in the Johnson days, that these weapons, which the United States regards as tactical, not strategic, would figure in SALT.

Imagine, then, the consternation of the Americans when the Russians insisted that U.S. forward-based aircraft, because they are technically capable of striking some Soviet cities, would have to be treated as one of the central systems, no different than long-range missiles and bombers. In vain did Washington later protest that these aircraft, although capable of attacking inland Russian cities on one-way missions, could not return to base; or that they posed no first-strike threat and had very little second-strike potential; or that the chief purpose of the forward-based aircraft is to counter the 650-odd Soviet medium- and intermediate-range ballistic missiles (MR/IRBM's) targeted on the cities of America's European allies. This latter point, Washington protested—also in vain—meant moreover that FBS was not an issue for bilateral talks, because the interests of other countries were involved. Nor could the Administration involve the Soviet MR/IRBM's in SALT, since these cannot reach American territory and thus wholly escape the central system definition.

Unprepared and off balance, the American delegation sought to extricate itself from FBS by moving on to something else. Smith elected an analogy, which left the Russians as it found them. Just as olives are removed from a bottle one at a time, he suggested, the delegations ought to identify the issues one at a time but avoid getting bogged down on any of them. This only confused the Russians, who do not pack olives in narrow-necked bottles.

The U.S. side then stressed problems of stability, which didn't seem to impress the Soviet delegation. Steering the discussion back to the problem of Minuteman, the Americans sought to explain that all elements of each side's strategic forces must be "survivable"; for one element—Minuteman, say—to become vulnerable would create dangerous anxieties, hence instabilities. The Soviets replied, in effect: Why are you so worried about Minuteman when your sea-based forces will always remain intact and available for the second-strike role? It was a *dialogue des sourds*.

What did comfort the arms-control bureaucracy in Washington

—and rightly so—was the disavowal by both sides of any intent to deploy nationwide ABM systems against "third countries." For third country, one can safely substitute China, the only other nuclear power whose intentions seriously troubled either Moscow or Washington. By rejecting nationwide defense against another power, the two were, in practice, rejecting the option of heavy ABM deployment against one another. This was progress.

Insiders remember SALT I for many reasons, among them some palpable signs of Moscow's Sinophobia. At one point, the Russians began talking somewhat vaguely about "provocative attacks" by third nuclear powers. The Americans recommended holding this question for another round. The Soviets agreed, but waited only for SALT II in Vienna to revive the putative problem of "provocative attacks."

Although it was a mixed performance, SALT I probably turned up more pluses than minuses. Granted the two sides parted as they met, still speaking a different strategic vocabulary. Granted, too, that the FBS issue did come as a nasty shock to the Americans, one of whom said: "We were so absorbed in our definitional problems we made no serious effort to anticipate theirs." Nevertheless, if the parties did not emerge from the thickets of nuclear strategy on the same path, they were at least in sight of each other. While each discovered that nothing had been categorically decided by the other, it was implicitly agreed that heavy ABM deployment was bad. In that sense, Moscow had come more than halfway toward accepting the favorite apothegm of Washington's assured-destruction school of strategy: "Offense is defense, defense is offense. Killing people is good, killing weapons is bad."

Briefly, SALT I was a useful curtain-raiser for the tougher sessions to come. Looking forward to these, both sides launched intensive preparations upon their return from Helsinki three days before Christmas.

During the 116-day recess between SALT I and II, Washington began to accept that the race for strategic advantage was impelled by the MIRV-ABM interplay. Each could beget the other. Stop one and any reasonable need of the other disappears. Although innumerable options and variants could be dreamed up, the pith of SALT still lay in four basic choices: (1) high ABM and high

MIRV; (2) low ABM and high MIRV; (3) a ban on MIRV, but not on ABM; (4) a ban on both. To a surprising degree, the four options ground out in Washington for SALT II embodied these choices.

This time they were lettered rather than numbered. Option A inhibited no American programs; it permitted both MIRV and all twelve ABM sites originally planned for Safeguard. Options B, C, and D each proposed that ABM's be either banned altogether or confined to National Command Authority—that is, to Moscow and Washington. The options of NCA or zero, Washington thought, should appeal to Moscow, since the Russians had suggested at Helsinki that the best choice lay between zero and limited coverage; for limited coverage, the Americans read "Moscow," which is what the Galosh ABM protects. In return for indulging Moscow's preference on ABM, Washington hoped to gain what it wanted most: a ceiling on the Soviet offensive-missile program and, beneath that ceiling a so-called sublimit on the number of SS-9's. The Soviets had about 300 of these monster missiles either deployed or under construction. Washington sought a sublimit of 250, but would have settled happily for agreement on 300.

The critical, though doubtless negotiable, U.S. number was 1710, the sum of America's 1054 ICBM's and 656 SLBM's. Each of the four options would hold Russian and American missile totals to that number. In all options, bombers were to be frozen at existing levels.

Washington called A and B the low options; C and D were the high options in the sense of being venturesome. Alone among the four, Option C would have banned MIRV. Option D's distinction lay in a bold scheme for effecting reductions in precisely the area of Soviet strength—land-based missiles—that most disturbed Washington. It provided that after settling on a ceiling of 1710 strategic missiles, each side would reduce forces to 1000 by 1978, a reduction rate of 100 per year.

All four options were shaped by an abiding concern with the potential threat to Minuteman of an SS-9 force equipped with MIRV's. Briefly, they represented a bald effort to achieve a lasting "hold" on the SS-9. Each option, for example, would have permitted "freedom to mix" but in one direction only: out to sea. (In the trade, this is called "one-way freedom to mix.") This meant that neither side could convert SLBM's to ICBM's, but each could do the reverse. Even with MIRV, it would be difficult for the Russians to give the smaller sea-based missiles a first-strike punch. The Administration was, in the words of one official, "trying to push them out to sea."

Each option also contained eleven "collateral constraints," the U.S. term for a set of technical prohibitions on various means of improving and modernizing forces. One would have given America the right to inspect Tallinn air-defense sites to make sure they weren't being upgraded into an ABM system. But the one to which Washington attached most importance would have denied both sides the right to enlarge or otherwise modify existing missile silos. Here again, the Americans sought to restrain the Russian's SS-9 buildup; if barred from altering silos, the Russians would be unable to replace smaller missiles with the huge SS-9. Such a constraint would add to the pressure to force the Russians away from the land, where their strength lies, and out to sea. The broad purpose of the collateral constraints was to frustrate any attempt by the Russians to elude the provisions of an agreement by technical ploys. And to that end, the constraints were very tightly written; indeed, so tightly were they written that, when a Soviet delegate plaintively asked whether painting the doors of their missile silos would violate the constraint on silo modification, he drew an affirmative reply.

By now, SALT was devouring the time and energy of many senior people in the government, not least Henry Kissinger. The Verification Panel, which he chaired, had direct responsibility for all the issues. The other members were Elliot Richardson, the then Under Secretary of State; David Packard, then the Deputy Secretary of Defense; the Chairman of the Joint Chiefs, Admiral Thomas Moorer; CIA Director Richard Helms; Gerard Smith; and John Mitchell, then Attorney General. Mitchell's presence attested to the domestic political content of SALT. If some of these men remained wary of SALT, they were intellectually drawn to its substance. One of them now describes his involvement with SALT as the richest intellectual experience of his life and certainly the most rigorous. Backing the panel was its working group and backing it were an array of subgroups in apparently endless motion, meeting on Saturday nights, Sunday afternoons, sometimes thrice daily.

The Verification Panel takes many but not all decisions, some of which are referred to the senior body, the National Security Council. The really tough choices are presented to the NSC, but the decisions are taken by the President and Henry Kissinger, sometimes before a meeting, sometimes afterward. One who has closely observed the process says: "Kissinger presents the NSC with a review of the Verification Panel discussions, after which Nixon raises a few questions, offers some comments, and conveys a mood. Then everyone goes away, and a decision is announced in the form of an NSDM. The decision is rarely announced in the meeting itself."

SALT II merits a niche in history because of two White House decisions involving, inevitably, MIRV and ABM. The MIRV decision aroused great bureaucratic passions, but in the end probably affecting nothing. The critical ABM decision, on the other hand, slid by largely unremarked, but was to cause the Administration more difficulty, if not embarrassment, than anything else it did in Vienna and Helsinki.

The first decision turned on how to verify Option C's ban on testing and deployment of MIRV. As written, the option provided for verification by national means, the only approach acceptable to the Russians. As Option C wound its way through the working groups and eventually into the Verification Panel, this language remained intact. But then, following an NSC meeting, it was broadened to include verification by on-site inspection.

The larger part of the SALT bureaucracy took it badly. It angered many that the mass of analytical work lying behind the original language could be so abruptly upset. Others feared that the White House had scuttled a first and last chance to turn back the clock on MIRV. The United States was soon to conclude MIRV testing, and would actually begin to deploy Minuteman III in June and Poseidon seven months later. Time, it seemed, had all but run out for those who saw MIRV as an agent of instability second only to the ABM. The prospect of Moscow accepting a ban on MIRV tests was bleak enough without attaching the one condition, on-site inspection, that would all but guarantee a categoric Russian *nyet*.

Just before the start of SALT I, Ambassador Dobrynin had passed the word that on-site inspection was not categorically ruled out. But, at Helsinki, it had nonetheless been ruled out categorically, and by the head of the Soviet delegation, Mr. Semenov; Dobrynin never again raised the issue. The Soviets strenuously oppose on-site inspection, partly because it is intrusive; partly because of an understandable aversion to parading their technological inferiority vis-à-vis the United States; partly because they suspect Americans of seeking targeting information not otherwise available or of just wanting to pry, and perhaps partly because of a concern that to disclose one thing could mean disclosing other things they prefer to keep secret.

A senior member of the Nixon Administration recalls that on the eve of SALT II "we had still not resolved some basic questions. One of these was whether an agreement verified by national means only was a better and safer alternative than no agreement at all. Our SALT position reflected this uncertainty."

The bureaucracy was looking at the MIRV issue analytically, while the White House saw it in subtler and more political terms. For the bureaucracy, the issue was whether a testing ban could be reliably verified by national means. Nobody doubted that the Soviets could get away with some cheating. Could they, however, cheat undetected on a scale large enough to make it worthwhile? The intelligence community, especially the CIA, thought not, favored the uninspected testing ban, and drew support from the State Department and ACDA, including specifically Rogers, Richardson, and Gerard Smith. Skirmishing against the idea was led by DDR&E, backed by various other parts of the Pentagon.

The related question was whether on-site inspection would contribute much to verifying a ban on MIRV deployment. Again, the bureaucracy split. Although the question is not really answerable, many if not most technicians believe that on-site inspectors could be easily deceived by determined efforts to cheat. Only if allowed to pry open the cover of a missile system and gaze upon its interior parts might an inspector be absolutely sure of how many and what kind of warheads were there. Yet such procedure would make a mockery of classification; few things are more closely held than warhead technology, and nobody doubts that Washington would resist as stoutly as Moscow so sweeping an invasion of privacy.

Obviously, Nixon and Kissinger were at least as aware as anyone of the pitfalls in on-site inspection and the Soviet loathing of the idea. Nobody can rank the considerations that inspired the

President's decision to attach the on-site inspection clause. He may have been impressed by the argument that a testing ban could not be safely verified. He may have worried that Soviet acceptance of a MIRV ban would damage relations with the Joint Chiefs, their congressonal allies, and some part of his more conservative constituency. Except for MIRV, America was doing little to improve its forces, while the Soviet expansion program was bounding ahead on all fronts. Thus, instead of stopping MIRV, Nixon and Kissinger may have elected to broaden the commanding U.S. lead in an exotic technology, an area that might eventually represent its sole advantage over the Russians. In that light, the decision to saddle Option C with on-site inspection could be reasonably seen as a convenient way to head off a MIRV ban.

That was how it looked to many bureaucrats. Some also saw the decision as partly tactical. The Joint Chiefs, along with various other parts of the Pentagon, had a preferance for the low options, A and B; these would impose few restraints on U.S. programs. The rest of the government preferred C and D. It struck some observers that Kissinger may have broken down this polarity by recommending to the President that he take the high options, but not the uninspected MIRV ban. In that light, on-site inspection would have been the price for Pentagon acquiescence on the high options.

The State Department and ACDA were troubled by the decision. Rogers and Smith much preferred the uninspected ban. So did Elliot Richardson, who had considerable standing in the White House. That these men, either singly or together, did not make a strenuous effort to reverse the situation suggests that the President —and doubtless Kissinger, too—had taken a tough position from which there would be no retreat.

It's clear now that Moscow would have turned down *any* proposal to ban MIRV testing. Option C was speedily rejected in Vienna. Yet had the Russians responded by asking the United States to drop on-site inspection as the price for their acceptance of the proposal, almost certainly Washington would have felt obliged to acquiesce. But the Soviet interest lay elsewhere. Just as U.S. leadership was determined to sustain MIRV, so Moscow was determined to master the technology.

The time to have stopped MIRV was August, 1968, before either side had started testing it. After that, it was probably too late.

Thus, the invasion of Czechoslovakia, by retarding SALT, may have erased whatever chance there ever was of blocking MIRV deployment.

The passion and controversy released by the MIRV affair were absent from the second critical SALT decision, which for a time troubled nobody. It seemed merely a question of presentation. Each of the four options contained the alternative of banning ABM's altogether or limiting each side to defending its capital. Early in March, 1970, the White House decided that instead of offering the Soviets an immediate choice between zero ABM or NCA, the delegation would put NCA forward first, and zero afterward.

On March 16, eight Senators and seven members of the House were invited to the White House for the most detailed briefing on SALT the congressional leadership was to receive until the President returned from Moscow more than two years later with the agreements themselves. The speakers were the President and Kissinger, flanked by Rogers, Laird, Helms, and General Wheeler. The Congressmen knew little beyond what was appearing in the press, and most of that was speculation: the tiny handful of journalists who knew anything at all wondered aloud whether the Administration would choose a comprehensive proposal—one that banned MIRV—or something more limited.

Detailed charts had been prepared illustrating Options A, B, C, and D. The President and Kissinger presented the charts and explained the options. They were asked numerous questions, some of them tough and challenging. Senator J. W. Fulbright and his since-defeated colleague, Albert Gore, gathered from the tone of the discussion that Nixon would choose the low options, A and B, and they urged him to go beyond these. When the President then announced that the high options, C and D, had in fact been selected, the response was positive, congratulatory, and, in a few cases, even enthusiastic. Nor did anyone seem put off when Kissinger, in explaining the ABM alternatives, disclosed that NCA was to be offered first, with Washington prepared to negotiate on zero if the Russians were.

The four options were reviewed for the last time on April 8 by the NSC. On April 10, six days before the start of SALT II, the White House issued NSDM 51, one of the more-historic SALT documents. It instructed the delegation to offer Option C first, D second. Of greater and lasting importance, NSDM 51 specified that in presenting either option the delegation should offer NCA before zero.

SALT II was to be the longest round, lasting 120 days, and except for the seventh (and last), it was the most episodic. SALT II also established an operating style that for the most part was to endure. Perhaps because of its length, SALT II brought the delegations closer together; something like working relationships were established. Otherwise, SALT II could not be judged productive. Curiously, the Administration's wariness of SALT had shifted to an attitude of confidence, at times approaching optimism. Yet little of what transpired at Vienna in the spring and summer of 1970 should have fostered optimism. Above all, SALT II provided some lessons on how not to negotiate with the Soviet Union on issues of surpassing sensitivity.

As in Helsinki, the delegations settled down to work after their new host government, Austria, had ceremoniously welcomed them on April 16. The Americans wasted little time in offering Option C, and their Russian colleagues wasted still less in refusing it. A MIRV testing ban policed by on-site inspectors was formally anathematized. The Russians, in turn, proposed a ban on MIRV production and deployment. This was not a serious proposition. MIRV's cannot be detected at the production and deployment stages, only while they are being tested. The United States said no.

Option D fared no better than C. It had, in the words of a senior bureaucrat, "a half-life of one plenary session." As with Option C, the Soviet reaction was unambiguously negative. Conversely, its reaction to NCA, which the American delegation, as instructed, also offered during this brief period, was not only positive but remarkably swift. It took the Kremlin less than a week to instruct the Soviet delegation to say yes to NCA.

Otherwise, the Americans were talking at a stone wall. After being greeted with C and D, the Soviets argued, in effect, that the United States was not making serious proposals, but merely staking out a one-sided position that would serve only American interests. Their language was elliptical, but the meaning was clear. With Option C, they felt that the United States sought to freeze them into a technologically inferior position and impose on-site inspection in the bargain. With Option D, they felt, understandably enough, that the United States was seeking to diminish the greatest source of Soviet strength, land-based ICBM's, and force them out to sea, where the advantage lies with America. "They were," says one American participant, "awaiting our 'real' position, and never mind that their 'real' position hadn't emerged, or that their negotiating position was more ambiguous—indeed, opaque—than ours."

This was disconcerting. The U.S. delegation had expected the offer of NCA to generate some discussion, during which it could present the zero alternative, much preferred by the State Department and ACDA. Now the United States was in the position of offering the zero alternative after Moscow had accepted NCA.

Tactically, the Russians had a greater advantage in the ABM discussion. They knew what they wanted and what they didn't want. They didn't want Nixon to deploy Safeguard, which had growth potential. They wanted minimal ABM deployment but the right to keep their Moscow defenses. The NCA proposal was one they might well have made themselves. And that, indeed, was a large part of its purpose.

The White House privately regards NCA as an intellectual blunder, and one for which it accepts full responsibility. The idea, thrown up after the first Helsinki round, was designed to meet the Soviet preference for limited coverage. The U.S.S.R., the Americans knew, would find it hard to abandon the Galosh system, whose real purpose, as they also knew, was to defend Moscow against a sneak attack by China. For the United States obligingly to confine ABM deployment to Washington would have the virtue of symmetry, a virtue that hopefully would carry over into offense and help achieve a common ceiling on strategic missiles.

Most untypically, the NCA option had been raised and settled in a single meeting of senior officials at the White House, and thereby quite escaped the analytical process through which SALT-related ideas normally have traveled. At the time, everything seemed to fit: NCA was probably negotiable with both the Russians and the Joint Chiefs, who had an aversion to zero ABM; most of the Pentagon preferred NCA to zero since it would keep up the ABM technology and provide some hedge against Soviet abrogation of a SALT agreement.

It wasn't until NCA had been offered at SALT II that its defects and snares were borne in on the government. The symmetry turned out to be more apparent than real. First, the Russian Galosh could offer some protection not just of Moscow but of 300 ICBM's deployed within the operating radius of the system. An American NCA, other than offering light protection to Washington, would defend little except a portion of the Atlantic Ocean. Here was a clear plus for Moscow of the sort that matters to strategists and systems analysists.

Of vastly greater importance was the specter of total asymmetry. In proposing NCA, the Administration risked saddling itself with an agreement that would leave the Soviet Union with a Moscow defense and the United States with nothing, for Congress, alas, might well deny funds for NCA. Its aversion to city defense had already helped persuade the White House to launch Safeguard as primarily a protector of Minuteman sites. Construction was starting on the two sites authorized by Congress. Would the Administration—indeed, could it—abandon these in the hope that a disaffected Congress would bestow its approval on a defense of Washington. Voter reaction to defending Washington was known to trouble many Congressmen. Appearances might suggest that the government was concerned only with protecting itself and cared nothing for the expendables living elsewhere. Briefly, NCA could well mean zero ABM for the U.S. and one site for Moscow.

The Administration was feeling discomfort. Its efforts to get a handle on the Soviet missile program, using NCA as bait, had gotten nowhere. NCA had been accepted, but the U.S. delegation, as instructed, was now also talking about zero. The Soviets, while not ruling out zero (they had mentioned it first in Helsinki), began to needle the Americans, saying, in effect: You propose one thing (NCA), and after we accept, you propose another (zero). Meanwhile, your leaders ask Congress for funds to build four more Safeguard sites. What is your real ABM position?

Nothing seemed to be working. That is what the delegation told Washington in a memorable message, called the SALT 80 cable. Dated May 20, the cable appealed for some recourse from Options C and D.

Smith and his fellow delegates returned from Vienna in mid-June, and a good deal of what one official called "stewing around" followed. On June 24, the Verification Panel exhaustively reviewed the possibilities, after which nothing happened for ten days, not visibly anyway. Then, abruptly, the White House surfaced NSDM 69, signed with a flourish by the President in his own hand and dated July 4, also in his own hand. NSDM 69 outlined yet another proposal, Option E. With a covering memorandum from Henry Kissinger, signed on July 9, the new position descended on the agencies, none of which had had advance knowledge of its content. Whereas the other options had been methodically shaped and honed by the entire SALT apparatus, Option E was strictly a White House affair; Kissinger, consulting closely with the President and one or two members of his own staff, was the architect.

Option E was a change in course, designed less as an instrument acceptable to all sides in Washington than as one that might be negotiable in Vienna. Gone was Option C's MIRV ban. Gone, too, were the phased reductions laid out in Option D. Instead, Option E proposed that both sides be limited to a total of 1900 strategic missiles and bombers, a number that would leave the United States with its 1054 ICBM's, its 656 SLBM's, and 190 B-52 bombers. Since the Pentagon was planning to reduce the B-52 force from the existing level of about 500 to 250, Option E would have meant a further reduction of 60 bombers and put the U.S. force in line with the Soviet Union's.

Option E was hardly a radical departure. Given the pace of the Soviet Missile buildup, the ceiling would have obliged Moscow to cut back some construction. Option E also sustained the effort to push the Russians out to sea. The so-called sublimit of 250 SS-9's was retained. So was the prohibition on modifying silos. Washington was still allowing conversion of land-based forces into sea-based, but not the reverse—that is, one-way freedom to mix. As for ABM's, Option E, like C and D, offered the Soviets NCA or zero as alternatives equally acceptable to the United States.

Some internal negotiation, lasting a few weeks, was needed before Option E could be put before the Soviets. At the same time, influential Congressmen were becoming both curious and impatient. Some wondered what had befallen the idea of a MIRV ban and missile reductions. Others were openly annoyed by the absence of consultation, the more so since they knew that the NATO allies were being well briefed. Apart from well-meaning gestures, such as a Senate Resolution proposing a mutual suspension of MIRV tests, there was little outlet for congressional frustration. It remained for the Senate Armed Services Committee, nobody's dovecote, to take a step that had to be reckoned with: At about the time the SALT delegation was "stewing around" in Washington, the Committee rejected an Administration request, already approved in the House of Representatives, to proceed with four new Safeguard sites for area defense, in addition to those already authorized for protecting Minuteman. The Committee later explained the decision in reporting the annual military procurement authorization:

> The Committee has decided to confine the authorization . . . of the SAFEGUARD program to those sites devoted to the defense of the deterrent. . . . In taking this action, the Committee wishes to establish the primacy of active defense to increase the survivability of the land-based deterrent. By striking from the authorization the House approved administration request [for] four area defense sites, the Committee affirms its conviction that there is no compelling need to move now to the deployment of an area defense of our population against Chinese Communist ICBM attack.[2]

The Committee was right in guessing that the long-term effect of its action might be "substantial."[3] Area ABM defense was now all but dead, and Safeguard's future as a big system along with it. Funds remained available for continuing the two sites already approved and for proceeding with two others. These, of course, were located near Minuteman bases, and most of the bureaucracy had by now conceded that Safeguard was unconvincing in the role of Minuteman's protector. So the White House worried—and with reason—that Safeguard might be shorn of two of the four remaining sites once the military authorization bill reached the Senate floor.

Still, the Administration was far from ready to give up on Safeguard, or on extending it. The bigger the system's potential, the richer its probable value as a bargaining chip in Vienna and Helsinki. The time for another congressional briefing had clearly arrived. Henry Kissinger arranged to make a rare, though hopefully secret, appearance on Capitol Hill; not even the staff members of relevant committees were informed of the meeting. The appearance was set for July 23, the day before the delegation was to make an informal presentation of Option E in Vienna. The place was a large reception room just off the Senate floor. Thirteen Senators and thirteen members of the House were invited.

The affair went not nearly so well as the earlier March briefing at the White House. A number of those invited failed to appear. The meeting was interrupted by numerous roll-call votes. Worst of all from the Administration's viewpoint, accounts of the event appeared the following day in the *Washington Post* and *The New York Times*, an intolerable breach of secrecy for which the executive branch blamed certain Senators. The Senate version held that the two reporters got their information by the expedient of eavesdropping at the door.

Both news pieces had Kissinger using SALT to sell Safeguard on the grounds that the system was an essential bargaining chip. According to the more specific *Washington Post* story, he said that continuing Safeguard was the way to persuade the Russians to limit their SS-9 program.[4] The story went on to say that Fulbright had reproached Kissinger for putting NATO ahead of the Congress with regard to SALT briefings.[5] The tone of the meeting was not good.

Back in Vienna, the delegations were fencing, reiterating the basic attitudes of their governments; as in May and June, there was a lot of highly technical discussion. The Russians had begun to chip away at the eleven "collateral constraints," most of which were directed only at them. The Americans were awaiting authority to put the new proposal before the Soviets, who did not have one of their own. Instead, they had some goals, but even these lacked precision and detail. They were letting the Americans do most of the running.

Their most memorable initiative during this first Vienna round had nothing to do with SALT, at least not from Washington's point of view. It did threaten to complicate matters, though. In Helsinki, Semenov had called attention to "provocative attacks by third nuclear powers," a subject the Americans managed to finesse. But on July 7, at a concert in Vienna, Semenov reopened the issue by putting it squarely to Smith in the form of a proposal, which was formally presented three days later.

A stunning glimpse of Moscow's China phobia was provided; on learning of plans for some "provocative" action or attack, the two sides—the United States and the Soviet Union—would take joint steps to prevent it or, if too late, joint retaliatory action to punish the guilty party. The Soviets, in effect, were proposing no less than a superpower alliance against other nuclear powers. Although clearly aimed at China, the proposal risked arousing NATO, whose membership includes two other nuclear powers, Britain and France. The Soviets never would explain exactly what might constitute provocative actions. Washington rejected the idea immediately and just as swiftly informed the other NATO governments, lest they hear of it through another channel and conclude that SALT really did foreshadow a great-power axis or condominium.*

Washington's flat negative had again deflected the issue of provocative attacks, but Semenov warned that more would be heard of it. It would surprise him, he said, if an agreement on limiting arms could be reached without an understanding on provocative attacks as well. Something, it seemed, would have to be done to silence the problem.

Option E is still known within the government as the August 4 proposal, the day of its formal presentation in Vienna. It had a more auspicious unveiling than C and D, but the Soviets remained wholly unprepared to talk seriously about limiting offensive weapons on American terms. With no counterproposal of their own, they sought to keep the ball in the American court. They quarreled mildly with Washington's ceiling of 1900 offensive weapons —the "aggregate" as the bureaucracy put it—and hinted they might come in with a number of their own. If they had one, it did not surface.

More disturbing, the Russians again raised the FBS issue, arguing that European and carrier-based aircraft would have to be treated as part of the American aggregate. This, of course, had been the surprise issue of the inaugural Helsinki round. And again, the Americans objected, as they would continue to object, that their

* Perhaps one day we will know whether Henry Kissinger, during his secret visit to Peking in July, 1971, told Premier Chou En-lai about Moscow's remarkable anti-China initiative.

forward-based systems had no place in a negotiation to limit strategic arms. Moscow was unmoved: it would continue to play FBS in a major key throughout the next round.

On August 14, ten days after Option E's debut, the parties recessed the talks, signed an inconclusive communiqué, and agreed to meet again on November 2, in Helsinki. SALT II had amassed a written record of more than 100,000 words, most of it consisting of the prepared statements of the two chief delegates, Smith and Semenov. Option E had enlivened the proceedings and quickened the tempo of activity. In addition to the twice-weekly plenaries, the Americans had arranged for experts on both sides to meet almost daily so that the Soviets could be entirely clear on what the new U.S. proposal really meant. The Americans wanted to put the ball in the Soviet court and keep it there for a while; specifically, they hoped for a considered and negotiable Soviet reply to Option E when SALT resumed in Helsinki.

Nothing the Soviets did or said in the closing days forcibly discouraged American hopes that Option E might be negotiable. And with congressional elections just ahead, the Administration chose to regard the SALT II experience as salutary and even encouraging. Washington, as one notable said at a background news conference, was "cautiously optimistic about the progress" of SALT.

The White House took special satisfaction from the performance of the system it had created for dealing with SALT. The Vienna round seemed to vindicate the idea that if one thing, or even two things—that is, Options C and D—wouldn't fly, the White House-centered system could react quickly without seeing matters paralyzed in long and painful internal negotiation, as might well have been the case in earlier days. Washington was, it was claimed, negotiating less with itself now than with the other side.

This was only partly true. Options C and D had shown a need for bureaucratic consensus. Option E, admittedly, was a more-reasonable proposal from Moscow's point of view, but, as it turned out, no more negotiable than the others.

At least twice in *A World Restored*, Henry Kissinger records Metternich's genius for keeping his options open. Flexibility is an undoubted advantage in negotiation, but so, too, are consistency and patience. That Options C and D were rejected outright by the

Russians did not necessarily constitute a reason to remove them from play. On the other side, Moscow's attitude on FBS, to say nothing of its refusal to go beyond a distressing level of generality in discussing most things, seemed no less unreasonable to the Americans. The Russians wanted an ABM agreement, yet were refusing to negotiate on radar controls, without which there could be no satisfactory agreement. Still, they would cling for some time to their position, while the Americans sought by one means or another to open serious negotiations.

Opinion divides on whether the White House should have offered the Soviets so many proposals in so short a time. When two negotiating parties are far apart, they normally hold for some time to fixed positions, inching but slowly toward each other and the eventual agreement or failure to agree. By offering the Russians two ABM alternatives in quick succession, the Americans all but closed the door on one of them (zero) before having made fully sure it prefered the other (NCA). By withdrawing Options C and D so quickly, Washington also lost any chance of acquiring something in return for giving them up.

People accustomed to dealing with the Russians worried that Washington's flexibility might confuse them, or tempt them, or end by doing both. Confusion breeds suspicion, and suspicion softens nobody's negotiating position. Alternatively, Moscow might have mistakenly assumed that Washington's interest in a SALT agreement exceeded its own and, if properly exploited, might return numerous concessions. Such was the concern of many Sovietologists within the bureaucracy.

Tedium has its place in the negotiating process, the more so when the negotiation harbors as many exquisitely sensitive and complex issues as this one. SALT II had its tedious intervals, but perhaps they should have been longer. Perhaps the parties would have been better prepared for the third and fourth rounds had they devoted more time in Vienna to explication and reiteration of basic positions, however conflicting. The Americans were setting a fast pace, while the Russians, though no less serious as it turned out, were exercising traditional and normal caution.

Put differently, the Nixon-Kissinger team's tight control did shorten reaction time in Washington. But in Moscow, as events would show, the decision-making process is more cumbersome, the reaction time longer. The Soviet military bureaucracy, as Washington discovered, was then playing a more-critical role in SALT than its American counterpart. And Soviet leaders, at this stage, seemed to agree only that they wanted to limit ABM's; the rest was being played by ear.

Vienna pointed up the stylistic differences, although these may have been more disconcerting than instructive to the parties. The Americans, it bears repeating, were struck by the lack of precision in Soviet statements and, indeed, by their reluctance, or lack of authority, to talk about most issues in detail. The Americans also were struck by the ignorance of the Soviet civilian delegates about their own weapons; even Semenov, heading the delegation, knew little about the numbers and characteristics of Soviet strategic weapons. The Americans, of course, did know and discoursed fluently about the military hardware of both sides, much to the annoyance of the military members of the Soviet delegation: At one point, Colonel-General Nikolai Ogarkov, who was listed as the second-ranking Soviet delegate but who is also the First Deputy Chief of the General Staff, took aside an American delegate and urged that he and others discontinue talking so specifically about Soviet military hardware; such matters, he said, need not concern his civilian colleagues.

All this hinted at Moscow's reluctance, or even its inability, to advance the pace; the Soviet Union's position was inchoate; its tactical preference, like that of a boxer in the early rounds of a long match, was for sparring with the adversary. Moscow was already suggesting longer recesses between negotiating rounds than Washington wanted. The Americans seemed already caught up in a momentum born of intensive preparation. They had come to Vienna with more advanced positions, more expertise, and a remarkable, if slightly uneven, analytical base. What they needed now was patience and consistency. That was the lesson of SALT II.

It was just as well that SALT III was the shortest round, lasting only forty-six days. The two sides were never so far apart. Washington had hoped for a negotiable Soviet response to Option E, one that would have permitted an agreement in principle by the end of the year. Hope dissolved quickly. In tone and substance, the biweekly meetings were about as inspiriting as Helsinki's brumous sky.

The Soviets arrived, still unprepared to talk precisely about issues that to the Americans cried out for precision. As before, they would neither confirm nor deny deploying the kinds and numbers of weapons that U.S. intelligence ascribed to them. Moscow's position had hardened during the recess. Looking back, it now appears that the Soviet leaders were split, though into how many factions and on what issues no one can say. Doubtless, they were negotiating a good deal more with themselves than with the Americans. Very probably, the leaders were slowly sorting out their differences and trying to reach a consensus on SALT before the start of the Twenty-Fourth Soviet Party Congress on March 30, 1971. Meanwhile, their immediate position would combine inflexibility, generality, and an unwillingness to neogtiate on issues about which they were still uncertain or divided.

The effect was to reinforce a suspicion among the Americans that it was they who were negotiating with themselves. A vexed American official unburdened himself in these words:

> We have tabled three proposals in minute detail. They complain bitterly about the degree of detail, yet they've learned a great deal about our programs. They've told us nothing. All we've gotten in return is general statements. And whatever they want in the way of agreement is supposed to be based on our acceptance of these general statements. The bulk of this negotiation is not bilateral but internal. We make presentations. They complain, because by objecting to the wealth of detail they get more of it. They'll say for example "We do not understand the following points." That obliges us to get into even more detail. Let's face it. They are learning a lot, but nothing else is happening.

In fact, the Soviet position was simplicity itself and perfectly suited to the tactic of keeping SALT more or less on the shelf for a time. A fundamental difference that had lain just under the surface was conveniently emerging. The Americans wanted to limit both offensive and defensive weapons, while the Russians wanted a simple ABM agreement, but had little if any interest in constraining offense. The White House, perceiving this, was doubly convinced that the only way to inhibit the Soviet buildup of the SS-9 and other missiles was to insist on tying offense to defense.

The Russians had two objectives, which for tactical purposes were linked. First, they wanted a formal agreement on NCA, on limiting each side to ABM defense of its capital city. The Americans, of course, had helped them immeasurably by first proposing NCA. Second, the Russians still insisted that any negotiable proposal would have to take account of FBS. On neither issue were the Russians particularly clear. Yes, they wanted NCA, but still refused to talk about the numbers or types of the radars that would be permitted, or the number of defensive missiles and other highly technical but essential conditions of an ABM agreement. The FBS issue was pressed with force and conviction; Moscow's aversion to a cluster of American air bases within striking distance of the motherland is genuine, long-standing, and quite unaffected by Washington's argument that these planes are tactical, not strategic, and essential to NATO war plans, notably to counter the 650 or more Soviet missiles targeted on Western European cities. Russians argue that such airplanes, by virtue of their proximity, are not tactical but strategic.

It was and is a good debating point; the Americans squirmed but conceded nothing on FBS. Probably they couldn't, not then at least, because here again the Russians put the issue on grounds that were neither specific nor even reasonable. They began by urging that all forward-based systems—both carrier and land-based —be withdrawn some unspecified distance from Soviet territory. Next they demanded compensation; in exchange for those airplanes that were not withdrawn, the Soviet Union would be entitled under a SALT agreement to deploy more strategic missiles. Still another variation of the theme was the notion that the United States should be penalized for its forward-based aircraft by being obliged to liquidate some unspecified portion of its actual strategic weapons.

Possibly, the Russians thought the FBS issue might just be negotiable on some such terms. If so, their leadership was investing its position with the kind of wishful thinking the Americans displayed in pressing Option E. ACDA and some closely involved members of the State Department would have favored a deal on

FBS; not so the White House, for whom concessions on this issue might have caused serious trouble both with NATO governments and with the Joint Chiefs. Hypersensitive questions would have arisen, among them the right of the United States to deploy aircraft carriers where it pleased and, in turn, its ability to intervene in local conflicts on the Mediterranean littoral, if only to show the flag. The anxieties of the Western Europeans were a major consideration, as Henry Kissinger observed in relating the SALT history to 130 members of Congress after the signing of the Moscow agreements in May, 1972. About FBS, he said:

> The Soviets believed that strategic means any weapons system capable of reaching the Soviet Union or the United States. This would have included our forward-based aircraft and carrier forces, but excluded Soviet intermediate-range rockets aimed at Europe and other areas. We opposed this approach since it would have prejudiced our alliance commitments and raised a distinction between our own security and that of our European allies.[6]

Toward the end of SALT III, Moscow dressed up its position by formally proposing the separation of offense from defense and an ABM agreement based on NCA. The Americans, who were still fine tuning Option E and hoping it might even be negotiable, demurred and insisted that agreement on ABM's alone was unacceptable. To this, the Russians declared a willingness to negotiate limits on offensive weapons if the forward-based systems were included. They would not deal with offense on any other basis. Since Washington was unwilling to give ground on FBS, the obvious thing to do, argued the Russians, was to begin by agreeing to limit ABM's, a goal both sides professed to seek. Washington refused.

At best, it was an impasse. At worst, SALT was having a perverse effect, planting doubts and uncertainties instead of promoting some understanding on each side of the other's position. Suspicion and mistrust were being fed, not dissipated. Again, the Russians were almost certainly confused, if not startled, by the versatility of the Americans in seeking to contain the Soviet Union's natural and preferred source of strategic power, its large land-based missiles.

Some Kremlin-watchers in this country doubted seriously that the Russians would be content with parity. The rate of Soviet missile construction backed by a tough ABM-only SALT position aroused concern that Moscow was seeking to strip the United States of the right to defend itself against Soviet strategic power, the scope of which, in numbers of missiles and in megatonnage, would greatly exceed that of the United States unless somehow braked by the kind of agreement that now seemed utterly non-negotiable. FBS was seen as another in a long series of Soviet initiatives aimed at dividing the United States from its allies. Growing tensions in the Middle East and Cuba, plus a disturbing Soviet naval buildup in the Mediterranean, added to the gloom. The Berlin agreement that actually did lie ahead seemed at this time unattainable; again, Moscow was being tough and uncompromising. To the degree that SALT relies on some identity of great-power interest, the prospect of any near-term agreement seemed even more doubtful than when the talks had begun a year earlier. "Tensions with the U.S.S.R. in other areas cannot fail to have a negative influence," said Gerard Smith in December, breaking his two-year rule against giving press interviews.[7] Relations between Washington and Moscow were on the downslide. Their identity of interest was narrowing, or so it seemed.

On December 22, four days after the close of SALT III, Secretary of State Rogers said that the talks "had not proceeded as fast as we hoped they would," adding that "it may take a little more time than we wished" to get an agreement. And a "knowledgeable informant" explained to *The New York Times* in mixed metaphor that the negotiators in Helsinki "passed like ships in the night, sparring rather than coming together on issues."[8]

Skepticism, caution, and suspicion come naturally to those in Washington who deal with the Soviet Union. The effect of three rounds of SALT was to sharpen the tendency to expect the worst. A large part of the bureaucracy, if not downright critical, was second-guessing the White House. Option E, although apparently nonnegotiable, was anything but popular with those who worried most about protecting Minuteman. Whereas Options C and D would have done something about this—the one by banning MIRV tests, the other by reducing Soviet missile strength—Option E would have deprived the United States of the right to defend

Minuteman without necessarily removing the alleged threat of a first strike. A greater and more reasonable concern was that in offering NCA, the White House had played its high card—an ABM limitation—with little assurance of getting in return an agreement on offensive weapons.

More specifically, the bureaucracy worried, and with reason, that informed opinon might force the President to accept an ABM-only agreement, thus depriving the Russians of any incentive to talk seriously about limiting offensive weapons. Thanks to a leak in Washington, the essense of the Soviet position crept into the American press, an event that enraged the two delegations in Helsinki. A *New York Times* editorial of January 17, 1971 said just what the Administration and most of the SALT bureaucracy least wanted to hear:

> The Soviet Union's suggestion of a preliminary strategic arms agreement restricting antiballistic missile (ABM) defense in both countries deserves an immediate, favorable American response without waiting for resumption of formal talks. . . .
>
> A meaningful agreement on offensive delivery systems is proving difficult to negotiate. The Soviet Union wants all American tactical bombers in Europe counted in the numerical limitations, something the United States justifiably refuses. . . .
>
> It would be self-defeating to endanger a possible ABM agreement by insisting that offensive weapons limitations must be linked to it.

The editorial was an early warning, an expression of an attitude that took hold quickly in liberal political circles and in much of academia. Even the best-informed people knew little about SALT, except for what was contained in the editorial, plus the Administration's reluctance to ban MIRV's, which were just beginning to be deployed. They needed to know nothing more to become convinced that if MIRV could not be halted the negotiators should speedily agree to squash the single greatest source of instability, the ABM.

All the pressure was on the Nixon Administration. The momentum of its SALT preparation had been artfully diverted. The Americans had done most of the running, but the Russians, with their solitary proposal for an ABM-only agreement, had maneuvered them onto the defensive; much of influential opinion in the United States was falling in behind the Soviet position.

Washington was mildly cheered, although not for long as it turned out, by a curious, though seemingly genuine, slowdown of the SS-9 program. On October 9, 1970, Defense Secretary Laird had announced that more than 300 SS-9's were deployed or under construction; but on December 16, he revealed that the program was slowing down. The Russians, it turned out, had halted work on 18 SS-9 silos started eight months earlier and had not begun any new construction for either the SS-9's or the smaller and more numerous SS-11's. The Soviet ICBM program, it seemed, had finally leveled off at a number in excess of 1500, including 288 SS-9's.

The real and lasting dividend of SALT III, however, lay well ahead and could not be predicted. It was the reward sometimes bestowed by patience. Finding itself in an awkward position, the Administration kept its poise. A hard political logic was pushing the United States toward an agreement innocent of any constraint on offensive weapons. Washington refused to bend to this logic; the White House would continue to insist that any deal on SALT would have to link offense with defense. And the White House was to be vindicated. Nobody was distracted by the irony that in first proposing talks in 1967, Washington wanted to limit or ban ABM's and cared little about offense, while Moscow was then concerned about America's commanding lead in offensive missiles and determined to cling to the ABM option.

"I barricade myself behind time, and make patience my weapon," said Metternich, a figure thought to have had more than a little influence on the formation of Henry Kissinger.[9] Three months would separate SALT III from the next round. SALT IV was due to start in Vienna on March 15, just two weeks before the opening of the Twenty-Fourth Soviet Party Congress. Both capitals would have time to wrestle with internal political difficulties thrown up by SALT, as well as to think about how to break the stalemate without harming their basic positions, which with time had grown farther apart. SALT IV would become the focus of intense activity, most of it carried on in Washington and Moscow rather than in Vienna.

For the Kremlin, there remained the apparently difficult problem of moving to more negotiable ground and carrying along all of the party leaders and the military. On the surface, Moscow seemed unwilling to bend. Its public silence on SALT was broken on February 4, 1971 when *Pravda* issued a heavy broadside against U.S. strategic policies and its SALT position. Special exception was taken to Safeguard, to MIRV, and, finally, to forward-based aircraft and Washington's unwillingness to discuss those of its weapons deployed overseas. Two days later, on February 6, the Washington correspondent of *Izvestia* charged that Gerard Smith, while secretly briefing the Senate Foreign Relations Committee, had taken a negative view of the Soviet proposal for an ABM agreement. The article said that "the idea of concluding such an agreement [on ABM's only] has evoked great interest in American political and scientific circles, and the Senators listening to Smith were puzzled by his extreme negative approach to such a practical step."

A Soviet diplomat of some consequence, interviewed during this period about why his government favored an ABM-only agreement, made the following points: The ABM is not the most dangerous weapon; Safeguard is "no good, won't work," and therefore doesn't worry Moscow, which is emphasizing defense because it is the easiest place to begin. Defensive weapons, he continued, are less developed, therefore simpler to limit than the more advanced offensive weapons, which, because they are "more difficult and much more provocative," will require more time. How much time? It may take "a couple of years," he said, to reach agreement on offense. He was utterly vague on what kind of limits might eventually be placed on offensive weapons.

In Washington, dovish circles were unhappy because the Administration was both deploying MIRV and refusing the half-a-loaf ABM agreement. Hawks were unhappy, because nobody seemed sufficiently sensitive to Minuteman's inevitable vulnerability to a surprise attack. Many bureaucrats shared this anxiety and also complained that the Russians, with little effort and nothing really negotiable on the table, had seized the initiative. Still others worried that the White House, having acquired patience, would cling overlong to Option E, which clearly wouldn't do.

Instead the White House lost no time in mounting a subtle yet direct assault on its SALT dilemma. And it was to take an even more-direct hand in the action, little of which was publicly visible and the essence of which was concealed from the SALT bureaucracy, from most of the Administration, and even from Kissinger's own staff.

The problem was how to change direction without discarding or compromising the essentials of the American position. First, the Administration and the bureaucracy had to be assured that the Soviet offense could not plausibly threaten the American deterrent or, through sheer magnitude, undercut American foreign policy. By now, the Russians had either deployed or under construction about 450 more ICBM's than the Americans, plus about 350 missiles on nuclear submarines, with many more of these on the way. They had also recently concluded extensive tests of multiple warheads for both the SS-9 and SS-11. Critics such as Henry Jackson, a presumed presidential candidate, along with many bureaucrats, felt strongly that Minuteman had to be defended. Obviously, the NCA and zero ABM options would mean abandoning Minuteman defense. And Safeguard by now was shorn of credibility as a reliable protector of ICBM sites. Some analysts, mostly in the Pentagon, also worried that missile-firing Soviet submarines could in just a few minutes catch American B-52 bombers on the ground and destroy command centers and communication links.

The bare bones of the White House position turned up in the President's annual State of the World message to Congress, a Nixon-Kissinger innovation. This bulky document, released on February 25, had quite a lot to say about strategic arms, including a clear rejection of Moscow's quest for an ABM-only agreement. "To limit only one side of the offense-defense equation could rechannel the arms competition rather than effectively curtail it," said Nixon. The document noted the apparent slowdown of the SS-9 program, calling it "unclear" and "ambiguous" and seeming to solicit from Moscow a signal that a limitation on giant missiles was negotiable. Moscow was put on notice that movement toward a first-strike capability would cause Washington "to react appropriately." Was the Soviet Union, Nixon asked, really prepared to settle for "strategic equilibrium?"

The statement said that the United States would have to proceed with a "minimal" ABM program, but it also hinted that a zero ABM agreement might be negotiable. In fact, the Administration was seeking funds to proceed with four Safeguard sites. Safeguard in the role of a bargaining chip remained basic to the White House strategy.

The White House also had underway, perhaps belatedly, a series of "survivability" studies aimed at measuring the actual vulnerability of the U.S. triad of ICBM's, SLBM's, and strategic bombers. The studies pointed up an inexorable, thought not immediate, threat to Minuteman. Safeguard was seen to offer negligible protection to those missiles it might defend. Concern about the B-52 bombers was eased by analysis showing that, to catch them on the ground, the Russians would need to develop something called a depressed trajectory missile, and so far as Washington knew, they were not even working on such a weapon. In any case, the Air Force was starting to disperse the bombers by moving many of them away from coastal bases.

Any potential threat to U.S. nuclear submarines was established as even more remote. Soviet antisubmarine warfare techniques lag well behind America's, and it is still hard to envisage either side deploying a reliable system, or systems, for canceling out the other's sub-launched missiles.

It couldn't have been more than a few days after releasing the State of the World Message that Nixon got his signal—and a harsh one at that—as to whether the Soviets were finished building big missiles, or just taking a breather. The message came not from Moscow but from U.S. intelligence, which had spotted some very large new holes situated in Soviet SS-9 fields, all of which are in central Russia, east of the Ural Mountains. There are six of these fields, spread more than 1000 miles in an oval.

It fell to Democratic Senator Henry Jackson, a conspicuous advocate both of Minuteman defense and of a high strategic profile, to make this information public. On March 7, Jackson appeared on the television program "Face The Nation" and disclosed the gist of a high-level briefing, as presumably he'd been expected to do. He had a lot to say:

> It will come, I think, as a shock to a lot of Americans, after much discussion here that they'd level off on the deployment of the SS-9's, to know that the Russians are now in the process of

deploying a new generation, an advance generation, of offensive systems. . . . We do not know quite what it means, but I can say to you that these are huge new missiles . . . big or bigger than the SS-9's. . . . The indications that we have are that the new system is something superior to the SS-9, not necessarily in yield, but in quality. It may be related to MIRV'ing.

I am sure, or reasonably sure, that the Russian use of this huge buildup will come not in the form of a first strike on the United States, but to use this growing power to take greater and greater international political risks in the 1970's. . . .

What I'm saying here now is that . . . the need to limit offensive systems is critical. This is why I think the President is right. We must do both; to limit just the defensive systems makes no sense at all.

It was a rude shock. For Moscow, abandoning the eighteen older SS-9 silos had been a matter of *reculer pour mieux sauter*. Jackson had accurately reflected the Administration's concern, though not its disarray and uncertainty. At this stage, U.S. intelligence could not reliably forecast either the scope or the nature of the new buildup. Unlike the Americans, the Russians normally dig holes and build silos *before* testing new missiles.

Soon more new holes began to appear in SS-11 fields in western Russia. The buildup would continue on into July; in the end, American intelligence counted ninety-one new holes; of these, twenty-five are in SS-9 fields and designed to house a missile at least that size, while sixty-six others resemble the SS-11. In Washington, some parts of the bureaucracy thought (or hoped) that the Soviets were not altering their missiles, but adopting harder silos. Others thought that Moscow was preparing silos to accept a MIRV'd version of their missiles. Still others believed that the new holes were a portent either of an entirely new and more-powerful missile or of new and more-efficient launching techniques, or both.

As articles about the new holes began to appear in *The New York Times* and the *Washington Post*, Administration critics fretted that the story was probably exaggerated, designed to promote Safeguard and to vindicate the rejection by the White House of an ABM-only agreement. In fact, nobody would know for a full year what sort of weapons would go into the new holes, but their immediate effect was to banish any lingering hope that the Administration would take an ABM-only agreement.

In conducting sensitive diplomacy, the government operates in what are called the "front channel" and the "back channel"; in the case of SALT, the front channel for the most part means instructions sent to the delegation, reports from the delegation to Washington, and so forth. Front-channel messages are often highly classified and sometimes restricted to a small handful of people. The back channel may involve utterly private contacts between two individuals—say Henry Kissinger and Gerard Smith in the case of SALT; or it may mean secret contacts between an American official and another government, about which only the President and possibly one or two of his senior officials are informed. Kissinger's initial contacts with China are a good example of back-channel activity. So, too, is the White House SALT initiative taken in January, 1971; five months later, it produced the first, perhaps the major, breakthrough on SALT. Nearly all this activity was carried on in the back channel by Henry Kissinger, who kept fully informed only his constituency of one.

It began with a meeting on January 9 between Kissinger and Soviet Ambassador Dobrynin in which Dobrynin was told that the President would insist on a link between offense and defense. Months later, columnist Marquis Childs reported that Dobrynin also saw the President on the ninth and was given a personal message to be delivered to Premier Alexei N. Kosygin.[10] This was the first in a series of Nixon-Kosygin exchanges aimed at "breaking the stalemate," as the President later put it. The security on this correspondence was, and is, remarkable. Even after the breakthrough in May, senior members of the Administration were not permitted to see it unless they had an absolute need, as in the case of Gerard Smith. The same restriction applied, for the most part, to Kissinger's staff.

Kissinger and Dobrynin swiftly agreed that the key issues were the American insistence on dealing simultaneously with offensive weapons and the Soviet commitment to the FBS issue. They also agreed to open the back channel on SALT. They met again toward the end of January, with Dobrynin expressing Moscow's "sympathy" and indicating that his government wanted their pri-

vate talks to continue. After this, the two discussed the kinds of
offensive systems that might be included in the agreement. A
breakthrough of sorts was made during the second week of February. The Politburo, Dobrynin announced, had authorized him
to tell the President that the U.S.S.R. wanted a SALT agreement.
Dobrynin added that Moscow preferred a straight NCA deal on
ABM's, but would settle for something else. Kissinger was then
taking the line that it was unfair to ask the United States to dismantle an ongoing Safeguard program, while the Soviet Union
maintained its Galosh system defending Moscow. Some sparring
ensued. Then, in March, the Soviets began to "backpedal," as one
American put it. In both the back channel—that is to say, Kissinger and Dobrynin—and in the front channel—in the talks in
Vienna—Moscow abruptly reprised its ABM-only offer.

March and April were the gloomiest months. Moscow's back-
pedaling coincided with the discovery of the new holes. Months
earlier, during SALT III, the U.S. delegation had tried to find
out from the Soviet delegation what the SS-9 slowdown meant.
The poorly informed Russians in Helsinki were unable to com-
municate a clear signal, but a nonofficial Russian did offer some
encouragement. He was Georgi A. Arbatov, Director of Moscow's U.S.A. Institute and a senior adviser to the Soviet leadership on American affairs. Arbatov is a familiar figure to both
academic and bureaucratic circles in America. He writes authori-
tative articles in *Pravda* and for his own institute's journal. He is
known to have Brezhnev's ear. In short, Arbatov is taken seriously,
the more so perhaps because of Moscow's penchant for delivering some messages out of official channels. During one of his
frequent trips to America, Arbatov put it about in Washington
that the SS-9 slowdown could be interpreted as a willingness in
Moscow to negotiate on big land-based missiles. The new holes,
while not necessarily belying him, inspired doubt; they also inspired a debate on Minuteman's vulnerability, which was described
by one participant as "cathartic."

Kissinger was feeling pressure as he entered the back channel
with Dobrynin in January. Moscow clearly aimed to have superior numbers in offensive missiles. Thus, Option E would have
to be scrapped, and with it any hope of agreement on "equal
aggregates," that is, strict parity in numbers of offensive missiles.

(The new holes only made this perception clearer.) The Administration was faced with three requirements: somehow to escape the trap it had laid for itself in offering NCA; to sidetrack FBS; and, of course, to secure a limit on the SS-9 (and any even more horrendous siblings that might lie ahead).

In December, 1970, Kissinger had ordered his staff to prepare a new look at the offensive side of SALT. He had an idea of his own about defense. The staff memorandum arrived on his desk on January 11, two days after the back channel, unbeknownst to the staff, had been opened. It suggested some variations on one single theme: a proposal to freeze offensive weapons at existing levels. Although at least one of the variants was rigged in a way to deny the Soviets numerical superiority, the freeze idea merely underlined the handwriting on the wall. Any agreement on offensive weapons, especially if it were to exclude forward-based systems, would have to grant Moscow in return a sizable edge in strategic missiles.

One of the variants proposed discarding Safeguard in return for Soviet agreement to halt further deployment of all offensive missiles, both ICBM's and SLBM's. Kissinger, still keeping his own counsel, was unimpressed by this idea. The White House, as noted, would cling to Safeguard, and not just for its bargaining value. Neither NCA nor a total ban on ABM's was in the cards. NCA really meant zero ABM for the United States, since Congress was unlikely to authorize funds for it. And zero ABM was regarded—above all by the White House—as unacceptable to the Russians, who would balk at dismantling Galosh. All this foreshadowed intensive bargaining for a deal that would leave each side free to keep all or some portion of its existing ABM program.

The freeze, on the other hand, either impressed Kissinger or conformed to his own thinking. But not for a few months would the delegation, or the SALT bureaucracy, or most of the Administration discover that.

The drift of Kissinger's thinking occasionally surfaced, though dimly. In a Verification Panel meeting on March 5, ten days before the opening of SALT IV, he wondered aloud why the United States didn't just propose a simple freeze of offensive weapons. David Packard, then the Deputy Secretary of Defense, answered indirectly by rehearsing the eternal problem of Minuteman's vulnerability. The new holes had just been sighted, and some officials worried that the Pentagon, fearing the worst for Minuteman, might even desert Option E, which was still before the Russians. Thus, Kissinger's aside drew little attention, if only because a simple freeze would do less to ease the Minuteman problem than even Option E.

On March 11, the White House issued NSDM 102, which instructed Gerard Smith to offer an ABM deal that would allow Moscow to keep Galosh and the United States to complete the four Safeguard sites for which funds were available. Since nobody expected the Russians to swallow such a disparity in the number of sites, the so-called four-to-one offer puzzled some and troubled others. In fact, the offer was designed as a holding action, while Kissinger explored the back channel with Dobrynin.

The Russians moved first. Less than a week after the start of SALT IV, their delegation repeated the ABM-only offer in the form of a draft treaty. *Both* sides would be limited to NCA and about 100 interceptor missiles each. The proposal was innocent of radar controls. The gloom, which by now was a fixed attitude, grew heavier. Any ABM agreement that failed to limit numbers and types of radars would be worse than no agreement. Each side would look upon new radars deployed by the other as possible evidence of a clandestine ABM buildup. Such an agreement would promote, rather than quiet, fears and instabilities.

On March 26, Smith in turn offered the new U.S. four-to-one proposition, but without prejudice to the other two options —NCA and zero—which, he said, were still on the table. Semenov's position was mildly intriguing. Unlike Smith, who had been kept in the dark, he *was* informed of the back-channel Kissinger-Dobrynin talks, the locus of the real action. Thus, he understood that the four-to-one proposal was a negotiating ploy. He also knew that Moscow would not be prepared for any departures in either the front or back channels until after the Party Congress, due to start in four days, which he would attend. He rejected the four-to-one proposal out of hand, reiterating: You offer one thing (NCA); we accept, and then you come back with zero and now still another proposal. He had a point. Washington had put three ABM options before the Soviets. One closely involved American says: "We probably made them uncomfortable with zero, but with four-to-one we insulted them, or at least they professed to be insulted."

During tea breaks and in other informal contacts over the next few days, Soviet delegates asked why the Americans seemed to shrink from NCA after having first proposed it. The Americans were reluctant to admit that NCA would probably be aborted on Capitol Hill, so they replied, in effect: Granted you have a debating point. But this isn't a debate. We can't dismantle an ongoing program (Safeguard) any more than you can. So let's try for agreement.

The issue arose in the next plenary session on April 1. Standing in for the absent Semenov was Rolan Timerbaev, a Foreign Ministry official not even listed on the Soviet delegation. The four-to-one idea was again rejected. Timerbaev said that since the United States had offered three alternatives, his government had a choice. It had, he said, chosen NCA. The American delegation cabled that the Soviet statement indicated a rejection of the two alternatives to NCA.

One week later, on April 8, the Russian delegation announced that it had been instructed to confirm Semenov's statement of March 26 that four-to-one was unacceptable. At that point, matters bogged down. The Russians had nothing more to offer. Neither did the Americans; beyond instructing Smith to offer four-to-one, NSDM 102 gave the U.S. delegation little room for maneuver. So the delegations were left to their jejeune tasks of clarifying familiar and nonnegotiable positions. The Americans did shed many of their eleven original collateral constraints at this time. Some had already been discarded or loosened at Helsinki. Now they were all to go, except for the ban on silo modification. Otherwise nothing was happening.

"Le Congrès danse, mais il ne marche pas," said the Prince de Ligne. And Byron characterized the Congress of Vienna as a "base pageant." SALT is hardly a pageant of any kind. Still, comparison with the Congress of Vienna has been unavoidable because Europeans, especially the Viennese, liked to make it. Knowing nothing about SALT, they can discuss it in no other terms. And they are impressed by the contrast.

Harold Nicolson said of the first Congress: "The affluence of so many otiose visitors to Vienna created serious problems of housing, maintenance and expense. In order to distract their attention from the actual futility of their presence a vast program of entertainment was devised. This program, while it threw a heavy burden upon the Austrian exchequer and thereby rendered the Congress increasingly unpopular with the Austrian public, has left behind it the legend that the Congress . . . devoted its whole time to social festivity."[11]

The delegations wanted neither a dancing congress nor pageantry. This was made clear to the host governments. Both the Americans and the Russians worked most of the time and were not very visible. Still, the Austrians, like the Finns, were gratified by their presence. SALT imparted to politically aware Viennese some sense of involvement with larger affairs. And when a prominent figure like Senator Stuart Symington followed a visit to Vienna with an attack on the alleged reluctance of his government to reach agreement with the Soviet Union, as he did in April, 1961, Vienna was titillated and felt drawn back into exciting political currents.

The Austrian and Finnish governments went to considerable length and some expense to meet the needs and preferences of the delegations. Each maintained observers in the other's capital, and each closely coordinated such essential functions as security and handling of the SALT press with the other. Security involved special effort and expense. In Vienna, a security man was attached to the delegations and two bodyguards each were assigned to Smith and Semenov. Security agents were maintained in various hotels housing American personnel and in the single hotel occupied by the Russians. Vienna's famous sewers were regularly inspected, and access from these to the buildings where delegates either lived or worked was closed off.

In Helsinki, most of the American SALT delegation stayed in what may be the town's best address, a hotel called the Kalastajatorppa (one does learn to pronounce it), while the Russians made do in a less-grand establishment. In Vienna, the pattern was different. The Americans spread themselves around a number of first-class hotels, while the Russians, after some internal debate within their delegation, finally opted for a new hotel called the

Park, located in the sulfur spa of Baden, about 15 miles south of Vienna. The Park is very grand, indeed, with a heated swimming pool, sauna, and medical therapy unit. The choice of Baden surprised Austria, mostly because it was Soviet headquarters during the occupation years. The younger Russians had hoped to stay in Vienna, but Semenov and the other seniors were seduced by the Park's swimming pool–sauna combination.

In any case, the questionable symbolism of a return to Baden never mattered. The townspeople were quite indifferent to the Soviets as paying guests. Semenov, who shares the devotion of his American colleague Paul Nitze, for German culture, attracted little attention as he took the innumerable "Beethoven walks" that Baden offers.

Most mornings, the Russians were bussed into Vienna to their Embassy, where they not only worked but took their meals, thus denying themselves the pleasures of the Park's dining room, considered by many Viennese to be among Austria's best. The dining room and terrace-café remained open to the public, while the rest of the hotel—rooms, swimming pool and sauna, were declared extraterritorial during SALT sessions. A young assistant manager of the Park says that every Russian had a local newspaper and the Paris *International Herald Tribune* delivered to his room each morning.

Another building made extraterritorial by the first phase of SALT was the Strudelhof, an agreeable restoration of a seventeenth-century private palace, which was headquarters for the American SALT delegation. The Strudelhof lies just around the corner from the American Embassy. It was once occupied by Count Leopold Berchtold, who as Royal and Imperial Foreign Minister, signed the ultimatum to Serbia on July 19, 1914 that led to the First World War. Gerard Smith's office was the rosewood room in which Berchtold, according to his wife, not only signed the document, but did several redrafts throughout the night before, each time strengthening it.

The talks fostered special ties between Finland and Austria, two neutrals with a sharp eye for the international conference trade. Both are betting heavily on an era of expanded negotiation; both see themselves as hosting a great deal of it, especially conferences like SALT, which join members of the two blocs.

And although competitive, officials of each government openly admired the other's style in handling SALT. They eventually lost SALT to Geneva because the switching back and forth complicated things, obliging the Americans and Russians, for example, to spend a lot of money maintaining two sets of secure communications.

The Austrians evince special determination, arising in part from a sense of the past and a lingering affinity for world politics. It's been a long time since Vienna's writ covered sixty million European souls, but it still thinks of itself as more than a political backwater administering to seven million Austrians. There remains considerable tradition in the baroque palace on the Ballehausplatz that is Vienna's Whitehall and houses the Federal Chancellory and the Foreign Ministry. Early arriving Austrian officials with offices giving on the Ballehausplatz could watch benevolently as Gerard Smith made his way on foot in the morning from the Bristol Hotel to the Strudelhof.

None of them, including the most senior, were told anything about SALT. Like everyone else, anything they knew about that was traceable to leaks in Washington, to *The New York Times* or the *Washington Post;* these stories were invariably printed in the Paris *International Herald Tribune,* which was surely one of the reasons why every Russian at the Park Hotel read it.

The SALT press was marvelously cared for by both the Finns and Austrians; all needs were anticipated and swiftly met. Except at the beginning, however, these were not very great because there was rarely anything for the SALT press to write about. The number of journalists covering the Vienna rounds dwindled to about twenty, half of them American. After the plenaries, they would meet in a cavernous press center in the Hofburg, the old Imperial Palace, and await the arrival of Nedville E. Nordness, ACDA's Public Affairs Adviser. Nordness is an amiable veteran of the arms-control business, and the press likes him, even though he has never had anything to say.

In one typical briefing, on May 5, 1971, Nordness began by specifying the exact time the session began and the time it ended. The press, he then said, could "assume that serious consideration had been given to issues on which we were attempting to make progress. The climate," he added, "was unchanged from past meetings." An English journalist who wondered whether on-site inspection was a snag was enjoined to have "a good weekend." Someone, possibly in desperation, asked whether thought was being given to inviting Peking to join the talks. Nordness replied that SALT was a two-party affair, and, while the question of other participants was not foreclosed, it had not arisen. The briefing ended with the announcement that the next meeting would be held on Friday in the Soviet Embassy. Withal, Nordness tells reporters: "You are sitting on top of the most important story in the world." But he can't help them get at it.

Throughout, the local press paid little attention. The thankless job of covering the talks was left to foreign journalists, all of whom learned quickly that the only place to find a SALT story is Washington. During the first Vienna round (SALT II), an American wire-service reporter stationed there—and perhaps temporarily unhinged by SALT's utter inaccessibility—began extrapolating from SALT leaks appearing in *The New York Times* or the *Washington Post* and sending these products of his fancy as authentic stories. Although this bizarre practice created no difficulty with the Russians, since the stories were wildly inaccurate, it caused his colleagues in Vienna no end of trouble; they were constantly awakened in the dead of night by editors who felt understandably uncovered as the "stories" broke in the hundreds of newspapers subscribing to the service. The aggrieved reporters complained bitterly to Nordness, who ended the matter by explicitly warning the offending journalist to suppress his imagination.

As for the delegations, by the spring of 1971 they had created neither the spectacle of a dancing Congress nor the illusion of a productive one. Still, their systematic no-nonsense approach to the business and their passion for secrecy were applauded. And, despite the stalemate, they managed to keep open a useful dialogue, exploring and reexploring terrifically complex technical issues, each all the while probing the other for some sign of the wobbles on one or more of the intractable gut issues. The routine of twice-weekly plenary sessions was still maintained, but the delegations were shifting into a looser, more informal operational style. The plenaries were dry affairs dominated by Smith and Semenov reading prepared statements cleared at home. After a time, the plenaries were broken up by extended tea breaks during which delegates could talk more privately, hence often more frankly. A strong tendency to shift the bulk of the business into small working groups and "mini-plenaries" was underway and would continue. Both delegations were keen to turn over various issues to those delegates and staff experts best able to deal with them.

It was during SALT IV that the vested interest of the delegations in making some progress became clear. In a broad sense, they were becoming accomplices, seeking to narrow differences between their governments, looking for bargaining room. This other tendency indicated, among other things, that SALT had slid into deep trouble.

The makeup of the delegations and their staffs had changed very little. On the American side, Ambassador Llewellyn E. Thompson was too ill to attend SALT IV and was replaced as the State Department delegate by another career diplomat, Ambassador J. Graham Parsons. Otherwise, the starting team was intact, with Smith as Chairman, Paul Nitze as the Defense Department delegate, Lieutenant General Royal B. Allison representing the Joint Chiefs, and Dr. Harold Brown, the academic community. Raymond L. Garthoff was the chief executive officer and Smith's closest adviser.

On the Soviet side, there was only one change, but it was an important one. Colonel-General Nikolai Ogarkov, First Deputy Chief of the General Staff, was clearly the most important figure on the Soviet delegation, even though Semenov was the nominal leader. Ogarkov failed to turn up at SALT IV, and was replaced by a considerably less-powerful officer, Konstantin Trusov. A partial explanation emerged during the Party Congress, when Ogarkov was promoted from candidate member to full membership in the Central Committee. He was also known to be in the running for the job of chief of staff, soon to be vacant. Ogarkov, it seems, had become too important for SALT. Semenov, another candidate member, was not promoted. He and the other key figures in the Soviet delegation, P. S. Pleshakov and A. N. Shchukin, stayed on, as did Garthoff's opposite number, Nikolai S. Kishilov, listed as the delegation's senior adviser and, like Garthoff, an ubiquitous figure.

In many ways, Garthoff and Kishilov, although not delegates, were key front-channel personalities. In Washington, they were called by some the "point men," by others the "lightning rods" of the talks. They met frequently, sometimes to work out the linguistic problems arising from the bizarre SALT vocabulary; each is fluent in the other's language. Sometimes they met to explore new issues or new proposals, so that each delegation might have an impression of the other's initial position or attitude. Very often they would meet with one or two delegates from either side in an effort to remove or narrow differences on a single point. Sometimes they met to see whether a new approach might move an old issue off dead center.

The delegates began to see more of each other socially; they were now authorized to meet for tête-à-tête lunches and dinners. Smith and Semenov, usually accompanied by Garthoff and Kishilov, saw each other privately, as did Paul Nitze and Academician Shchukin, General Allison and General Trusov. On each side, various personalities (though not the seniors) had achieved a first-name relationship. From SALT IV onward, informal contact between the delegations increased steadily, just as the style of the enterprise became more flexible.

In Washington, as perhaps in Moscow, some people had mixed feelings about the more-intimate character of the talks. The U.S. delegation, although occasionally in full agreement, did not often present a united front in Washington, tending instead to reflect the biases of the major bureaucratic factions. Hence, a suspicion arose that in their contacts with the Russians, some Americans made much of that which they wanted to hear, while ignoring, or playing down, less compatible signals. And despite firm White House guidance—more specifically, from the Kissinger controlled Verification Panel Working Group—some U.S. SALT delegates could and did operate in back channels of their own, reporting privately by secure telephone to their principals in Washington. Especially in the later rounds (V, VI, and VII), a number of bureaucratic games were under way that the White House, however suspicious, could neither control nor effectively monitor. Bureaucracy, in short, was operating as it always does.

The second Vienna round (SALT IV), like its predecessors, recorded little progress and was really the last part of an extended prelude. SALT IV is memorable, though, for having produced an event that joined the front and back channels.

As intended, the Twenty-Fourth Soviet Party Congress tightened the control of the party's Chief, Leonid Brezhnev, who was committing himself to a full-blown policy of *détente* with the West. Agreement with the Americans on SALT abruptly became priority business.

Ambassador Dobrynin, like General Ogarkov, was promoted from candidate member to full membership in the Central Committee during the Party Congress, which he, of course, attended. Dobrynin stayed on for two additional weeks, and returned to Washington toward the end of April prepared to do serious business with Henry Kissinger. For the first time, Moscow was ready to talk about linking offensive and defensive weapons.

The back channel was flooded with activity. Kissinger and Dobrynin were now negotiating. They often met in Kissinger's office, and they had innumerable telephone conversations. The arresting Mr. Arbatov, who was also promoted at the Party Congress (to a watchdog group called the Central Auditing Commission), appeared in Washington during this period and saw Kissinger.

In broad outline, Kissinger and Dobrynin were talking about a formal ABM agreement and something less formal—an interim freeze perhaps—on some kinds of offensive weapons. Soon they were caught up in a frenetic effort to fill in some of the blanks and thus move SALT within sight of agreement.

For reasons nobody in Washington understands, the Soviet delegation suddenly jumped into the act. Semenov dined with Smith in Vienna on May 4 and, speaking from a written brief, noted that Smith had raised the issue of a joint freeze on ICBM's. Smith replied that he had not raised any such issue, and knew nothing about it; that was true. Semenov then proposed an ABM agreement, limiting both sides to NCA, with an understanding that ICBM construction would be halted afterward. This aroused some interest and considerable suspicion among the Americans. Moscow, it seemed, might be trying to snare the cherished ABM agreement by talking in vague terms about a limitation on offensive missiles, even while digging all those new holes.

Two days later, on May 6, another private conversation indicated a possible Soviet willingness to go beyond Semenov's suggestion and simply halt further ICBM construction. This same encounter also produced the first hint that Moscow was ready to accept the so-called sublimit on very large missiles like the SS-9, which Washington had pressed so assiduously.

This *was* interesting. The SALT bureaucracy in Washington, like the delegation, was intrigued by what seemed to be an important Soviet initiative. Curiously enough and unbeknownst to the delegates, they were overtaking their back-channel colleagues. Kissinger and Dobrynin were now feverishly negotiating an exchange of identical letters between Nixon and Kosygin, as well as a joint U.S.–U.S.S.R. announcement for release in two weeks' time. Dobrynin, with more authority than his colleagues in Vienna, had come a little farther than they in accommodating the American demand for "simultaneity," that is, for limiting offense and defense at the same time. Also, whereas his colleagues in Vienna were still rigorously pushing a straight NCA deal on ABM's, Dobrynin, while not yet abandoning that position, was showing signs of flexibility. Kissinger was urging some kind of "equality" on ABM's, which in effect would leave Moscow free to keep Galosh and the United States some portion of Safeguard.

Smith was immediately instructed to return to Washington. This was judged no time to risk allowing ambiguous signals in Vienna to complicate the back-chanel negotiation—the main event, as it were. Smith would return on Monday, May 10, along with Nitze, Garthoff, and General Allison. But first there was the ritual weekend outing of the two delegations hosted by the Austrian government.

The first one, held a year earlier, had been a great success. Delegates, wives, and staff personnel had been taken by boat to visit a Benedictine abbey, a baroque construction on the original tenth-century site. They had managed, according to Austrian authorities, a per capita consumption of 1.5 liters of wine; moreover, there *was* dancing, as one Austrian official coyly recalled, and while the affair could scarcely be compared with what Harold Nicolson called "the idle diplomatic lubricities" of Alexander and Metternich, a good time was had by all.

This time, the delegations were to visit Carinthia, Austria's southernmost province: Alpine, full of lakes, Roman ruins, and well-managed resort hotels. Everyone on every side—eighty-three Americans, fifty-five Russians, and thirty-two Austrians—seemed to be looking forward to it.

The Carinthia outing, although no less convivial than its predecessor, is memorable for another reason; it produced the most significant Semenov-Smith conversation to that date. While on a lake steamer during the second day (May 9), the two talked privately and at length with only interpreters present. Since they were obviously talking business, their hosts saw to it that the boat continued to steam around the lake for an unscheduled additional half hour until the conversation was completed.

The May 6 overture on linking offense and defense was repeated, and Semenov implied that a halt on new construction might well apply not just to large ICBM's, but to other offensive weapons as well. He also said that he was responding to a question put by Smith and wished it to be understood as such in Washington. Smith disputed that—he'd posed no such question—but said that he would be happy to take responsibility for it. They continued their talk on the train back to Vienna.

Semenov's reference to other offensive weapons was ambiguous, because he refused to be drawn out. The essence of the conversation, in fact, was positive but cryptic. Still, thanks to their Russian colleagues, Smith and a few others now had a strong whiff of what was happening in the back channel. He and Garthoff were not entirely in the dark as they returned to Washington. Yet it isn't clear exactly how much the Soviet delegation knew about the Kissinger-Dobrynin negotiation. That it knew a fair amount was clear. But why the Russians disclosed what they knew to the utterly uninformed Americans or, indeed, put forward propositions that were similar to, though far less precise than, Dobrynin's negotiating brief is unclear. One interpretation was that Semenov was instructed to take Smith over this ground just to see what, if anything, the United States delegation knew. Another saw the affair as evidence of a Dobrynin-Semenov rivalry, with neither willing to concede the chief responsibility for SALT. This, says one American official, "is called surfacing something in the front channel in order to contain the back channel." He meant that Semenov may have been trying to recapture the initiative. If in fact Semenov was trying to "contain" Dobrynin, he failed. Moscow, like Washington, was happier operating in the back channel. Smith's return to Washington coincided with the final week of the Kissinger-Dobrynin negotiation. The joint announcement was scheduled for May 20. Throughout that hectic week, Kissinger disclosed none of what was happening to his colleagues. Most senior officials concerned with SALT (Smith included) had no more than a day or two of advance warning. The Verification Panel met on May 18 with Kissinger in the chair; a number of issues were discussed, including the U.S. ABM position. Some people favored accepting the NCA deal and scrapping Safeguard in the hope that this would make the Russians more amenable on limiting offensive weapons. Still others wanted to press for zero, and some favored clinging to Safeguard and scrapping both NCA and zero ABM.

In fact, the ABM decision had, in principle, already been taken. Moscow, working through Dobrynin, had yielded its cherished NCA position and accepted the Kissinger preference for "equality" in ABM's, an as yet imprecise concept that would require a great deal of further negotiation.

The country, the Congress, and the world were agreeably surprised by Nixon's brief statement, read over radio and television at noon on May 20. In it, he hailed his agreement with Moscow as "a major step in breaking the stalemate on nuclear arms talks," which, he observed, "have been deadlocked for over a year."

The operative language read:

> The Governments of the United States and the Soviet Union, after reviewing the course of their talks on the limitation of strategic armaments, have agreed to concentrate this year on working out an agreement for the limitation of the deployment of antiballistic missile systems.
>
> They have also agreed that, together with concluding an agreement to limit ABM's, they will agree on certain measures with respect to the limitation of offensive strategic weapons.

Behind the statement, released simultaneously by Moscow Radio and TASS, the Soviet press agency, was the agreement laboriously worked out by Kissinger and Dobrynin in the form of an exchange of identical letters between Nixon and Kosygin.

Only a handful of Americans have seen the correspondence, but the gist is known to those directly involved with SALT. As intended, it did break the stalemate by removing the snags: the nonnegotiable elements of both positions. Besides letting Washington off the hook on NCA, the Soviets agreed to forget about America's forward-based systems, at least until an initial agreement had been concluded. They also bowed to Washington's demand for "simultaneity" in treating offensive and defensive weapons. The idea was that bargaining on offense and defense must follow a parallel course and be brought to a conclusion at the same time. Although Moscow agreed in principle, the "simultaneity" issue had not been silenced. Laying down the parallel course was to prove difficult.

Washington made a major concession by dropping its proposed equality in numbers of offensive weapons (the "equal aggregates" of Option E). Put differently, the Nixon White House, which began life leery even of parity, was conceding the Soviet Union a three-to-two edge in ICBM's. In the bargain, it was implicitly conceding that little, if anything, could be done to hedge against a potential threat to Minuteman posed by big Soviet missiles. Any kind of ABM agreement was likely to rule out a heavy and reliable defense of Minuteman.

The back-channel bargaining had been arduous, especially so, perhaps, for Dobrynin. He told Kissinger at one point that the back-up letter, as it's called, was the only document he knew of that had been worked on by the whole Soviet Government. And, at one point, Kissinger told him that Russians had been easier to deal with when the United States bought Alaska. To which Dobrynin replied that those Russians had not been obliged to contend with Henry Kissinger. Dobrynin also voiced the hope, presumably at some particularly tiresome moment, that Kissinger might one day be an ambassador in a foreign capital far from his source of power.

Their efforts had moved SALT onto negotiable ground. Still, some of the significance of the May 20 accord lay in what it failed to say about some things and in what it failed to say clearly about others. It was hardly a legal document. Various ambiguities remained. Nobody knew just which offensive weapons might be included in the simple freeze that had been agreed to. ICBM's would be, but SLBM's and strategic bombers were neither included nor excluded from the terms of the back-up letter or the Kissinger-Dobrynin negotiating history. Nor was there reference to Washington's first priority, the sublimit on very large missiles like the SS-9. Since the sublimit was basic to the U.S. position, the White House assumed that Moscow would regard it as an implicit part of the ICBM freeze. For those who worried most about Minuteman, the uncertainty on this point was disturbing. Another ambiguity turned on the Russian version ("pri") of the term "simultaneity"; it has less force than the English word. Finally, it was one thing to accept the principle of "equality" in ABM's, quite another to achieve it. One side was defending its capital city, while the other was planning to protect ICBM's at four different sites.

A part of Henry Kissinger's charm is a sardonic wit often, if studiously, turned inward. During a Verification Panel meeting held around this time, he got off a self-mocking quip that gave his critics in the SALT bureaucracy great pleasure. Reviewing the bizarre U.S. performance on ABM's, he observed that the Soviets had been offered three options (NCA, zero, and four-to-one). They chose the wrong option, he said, and we sent them back to choose another one.

SALT IV ended on May 28, and the American delegation went right to work preparing for the next round, due to begin in Helsinki on July 8. The May 20 statement dictated a whole new negotiating position. If words meant anything, both governments were bent on having a SALT agreement. A political thrust had developed that presumably would push the talks along. That was new. The back channel was open, and would be kept open by the supreme political authorities, if only to prevent another deadlock. That also was new.

The gloom had lifted, but there remained considerable skepticism. The huzzahs for May 20 were muted by warnings thrown up by various bureaucrats and Soviet specialists. Many of them felt that while it was useful and appropriate for Kissinger to be negotiating privately with Dobrynin, Nixon should have remained offstage. In publicly committing his office and prestige to a SALT agreement, he risked tempting Moscow to exact the greatest possible concessions. Nixon, after all, would be running for reelection in 1972. Anxious bureaucrats feared that the Russians would raise the price of a SALT agreement, once they decided that Nixon needed it. Not long after the May 20 statement, a closely involved American said: "May 20 was unfortunate on two counts. It was too narrow in scope, and it got Nixon's neck out. It will be an uphill fight to amend or stretch May 20. The Russians now assume that Nixon needs an agreement."

One year later, after the Moscow summit, the same figure, no less closely involved, took a different line. In another conversation about the May 20 affair, he argued that Nixon had been right to involve himself publicly. "The Congress and public opinion," he said, "had to be prepared for a SALT agreement that would make a distinction between offense and defense. We knew that an ABM agreement would be in treaty form and permanent, while the agreement on offense would be less formal and of limited duration. May 20 was the first step in preparing people for that."

Nonetheless, some of the wisest heads in Washington worried that Nixon had maneuvered himself into the role of supplicant, the worst of negotiating positions. They were unaware of two critical elements in the SALT brew. We know now, but didn't then, that Brezhnev had committed himself within his party to a policy of expanded negotiation and *détente*. Hence, within *his* constituency, Brezhnev's prestige was perhaps no less involved than Nixon's. Second, Nixon and Kissinger had long since opened a back channel with Peking. It, too, had become abnormally active.

On his twelfth day in office, Nixon instructed Kissinger to look into the possibility of a *rapprochement* with China. Peking had already sent some faint signals toward the new President. Five days later, the White House issued NSSM 14, calling up a China study from the bureaucracy.

There followed a series of small steps aimed at creating the conditions for a thaw. Washington issued a mild relaxation of trade and travel restrictions. Peking's surprise invitation to the American table tennis team and Premier Chou En-lai's remark that "a new page" in Chinese-American relations had been turned coincided with the Twenty-Fourth Soviet Party Congress. Soviet leaders must have been aroused by quickening movement toward the liaison they most feared. And if the handwriting was not on the wall, Kissinger put it there with harsh clarity by suddenly turning up in Peking on July 9, one day after the start of SALT V. Triangular politics had started. Indeed, the United States was playing at old-fashioned *Realpolitik*, hitherto an alien style. The SALT agreement reached on May 26, 1972 was the product of multiple purposes and forces of which none may have been more critical than Washington's revival of nineteenth-century power politics.

Relying on the back channel has obvious advantages, especially in dealing with Soviet and Chinese leaders, who place a high value on secrecy and respect the other side's ability to achieve it. Moreover, the arrival of the Xerox machine has made senior officials in Washington more cautious and, in fact, reinforecd the cabalistic instinct that lurks in high places of government. Front channel operations mean records; these can be spread over the entire government in a few hours and, from there, leaked to the press.

But the officials and civil servants down the line, who must interpret the results of back-channel dealings and try to work within them, may be severely handicapped by the secrecy and frequent absence of a written record. Complications arise, and the process of government can be made even more confused, frustrating, and difficult.

As might be imagined, the immaculate secrecy leading to the May 20 statement irritated many people already chafed by Kissinger's tight grip on SALT. If they could be compared to a crew, SALT was by now an unhappy ship, notwithstanding its brightened prospects.

If SALT III and IV were the gloomy rounds, SALT V was the rancorous one, at least in Washington, where the task of erecting a new U.S. position around the so-called parameters of May 20 taxed, if not exhausted, the patience of nearly everyone involved. Some relationships were already in disrepair, and the summer of 1971 was to open fresh wounds that only time and perhaps distance will fully close.

Preparing for SALT V meant filling in the numerous blanks of the May 20 accord in a way best suited to United States interests. The problem was defining these interests. A new look at both offense and defense was needed.

On the offensive side, the equation had become less complicated,

although that would change. The May 20 negotiations had specified nothing more really than a freeze on ICBM's. Seemingly,
there remained only to settle the sublimit on very large missiles,
now called MLBM's (Modern Large-Ballistic Missiles), a date
when the freeze would take effect, and some related technical
issues.

Those among Kissinger's staff who worked on SALT saw things
differently and argued that a limit on submarine-launched ballistic
missiles (SLBM's) should also be worked out, even though the
May 20 back-up letter didn't cover them.

Kissinger had not pressed for including SLBM's in the May 20
accord. With the Russians trailing the United States in both the
operational number and the quality of boats, he feared that making
an issue of SLBM's might produce another stalemate. Worse still,
springing the SLBM issue might provoke Moscow to revive the
FBS issue, now happily on the shelf. Also, at this point Kissinger
may very well have been prepared for a race in SLBM's, since a
SALT agreement would certainly freeze the Soviet advantage in
ICBM's.

His staff, or part of it, felt strongly that the risk was worth
taking. It behooved the Administration, they felt, to maneuver the
Russians into accepting as much as possible in this first phase of
SALT, because then as now, the prospects for Phase II seemed
unpromising. A SALT agreement that permitted the Russians
600 more ICBM's than the Americans, while allowing them to
build their submarine force up to a level of 80 or 90 boats over the
following five years, might set off serious opposition in the Congress. Much better, argued the staff, to obtain a limit on both
ICBM's and SLBM's.

The SLBM issue was thrashed out in high-level meetings on
June 18 and June 30. The Soviets then had 22 boats operational
and about 15 under construction, as compared with 41 U.S. boats
operational. But the Russians were building nuclear submarines at
the rate of 8 per year and, if they chose, could have virtually
twice the size of the U.S. fleet in five years. Washington
had no plans to increase the SLBM force; in any case, U.S. building capacity was fully absorbed in modifying Polaris boats to
take the MIRV'd Poseidon missile system. Since each Poseidon
carries 10 to 14 warheads, America was, in fact, increasing many

times over the destructive potential of each submarine without adding to their number.

The State Department and ACDA threw their weight behind the Kissinger staff. SLBM's, they felt, should be included. Smith, however, went beyond the staff, which was proposing to freeze the Soviet program at the magic number of 41. He argued in favor of stopping the Russians in their tracks and not allowing them to complete those boats under construction. Since they were ahead in ICBM's, Smith wanted to halt a dynamic Soviet program in an area where the United States still held a commanding lead.

The White House—that is to say, Nixon and Kissinger—bought the staff argument. The United States would propose a halt on SLBM's to take effect July 31, 1971. The Soviets would be allowed to complete those boats under construction as of that date, thus giving them an equivalent number.

Kissinger's astonishing visit to China in July strengthened the bias of his staff in favor of pressing the Russians on SLBM's. With the channel to Peking now wide open, the United States, they felt, was in a remarkably good position to bargain with Moscow. The Joint Chiefs, at this point, did not have strong feelings on the issue. That, too, would change. By autumn, the Chiefs were insisting so strongly on including SLBM's that any retreat from this position ran the risk of losing their support for a SALT agreement. In any case, the critical decision was taken following the second high-level meeting, on June 30. A new SALT position was outlined in NSDM 117 and signed by the President on July 2. The White House, after swallowing hard, decided to push for a limit on SLBM's. Moreover, the White House clung to this position, even when it appeared that Moscow would never agree. It was one of the few SALT positions from which the White House was never to budge. Indeed, in the weeks preceeding the Moscow May summit, the SLBM limit had become Washington's top priority item and the toughest piece of bargaining in the back channel, where it was finally worked out.

NSDM 117 also proposed a freeze on ICBM's as of December 31, 1971. Any new Soviet missiles that U.S. satellite photography did not establish as completed by that date would be banned. This was a bald effort to prevent the Soviets from filling the huge new holes in their SS-9 fields. In short, the White House was trying to hold Moscow to the existing 288 SS-9's and to head off deployment of something perhaps even more formidable. (No new holes were started after July, which suggested that the Soviets were serious about a freeze.)

NSDM 117 fell with a thud on the bureaucracy. The text had been prepared in haste—"in frantic haste," according to one participant—because of the pressure of other business (notably, the still-secret China trip) on Kissinger. Its fifteen or so double-spaced pages laid out a number of wholly new positions, about which the unhappy SALT bureaucracy had scarcely been consulted. Several weeks of confused and often bitter skirmishing lay ahead.

The delegation left three days later, on July 5, for the customary NATO briefing in Brussels; it would go on from there to Helsinki. At that point, NSDM 117 fell under a heavy attack, led by the delegation. Many of the positions were appealed. These included the language on radar limitations, as well as the definitions of "exotic" ABM's and the ideas of how to ban them. The freeze dates were also challenged, with the delegation arguing that all Soviet missile construction—land-based and sea-based—should be halted as of September 30. Not only was the delegation, if only for negotiating purposes, aiming to freeze Russia's numerical inferiority in submarines; it was also aiming to make certain that none of the ninety-one new holes—either the twenty-five very large ones, or the sixty-six smaller ones—would ever house actual missiles.

The appeals were reviewed, and NSDM 120 (dated July 20) was sent out. The delegation was conceded some points, but overruled on others, including the freeze dates. Then, abruptly, rancor and confusion were compounded by much the most sensational of the various SALT leaks. In government, it is still known as the July 23d leak, named for the day it appeared on the front page of *The New York Times;* it's also known as the Beecher leak, for William Beecher, the reporter to whom it was confided. July 23d, alas, happened to be the day when the American delegation was beginning its presentation of the new U.S. position to the Russians. The Beecher article performed the same service, laying out the essentials and even revealing one of the American fall-back positions. The article contained a major inaccuracy: a statement that the U.S. freeze would not permit Moscow to complete those submarines under construction. This, of course, was the delegation's position, stoutly backed by some elements in the Pentagon, Beecher's normal beat. It was not, however, the official position.

Beecher's dubious coup was that rare event to which most of the government had the same reaction: rage. But since nobody knew the source of the perfidy, or the motive, the affair nourished the already abundant hostilities between various parts of the SALT apparatus. One deeply involved official said: "It could not have come at a worse time. To parade the U.S. position in a newspaper even before we'd been able to show it to the Russians was a major disservice to the SALT talks. If I knew who it was, he'd have a half-hour to clean out his desk and leave the government."

An investigation followed. The FBI spent four months trying to run down the source of the leak. Its agents questioned many people known to have talked to Beecher, whose contacts extend beyond the Pentagon. The security offices of the involved agencies joined in. At one point, *The New York Times* itself reported that two White House staff members spent five months trying to locate the origin of this *cause célèbre* and to find the means of preventing further leaks.[12]

Unless the President and Attorney General have information available to no one else, the daring culprit is still unknown. Nor can anyone, even now, establish his motive. Some think it was an effort inspired in some part of the Pentagon to sabotage the talks. Others saw Beecher as used by someone operating in behalf of some high official who wanted to freeze the U.S. position—to discourage any fallback—by going public with it. In fact, these are nothing more than random guesses.

Meanwhile, Washington's truly nasty problem was to find a position on defense—on limiting ABM's—that the various parts of the town could live with and that might be negotiable. To date, no other issue had created such contention, and, in July and August, it pushed the major players of the SALT drama to a new peak of bitterness and frustration. As if the ABM issue weren't complicated enough, each player in his own way managed to make it even more so. In Helsinki, the talks were devoted almost entirely to ABM's, not because the Soviets were reneging on the simultaneity principle, but because they continued to treat defense as the first order of business. Agreement in principle on ABM's would presumably clear the path for serious conversation on offense. The delegation went along with this approach, partly because it was unhappy with the U.S. ABM position and hoped, one way or another, to change it. Not that the delegation had a unified position of its own. Rather, its members were split; nearly everyone had his own preference. The delegates were linked only in their opposition to the White House position, which some regarded as disingenuous nonsense.

Once released from the NCA trap by the May 20 agreement, the White House had decided to build its ABM position around Safeguard. The President, after all, was committed to the program. It had bargaining value, and there seemed no altenative. Most of the bureaucracy, as one participant in the debate recalls, "was dragged along kicking and screaming."

A novel formula was concocted, and became known as "three or one." Each side could choose between defending its capital city with 100 antiballistic missiles, or defending its ICBM's at three different sites with 300 antiballistic missiles. The first alternative, of course, was NCA and represented what Moscow was already doing. The second represented essentially what the Administration planned to do. The idea was rather disingenuous, because by then everyone knew that the Soviets would not dismantle Galosh, as they'd have had to do in order to adopt alternative two. In effect, the Administration was rigging a position that would have left the United States with three ABM sites, the Soviet Union with one.

A case of sorts could be made for such a disparity: If the Russians were to have more ICBM's (and perhaps SLBM's), why shouldn't the United States have more ABM's to defend itself against them? Also, the Galosh system, besides defending Moscow, affords some protection to about 300 ICBM's deployed within its operating area. This is called overlap, and American strategists fear and detest it. Overlap mixes area defense, which is unstable, with missile defense, which is thought not to be.

The case against three or one was more persuasive. For Moscow to agree, however unlikely, would surely have required Washington to endorse implicitly a permanent Soviet advantage in offensive missiles. Nowhere in government were there people left to argue seriously that three Safeguard sites would have any strategic value, whereas a large Soviet advantage in ICBM's, especially when MIRV'd, would be a different story. The Pentagon would have relished the twelve-site Safeguard system originally planned. But the military, by and large, were unimpressed by the three-or-one deal (still less by two or one, the fallback position). Briefly, a two-or-three-site Safeguard system bereft of growth potential had some appeal, but not much.

Others would argue that three or one was a poor idea, because it was nonnegotiable and merely delayed bargaining on issues of more concern to Washington, especially SLBM's. The answer to the question of what the Administration should have proposed to do about ABM's in the summer of 1971 is not difficult. There were two fairly obvious choices. First, it could have proposed that both sides maintain ongoing programs, but nothing more. Neither would dismantle anything. The Russians would have held on to Galosh, while the United States would have kept working on the two Safeguard sites then under way. The Grand Forks, North Dakota, site was more than half completed; work on the second site, near Malmstrom Air Force Base, Montana, had started but was paralyzed by strikes. Or, the Administration could have proposed a simple "one-for-one" deal, permitting the Soviet Union to keep Galosh and the United States the Grand Forks site. Besides being eminently negotiable, such an arrangement would have established parity in ABM's, a principle that Washington might then use to effect in SALT's second phase as a rationale for bargaining down the gap in ICBM's. The only real difference between one Safeguard site and two is financial, since neither is worth much.

In politics as in life, the best is often the enemy of the good. Instead of urging either of these sensible alternatives on the White House, some of the SALT delegation, backed by various parts of the bureaucracy, reopened the zero ABM option.

Zero made sense in the abstract. If there were no ABM's, the question of cheating would virtually disappear. There would be no ABM radars to survey, no ABM tests to monitor; there would be no ABM hardware to move about, thus nullifying fears of transportable systems. The trouble is that zero was never really an option. Admittedly, the Russians did mention it during SALT I, but they retreated steadily from the idea thereafter, always indicating that to dismantle Galosh was out of the question. Still, much of the civilian bureaucracy clung wistfully to the one option that could reliably excise the menace of ABM's once and for all. Most of the military felt differently and preferred to keep at least one site, whether NCA or Grand Forks, as a means of achieving some operational experience with ABM's and as a platform, however flimsy, on which to build if a SALT agreement fell apart.

The fight over zero is recalled by one who watched it as the "most vicious" bureaucratic struggle of SALT, arousing even more passion than the futile effort of the previous summer to remove the on-site inspection clause from the proposal to ban MIRV tests. Just confronting the issue irritated the White House, which bore some of the responsibility.

Smith was instructed by NSDM 117 to explore the three-or-one deal, and to fall back on two or one after a decent interval of sparring. He was also separately authorized to approach Semenov privately on zero, which he did. Semenov replied by asking for a specific proposal that he could transmit to Moscow. On August 2, General Allison reported a conversation held during a lunch he had hosted for his opposite number, General Trusov, and four other Soviet officers. The U.S.S.R., he cabled, would not dismantle Galosh. Smith and Semenov met twice again, and on August 5 Smith reported Semenov asking for specific details, including what kinds of radar would be allowed in a zero deal. Still another telegram was sent reporting a conversation with two other Russians, Timerbaev (Semenov's number two) and Kishilov. By this account, Timerbaev referred to the Allison-Trusov luncheon, and said that Trusov was emphasizing his personal views, not the views of the Soviet government, which were established in instructions and conveyed by Semenov. Soviet interest in "seriously exploring a possible zero-level ABM agreement stands without change," said the telegram.

On July 31, the delegation, with Allison dissenting, urged formally proposing zero. And on August 4, ACDA drafted a cable authorizing Smith to put such an offer before Semenov, but privately. (Possibly, they didn't want to arouse Trusov and his allies.) Normally, a cable like this is dispatched once the White House staff and the appropriate agencies approve it. If a single agency objects, the cable normally goes out anyway, with the dissent recorded. This cable did not clear the government, because the Joint Chiefs and the Office of the Secretary of Defense both dissented strenuously. Suddenly, the Pentagon was in full cry against all the earlier ABM proposals and was urging a brand new position.

In the space of a week, a few telegrams from Helsinki had set the Pentagon against everyone else and put the White House in an awkward spot. The Office of the Secretary of Defense's dissent arrived on August 6. A meeting of the Verification Panel was called for August 9.

As always, Kissinger was in the chair. There were two subjects: zero ABM and "exotic," or future, ABM's, about which another battle was brewing. One who observed says: "Henry took a tougher line than usual. He was very acid." The record supports this. Kissinger and the President had to decide whether to overrule a very tough Pentagon dissent (about three and a half pages worth) without having what they regarded as a reliably clear signal from the Russians on the zero proposition. Also, by one account they were confronting appeals from the delegation on fifteen other items.

Kissinger didn't mince words in offering his colleagues some reflections from the Oval Office, plus a few of his own. The President was described as surprised that so much time was being spent on matters he regarded as already settled and as being restive with all this nit-picking of his decisions. These fine Talmudic points, said Kissinger, have moved out of the realm of guidance. He was worried, he said, about having the greatest seminar on arms control in history and no agreement.

Stiff resistance to zero was expressed by David Packard from The Department of Defense and by Admiral Moorer representing the Joint Chiefs. The State Department, represented by Under Secretary John Irwin, aligned itself with ACDA and backed zero. Packard and CIA Director Richard Helms felt that in trying for zero the United States risked giving up leverage for bargaining on offensive weapons. Kissinger asked Helms if he thought Moscow would dismantle Galosh; Helms said he didn't think so.

Kissinger saw Dobrynin at least once between July 31 and the August 9 meeting; nobody doubted that their conversation covered the zero issue. And while Kissinger never discussed his back-channel talks, he said repeatedly that zero ABM's was not consistent with the May 20 agreement. He seemed to suggest that Dobrynin, on behalf of Moscow, had ruled out zero.

The Soviets, Kissinger finally said, must be told that now is the time to get "the damn thing" (the May 20 agreement) moving. The fight on zero was over. The Pentagon was willing to accept the current White House position. Three days later, on August 12, NSDM 127 was issued. It reaffirmed the three-or-one ABM position, and added rhetorically that a ban on all ABM deployments "remains an ultimate U.S. objective and will be a subject for negotiations after we have reached an agreement on defensive limitations and an interim agreement on offensive limitations."

Perhaps more important than disposing of the zero issue was the discussion on August 9 of futuristic ABM's. Strictly speaking, these are not ABM's because the interceptors would not be ballistic missiles but other more exotic devices, like lasers, charged particles, or electromagnetic waves. Within government, they are lumped together under the term "exotics." While it would take many years, certainly more than a decade, to develop, test, and deploy any one of the exotics, heading them off during SALT was priority business; happily, it was largely accomplished.

NSDM 117 of July 2 proposed to ban exotics by specifying that everything not allowed in a SALT agreement was forbidden. The delegation split on the issue and sent an appeal. NSDM 120 of July 20 did not cover exotics, so the issue was left hanging until the August 9 meeting during which the State Department, the CIA, and ACDA each urged a ban on everything of an exotic nature. The Joint Chiefs opposed the ban, while OSD favored banning novel interceptors but not some of the related hardware, like sensors. The White House staff wished to ban everything except certain research and development; the staff reasoned, that for verification purposes, it would be best to have some grasp of the technologies in order to know what to watch out for. ACDA officials conceded that a ban on research and development of exotics could not be verified.

The discussion was about as arcane as might be expected. The President's scientific adviser, Dr. Edward David, was called in and imparted, as one observer put it, a "Buck Rogers flavor to the meeting." At one point, he unveiled the prospect of a "carbon dioxide laser with a recirculating medium," to which Kissinger, doubtless speaking for everyone, confessed to knowing about carbon dioxide but about recirculating mediums, not at all.

The White House staff prevailed. NSDM 127 banned everything other than research and development on fixed land-based exotics. There remained to convince Moscow that the great powers should remove exotic future threats to stability, as well as the immediate ones.

The tempest spent itself quickly after August 9. The disaffected had lost the day; signs of rebellion disappeared. Yet, while the meeting had cleared the air, it couldn't efface the bitterness and tension that were agitating the conduct of SALT. The White House, confident again of its control, cared little and, indeed, felt confirmed in its suspicion that on some issues the delegation was unreliable. On zero ABM, for example, the White House believed, whether fairly or unfairly, that people in Helsinki heard what they wanted to hear. "Those who favored zero heard zero," as someone put it, "while those who didn't want to hear zero from the Russians didn't hear it." Summing up the events surrounding the August 9 meeting, one official said with more bitterness than resignation: "We dissipate our energies negotiating between ourselves."

Compared to earlier rounds, the SALT V talks in Helsinki were showing some progress, though not yet on major issues. The Soviets still avoided discussion of offensive weapons. They were reluctant to be diverted until some progress on ABM's had been recorded. The extravagantly complex ABM issue probably did require more attention, but the Americans were anxious to discuss offense, chiefly to insinuate SLBM's on to the agenda. For some time, they were stonewalled. Semenov protested vigorously that SLBM's had not been covered by the May 20 agreement. He was well aware that Smith had not been told beforehand about the May 20 affair, so Smith informed him one day that he had read the secret correspondence relating to May 20, which did not necessarily exclude SLBM's. Semenov took a somewhat more subdued line on the SLBM issue after that.

Impressive momentum had developed behind the process of loosening the talks. SALT V was considerably less stylized than even the preceding round, when the trend had already been in this direction. Plenary sessions were fewer and mattered less. The real work was being done in mini-plenaries, troikas, small working groups, and tête-à-tête conversations. Smith, Nitze, and Allison were the key figures on the American side, Semenov, Trusov, and Shuchukin on the Soviet. The roles of Garthoff and Kishilov, the point men and trouble shooters, had become even more wide-ranging. Kishilov, for example, went to Moscow during SALT V, and, after returning to Helsinki, approached Garthoff on the issue of ABM radar controls, a critical problem that the Soviets had always been reluctant to treat seriously, or even at all for quite some time. Kishilov and Garthoff became a committee of two on radar controls, and before the end of SALT V had already worked out in rough draft some of the necessary language on this immensely complex issue.

This was a hopeful sign. There were others. The push for loosening the talks was inspired more by the Soviets than the Americans. The Russians were negotiating seriously and with more precision than before, even if the promised link between offense and defense had yet to be made. And even here, during the last week of SALT V, Semenov made what one American called a "good record" by indicating his government's acceptance of the need to put together an offense-defense package.

One modest achievement was chalked up during SALT V: the Soviet need to do something about so-called provocative attacks by third powers had been harmlessly—indeed, usefully—satisfied by two related accords known as the Accidents and Hot Line Agreements. The first obliges the parties to notify each other immediately in case of events that could be misinterpreted as, or lead directly to, nuclear war; these include accidental or unauthorized use of nuclear devices, detection by missile warning systems of unidentified objects, and the like. The second agreement provides for specific measures to improve the direct link between Moscow and Washington; these include two additional circuits using satellite communications.

Neither in Helsinki nor in Washington did anyone feel that great progress toward an ABM agreement was being made. But the Moscow summit in May 1972 would show that the two sides were much closer together in September 1971 than they knew.

Weeks before SALT V ended on September 24, the Americans had fallen back from the three-or-one notion to two or one. The Soviets, unimpressed, were insisting on parity. After toying with various concoctions, the Soviets formally counterproposed a one-plus-one arrangement, just about what was to be agreed to later in

Moscow. It meant that the Russians would have Galosh plus something else, while the Americans would have its Grand Forks Safeguard site plus NCA. The Americans said no, partly because they were not ready to accept parity in ABM's until the link with offense was in place, partly because the offer revived NCA, and partly because of the proposal's considerable ambiguity. The Russians' "something else" seemed to mean ABM protection of some portion of its ICBM force—something roughly equivalent to one American Safeguard site.

The U.S. delegation immediately asked if the second Soviet ABM site would be located in the SS-9 fields east of the Urals. An ABM installation in this sparsely populated region would trouble Washington far less than one located in the SS-11 fields in western Russia, where it would provide a fair amount of area defense, especially if tied in with Galosh. This, as noted, is the overlap problem which so disturbs nuclear strategists. A second Soviet ABM site in western Russia was utterly nonnegotiable. But, as SALT V ended, the Soviets were still refusing to say where the second site would be located.

Despite some measurable progress, the events of the summer left a heavy deposit of despondency, frustration, and resignation—at least, within the SALT bureaucracy. Then as now, the military complained that the Minuteman vulnerability problem was being short-changed. Everywhere, people worried that the link between offense and defense was still promissory. Some were disturbed that the May 20 agreement hadn't really shelved NCA; the last Soviet proposal hinted as much.

It also suggested something more interesting. The Americans, thanks to their patient exposition of the virtues of missile defense, as distinct from area defense, had sold the concept to the Soviet military. Moscow's one-plus-one proposal was a sign of this. The keen interest in ICBM defense suddenly shown by General Trusov and his fellow officers in Helsinki was another. What's more, with Safeguard in declining fashion, both Americans and Russians had begun to discuss the merits of hard-site defense. All this was disturbing to those who hoped to choke off ABM's at a low and virtually meaningless level. It seems marvelously ironic that after years of neglect the hard-site alternative came alive just as the great powers were moving toward an ABM treaty.

Finally, in government as elsewhere, ignorance breeds frustration and confusion. The delegations had been working in the front channel, but nobody doubted that the back channel was very much alive, as indeed it was. Nixon, who was in direct contact with Brezhnev, now seemed committed to a summit conference in Moscow following his trip to Peking. His intention to crown these "journeys for peace" by signing a SALT agreement was taken for granted. But just what the agreement would contain was a source of deep anxiety to some skeptical bureaucrats, who suspected that Moscow would steadily raise the price as the summit meeting drew near. Nixon and Kissinger, they feared, had maneuvered themselves and SALT into a bind.

SALT VI was prelude; but to what, wondered the government. A divided Administration approached the resumption of talks on November 15 nervous about where it had gotten to in SALT, how it had gotten there, and what would happen. The concern was general. Other Western governments complained that the White House was ignoring Alliance problems in favor of the new triangular politics, which might produce little more than a bad SALT agreement and increased tensions, if not open splits, between Europe and the United States. "If Nixon is diddled and has to negotiate himself in Moscow, it would be terrible," observed one Washington-based diplomat. "Nixon is running a great risk." And Henry Kissinger, he complained bitterly, "is consumed by *follie de grandeur*."

Many officials also worried aloud that a "soft" SALT agreement would erode the future U.S. bargaining position with the Soviet Union. By this they meant that, in return for very little, the United States would have played its best cards.

Some of the concern was well founded. Such traditionally primary concerns as relations with Europe and Japan had been eclipsed—for how long no one could say—by summit diplomacy. The old conventions of *Realpolitik* were ascendent. Triangular politics is a euphemism for a policy aimed at moderating relations with Russia and China partly by playing them off against each other. There would be no major concessions or movement on SALT—not, at least, by the Americans—until Nixon's February trip to China, which, among other things, would "keep the Russians honest," as one official put it.

It was a complicated game plan, as the President himself might have put it. The weeks preceding SALT VI were crowded with activity and pronouncements, all of them bearing directly or indirectly on SALT. On October 7, Nixon disclosed plans for Phase II of his economic stabilization program. At the very end of his televised address, he digressed, saying that 1972 "can be a year in which historic events will take place on the international scene, events that could affect the peace of the world in the next generation, even in the next century."

This language inspired one high-level Administration official to unburden himself anonymously to the *Washington Post:* "You just can't keep talking about a generation of peace, about the era of negotiations as the President has, then go to Moscow and not come back with agreement."[13]

A few days later, on October 12, Nixon opened a news conference by announcing that the Moscow summit was laid on for May. He also revealed that Kissinger would soon revisit Peking, this time to work out a date and other details for the presidential trip. Kissinger left on October 20.

The White House was betting that Brezhnev's interest in a successful summit matched its own; that from his point of view a SALT agreement would put China's role and Chinese pretensions in perspective as nothing else could. Nixon could go to Peking, but the major business on the East-West agenda could only be performed by the superpowers, in some cases working with their allies. The Berlin negotiation offered a first and splendid example of spin-off from triangular politics. The four-power ambassadorial talks aimed at improving Western access to the city and formalizing its legal status had been stalled since their beginnings in March, 1970. Then, early in August, 1971, the Russians pressed for marathon sessions; by the end of the month, an agreement had been pinned down at the ambassadorial level. There is little doubt that Kissinger's first China trip and Nixon's commitment to go himself aroused Brezhnev to hasten the sluggish pace of his *détente* diplomacy. Few concepts are more detested in Moscow than that of a multipolar world.

Perhaps only Nixon and Kissinger fully understood the pressures on Moscow, because only they were aware of what was happening in the back channel. On SALT, for example, their colleagues had to measure judgment by what they perceived to be happening in

Vienna. And opinion in Washington was sharply split. Many officials and bureaucrats worried that decisions on all the major SALT issues had yet to be fought out within the Administration, which, they felt, had not at this late stage worked up its position or a set of precise negotiable objectives. Others felt that progress in Vienna was good enough to suggest that nothing impeded a quick march toward agreement save foot-dragging in the White House—more specifically, a reluctance by Nixon to ruffle Peking before his trip by concluding a major negotiation with the Soviet Union.

Both viewpoints had some validity. The U.S. SALT position was still not fully formed in the winter of 1971–72. Nixon and Kissinger were concentrating on the China trip and holding off on big SALT decisions. Their calculation, of course, was that a "good" China trip would put added pressure on the Russians to be amenable on SALT. Progress in Vienna, under these circumstances, *was* good. The delegations had quickly begun to draft language for a joint text on both the defensive and the offensive agreements. They had settled many of the minor issues and left brackets around the unresolved major problems. These included ABM levels, radar controls, the duration of the offensive agreement, the freeze dates, and the SLBM issue.

The plenary sessions had finally been wholly superseded by a pattern of troikas, working groups, and working lunches. The so-called mini-plenaries were used to record agreement, or agreement in principle, worked out in these other highly informal settings. With the plenaries all but scrapped, some Americans and Russians rarely saw each other.

The stress was still on defense. The two sides were sparring, each seeking a one-site advantage in ABM's. The Americans had changed course and were arguing that both sides should simply complete what they had, a notion that would have left the Soviets with Galosh and the United States with the two Safeguard sites then underway. The Russians were pressing a different two-to-one arrangement, arguing that, besides defending Moscow, it, too, should have one site for defending ICBM's. Their proposal would have left the United States with just the Grand Forks Safeguard site.

Early in December, a heavily involved U.S. official said of the two positions: "The Russians have something of value to them—their Galosh, which at least has some anti-China capability—while we have two Safeguard sites that protect nothing." He and others were intrigued by diverging attitudes on the Soviet side. General Trusov and the other military people were becoming steadily more enamored of the American hard-site concept for defending ICBM's. Indeed, by then, some of these officers were using the American term "hard site" instead of a Russian equivalent. They had obviously learned a good deal about hard site from their opposite numbers on the American side. Soviet civilians, on the other hand, still had not given up on an NCA arrangement. "They not only want us to have NCA, but seem almost insistent," said one American. Why? "Probably, they want to see Washington protected against accidents or what they call provocative attacks, and they feel that they know the Chinese better than we do. In any case, their suspicions of China are deeper and certainly more irrational than ours." Another closely involved American said: "They can't seem to understand why we are less concerned with protecting our leadership than in protecting a small portion of our missile force. They argue the point in terms of stability; leadership, they say, must be protected."

Although the basic ABM agreement would be left for an eleventh-hour White House decision, the delegation managed a major breakthrough toward the end of January when the Soviets accepted the U.S. position on exotic systems. Back in the summer, Moscow's attitude, as reflected by its delegation, had been sympathetic. Then, in the autumn, it hardened, probably under pressure from the military bureaucracy. Washington was accused of injecting an entirely new issue. Moscow would not agree to a ban on future defensive systems, except for those that might be space-based, sea-based, air-based, or mobile land-based. The U.S. delegation persisted and was rewarded. Land-based exotics would also be banned. The front channel had produced an achievement of incalculable value.

By now, much the most-sensitive issue turned on whether SLBM's would be covered. The Americans were proposing parity in numbers of boats and rough parity in numbers of "tubes," that is, the launchers themselves. The Soviets argued a need for having more boats because of the heavy geographic penalty on their sea-based operations. As noted, the transit time of Russian submarines from port to their stations in North American coastal waters is very long; nor do they have forward bases, as the Americans do at Holy Loch and Rota.

As on other matters, the Soviet delegates—at least, the civilians —were poorly informed; they didn't know the numbers of submarines they had operational and under construction. They didn't know that soon their government, given a construction rate of eight per year, would have more boats than the United States. So in January, 1972, more than two years after the talks had started, Gerard Smith took Semenov aside and gave him the relevant numbers on Soviet submarines.

Asserting a need for superior numbers of submarines, however deeply felt, may then have been a tactic designed to discourage the Americans on an issue to which Moscow never expected them to cling. In any case, the SLBM problem was well beyond the competence of the delegations. It was, *par excellence*, an issue for the back channel, where it was eventually, though laboriously, resolved and even then not fully settled until the very day the SALT agreements were signed.

The front channel fared better in coping with an older, less complex, but equally sensitive issue—the sublimit on very large missiles like the SS-9. As SALT recessed briefly for Christmas, the Soviets were still balking at the sublimit, the Americans still pushing, but without much hope. A failure to get the sublimit was among the gloomiest of prospects. Signing a SALT agreement bereft of this his highest priority could have cost Nixon the support of the American military and perhaps other parts of the government, as well. No one can say whether he'd have taken the risk. Happily, Moscow removed it in January by agreeing in principle at Vienna to language that gave the Americans their sublimit.

One may well wonder why the Russians accepted a limitation on their biggest missiles at this precise moment. Surely they were tempted to hold this concession for the tough back-channel bargaining that lay ahead. A reasonable guess is that they were sending the White House a signal. Nixon was now giving Moscow more to worry about than China. Looking ahead to a SALT agreement that would leave the Russians with more offensive missiles, the White House began thinking in the autumn about improving strategic forces and sharpening their "visibility," as one Kissinger staff aide put it. This meant spending money. Nixon's new defense budget sought an increase of $1.2 billion in spending on strategic arms. This, it should be noted, was the first time in years that Washington had hiked the strategic-arms budget. As it entered an election year, the Administration was notifying the country and the world that neither a SALT agreement nor Soviet arms production would leave the United States lagging behind or even appearing to lag behind.

Much the largest part of the increase would be absorbed by ULMS, the Navy's Underwater Long-Range Missile System, and by Trident, the submarine not yet out of the design stage that is supposed to carry ULMS. It was proposed to accelerate ULMS-Trident by making available $942 million, compared to the $105 million allotted to this program in the preceding year.

Accelerating Trident was intensely controversial within the government. The strongest push came from the Navy and Admiral Moorer, Chairman of the Joint Chiefs. The Air Force backed the Navy; so did Secretary of Defense Laird, and with steadily increasing force. Some members of the White House staff vigorously fought the idea, trying to hold spending on Trident to about $300 million. Instead of "freezing the design" of Trident, perhaps prematurely, they proposed, as did others in the government, that the Navy build more Polaris-type boats. These could accommodate the first-generation ULMS missile, thus removing any short-run need for a new submarine. But the Navy and Moorer wanted the new submarine and got the funds needed to accelerate the program. The first Trident submarine may join the fleet in 1978, instead of 1981 as originally planned.

Moscow was known to be unhappy about ULMS, whether deployed on Polaris-type boats or on a wholly new submarine. Soviet submarines and the SLBM's they carry are already conspicuously inferior to America's. This is another, though unstated, reason why the Soviets would seek a formal right to deploy more nuclear submarines than America.

Finally, an even more ominous prospect loomed before the Soviet leadership in January, 1972. The Pentagon, concerned as always with Minuteman vulnerability, was pressing to keep the option of hard-site defense. Laird had taken on the leadership of this enterprise, and was urging hard site both on Congress and on the President. In mid-January, he told Nixon in a letter that he was "deeply disturbed about our SALT position," which he felt would leave Minuteman inadequately defended and hence make an agreement more difficult for Congress and the public to accept. The Pentagon, it turned out, wanted to write into the SALT agreement the option of deploying hard-site defense in three years.

By now, some part of the Soviet military establishment was also intrigued by hard site and was doubtless applying who-knows-how-much pressure on the leadership to do something about it. But Moscow's interest, as it made clear, lay in setting a very low limit on ABM's. Hard-site defense would confound such a goal as nothing else could. An effective system would require numerous installations and thousands of interceptor missiles. Quite possibly, the Soviets decided in January that accepting a limit on their big offensive missiles would lighten pressure on the White House to approve hard site; this in turn would lighten pressure on Moscow to do something it did not want to do.

SALT VI ended on February 4, with both sides looking ahead to the next and decisive round—above all, to the summit conference and a SALT agreement. Nixon was under pressure in an election year to obtain the agreement to which he was personally committed. Brezhnev was under pressure to give more substance to Moscow's trumpet calls for *détente* so that the dividends might start coming in. He and Nixon were spending some additional money on strategic arms, partially to impress each other, but each was hoping to discourage another round in the arms competition and the heavy spending that would go with it.

Nixon and Kissinger were preparing to go to China. Dobrynin had just returned from a long trip to Moscow, where he presumably drew fresh instructions for SALT. With a "good" China trip behind them, Nixon and Kissinger looked to reopen the back channel with Moscow. Kissinger and Dobrynin were expected to start negotiating the broad lines of a SALT agreement, while the delegations would supply precise language and otherwise fill in the blanks. Although this, indeed, was the scenario, it was to be considerably less simple than it seemed.

Kissinger wasted no time. En route to China in February, he instructed his staff by telephone from Guam to prepare some precise recommendations on the major SALT issues. Their chief recommendation was to accept equality in ABM sites as a means of obtaining a Soviet agreement to limit both SLBM's and land-based mobile missiles. The staff felt that a good offer on ABM's would capture one or the other—SLBM's or Mobiles—and possibly both. The delegation agreed that such an offer should be made, but expressed pessimism that Moscow would bend on SLBM's.

Part of the staff urged a simple one-and-one ABM proposal, leaving the Soviet Union with Galosh, the United States with the Grand Forks Safeguard site. Kissinger and other staff members seemed to favor a two-and-two arrangement, which would leave the United States with both the Grand Forks, and Malmstrom Air Force Base Safeguard sites, and Moscow with Galosh and a single ICBM defense site.

SALT VII would begin in Helsinki on March 28, which allowed about three weeks for working up a position. A meeting of the Verification Panel on March 8 was largely absorbed by an inconclusive discussion of hard site. The NSC met on Friday, March 17, with all participants agreed that SLBM's should be in the agreement. The Joint Chiefs were by now tough and articulate on this point.

By March 23, the White House had decided, and set forth its position in NSDM 158, dated that day. The Americans would propose equality in ABM's—specifically the two-and-two arrangement—provided the Russians agreed to put SLBM's into the package. Otherwise, Washington would insist on a two-to-one arrangement, leaving the United States with a one-site advantage in ABM's (for whatever that might have been worth). The delegation was given no fallback position. If, as expected, the proposal met resistance, Smith had instructions to return to Washington within three weeks to make new recommendations.

He and the other delegates were not pleased by these instructions. They wanted fallbacks. They wanted to be able to conclude the agreement before the Moscow summit so that Nixon would have only to sign it. Much of the government felt the same way.

The White House had two purposes in denying the delegation a fallback position. First, it wanted to create an aura of "hanging tough on SLBM's," as one participant put it, since Moscow still doubted Washington's strength of purpose on this issue. Second, it feared another leak of the Beecher variety and wanted no fall-back positions committed to paper. Indeed, so profound was the concern with security that only four copies of NSDM 158 left the White House; these were delivered to Secretaries Rogers and Laird, to Gerard Smith, and to Richard Helms.

The delegation left for Helsinki the day after NSDM 158 was signed. Smith quickly made a number of minor concessions to the Soviet position. Then, acting on his instructions, he put forward the new proposal linking ABM's and SLBM's. At that point, he had exhausted his authority and could only argue the case. The Soviets were disconcerted by the tough unyielding line on SLBM's. They had apparently assumed that Washington would drop the SLBM issue as the summit drew near. On Friday, April 14, Semenov, Trusov, and Shchukin, the major figures of the Soviet delegation, were recalled to Moscow. This was a surprise, not least to the Finnish Government, which had arranged a joint outing to Lapland that weekend.

The Americans were champing at the bit. They had nothing more to offer and, in any case, nobody to negotiate with. On April 14, they cabled a recommendation to Washington to hold firm on SLBM's, but to accept a Soviet ABM proposal, which called for one-plus-one. This would allow the United States to keep the Grand Forks site and to build an NCA system, while allowing Moscow to keep Galosh and to build one ICBM defense site. Moscow disliked Washington's two-and-two offer because it would have allowed the United States to defend twice as many ICBM's. For reasons of their own, the Russians found this unfair.

The ABM agreement was to be a treaty of unlimited duration, with a standard provision for review at five-year intervals. The agreement on offense was to be an interim arrangement, but the parties were at issue on its duration. The Soviets had alternately proposed eighteen months and two years. The Americans couldn't agree among themselves. The Joint Chiefs, like the Russians, wanted the shortest possible interim agreement. The White House staff was urging five years. It would take the United States even longer than that to deploy any of the new weapons it was considering. More important, argued the staff, to accept the Soviet proposal would be to accept the near equivalent of an ABM-only agreement. The delegation, except for Paul Nitze, favored three years. He, too, wanted five. Like SLBM's, this was an issue for the back channel.

It was put about Washington that an important meeting, presumably on Vietnam, would be held at Camp David on the weekend of April 22–23. Everyone, including most cabinet officers and the White House staff, assumed that such a meeting had taken place until it was announced on Tuesday, April 25, that Henry Kissinger had just returned from Moscow, where he had been negotiating with the Soviet leadership over the past four days. As usual, the secrecy had been immaculate. He had taken along his senior deputy for the Soviet Union and Europe, Helmut Sonnenfeldt, his principal deputy for Vietnam, two other staff members, and Ambassador Dobrynin. Nobody, it seems, remarked the absence of any of them. The Camp David cover story worked so well that some people (including Smith in Helsinki) with a need to talk to Kissinger tried telephoning him there.

He wasn't starting from scratch in Moscow. Besides the periodic meetings with Dobrynin, about a dozen messages had passed between Nixon and Brezhnev. Among other things, the trip showed a keen awareness on both sides that summit meetings are notoriously accident prone. The Paris summit in May, 1960, fell to pieces on the wings of Captain Powers's U-2. Thirteen-months later, Kennedy was greeted by Khrushchev in Vienna with a Berlin crisis. Johnson's Moscow trip, like the gallant Prague Spring, was a casualty of the invasion of Czechoslovakia. And in late April, 1972, the ground beneath Nixon's Moscow project began to tremble.

The damage to four Soviet ships by American aircraft bombing the Haiphong harbor had been protested, but in a low key. Still, North Vietnam's spring offensive was going very well at this time. Nixon, it was feared, might feel obliged to take steps that Hanoi's chief ally and arms supplier would find inconsistent with summitry. Fortunately, Vietnam was not the only major drama then playing the theater of world politics. The West German Bundestag was moving slowly and with great uncertainty toward a vote on ratification of a nonaggression treaty with Russia. Chancellor Willy Brandt's majority in favor of the treaty was so thin as to seem more apparent than real. Brezhnev and his immediate colleagues wanted few things more than this treaty, seen as a stride toward broader Soviet access to Western European technology and commerce, and, perhaps, political influence as well. To cancel the summit meeting risked losing both a SALT agreement and the treaty with West Germany. Western diplomats in Moscow doubted that the leadership would accept that risk, whatever happened in Vietnam. They were right.

Measured by the time that Kissinger and his Soviet hosts spent discussing it, SALT probably ran a poor second to Vietnam. A great deal was accomplished, however. Indeed, it wasn't long after that a SALT agreement, or agreements, could be perceived in silhouette.

Brezhnev took the initiative by presenting Kissinger with two memoranda, a three-page statement dealing with offense and a one-page statement on ABM's. The statement on offense was to break the back of the SLBM issue. Moscow would accept a freeze in return for numerical superiority in submarines and tubes. The now-famous numbers were 62 submarines and 950 tubes (compared to America's 41 boats and 656 tubes). Here, indeed, was something for Washington to chew on. Some of the language on SLBM's was vague and, if accepted, would require considerable negotiation. But clear profit turned up in a Soviet willingness to meet the White House preference for an interim agreement that would last for five years.

The ABM statement rehearsed the one-plus-one proposal that Semenov had been pressing in Helsinki, and specified that no more than 100 interceptor missiles could be deployed at any of the sites. Although Kissinger had no great difficulty with this approach, it, too, would require considerable negotiation in Helsinki. The statement ignored geographic constraints, and the Americans still insisted that a second Soviet site would have to be located east of the Urals, well away from population centers. Also, the horrendous problem of radar controls was still far from thrashed out.

Kissinger's visit coincided with a sensational piece of news. On Saturday, April 22, the CIA informed the White House and appropriate agencies of government that the Soviets were preparing to test a new ICBM larger than any other, including the SS-9. Washington now knew what Moscow intended to put in those 25 huge new holes located in the SS-9 fields. The Americans also assumed that the new missile would eventually be MIRV'd, and would replace the SS-9 force. Thanks to an improved launching technique (detected by U.S. reconnaissance systems), the new missile could possibly double the yield of the SS-9.

On the following day, a full and accurate account of the CIA's disturbing report turned up on page one of *The New York Times* under the byline of William Beecher. This kind of bad news travels fast in Washington, though usually not quite that fast.

Beecher's source was presumably no friend of the SALT agreement that would be signed in a month's time. Yet as much as anything else, the new missile argued for getting the agreement and freezing Soviet ICBM's at 1618, the number operational plus the 91 new holes.

A Verification Panel meeting was scheduled for Friday, April 28. Smith and Allison returned instantly from Helsinki. Kissinger's first task was to prepare the bureaucracy for a deal on SLBM's that he and the President had apparently decided to make along the lines discussed in Moscow. A question of no great relevance but some fascination arises at this point. Did Brezhnev spring the offer of 62 boats and 950 tubes on Kissinger? Or did Kissinger, plying the back channel with Dobrynin, suggest something similar and hence invite the proposal he got in Moscow? At this stage, the question cannot be answered; probably no one working in government could say for sure—other than Kissinger, who does not discuss back-channel activity. He and his staff had concluded before the April trip to Moscow that the Soviets, if they agreed to an SLBM deal, would insist on superior numbers. Analysts had already calculated that Moscow would need roughly 20 more boats than the United States in order to keep as many on station. So there is the possibility that Kissinger invited the proposal. On the other hand, the figure of 950 tubes made absolutely no sense to the Americans. Most Soviet submarines carry 16 tubes; some are being modified to take 12 new and larger SLBM's. Mathematically, however, there is no combination of 16 and 12 multiplied by 62 boats that will produce the figure 950. This may suggest that the Soviets know something about their SLBM program, or their plans for it, that United States intelligence has yet to learn.

The Verification Panel meeting of April 28 would be critical. "The problem," said one observer of the meeting, "was how do you put into the front channel a deal worked out in the back channel?" Kissinger ordered up a paper for the meeting with estimates of the numbers the Soviets *might propose* if they agreed to a freeze on SLBM's. The figure of 62 boats turned up squarely in the mid-range of possibilities.

Even for Henry Kissinger, this was playing the SLBM issue very close. As the Verification Panel met, only Nixon and Kissinger, certain NSC staff members, and some, though probably not all, of the principals knew that Brezhnev had put forward an SLBM proposal with precise numbers.

At one point during the meeting, Kissinger and Admiral Moorer held an exchange that probably settled the SLBM issue, even if nothing was formally decided. Nixon needed the support of the Joint Chiefs for an agreement freezing Russia's numerical edge in both ICBM's *and* SLBM's. Moorer wanted White House support for speeding up the Trident submarine program. Trident, in a sense, was bait. The meeting soon established the Pentagon's strong preference for awaiting Trident's availability—in 1978 at the soonest—to building more Polaris/Poseidon boats. The Navy worried that not accelerating the Trident program could mean losing it in Congress.

Kissinger asked Moorer how many submarines the Soviets could have by 1978 in the absence of an agreed freeze. The answer was at least 80. Kissinger then made a number of points, among them the desirability of an agreement that held the Soviets well beneath the level of 80 submarines, especially if Trident could not be put to sea until 1978.

The meeting soon adjourned. It was resumed in a more restricted group the following day. But the meaning of the exchange between Kissinger and Moorer was clear to those who heard it: The Navy would have Trident, assuming congressional approval, and the President would have the support of the Chairman of the Joint Chiefs of Staff for an SLBM deal that gave the Soviets nearly half again as many missile-carrying submarines as the United States.

The climactic meeting was held in the President's office on Monday, May 1. It lasted nearly two hours. Besides Nixon and Kissinger, the participants were Rogers, Laird, Smith, and Moorer. Notes were taken by General Alexander M. Haig, Jr., Kissinger's chief deputy. A fly on the wall might have been confused by what seemed a reversal of roles. Admiral Moorer supported the asymmetrical submarine deal, while Smith and Rogers were dubious and seemed reluctant to formalize such disparate numbers. Smith especially disliked freezing the disparity for five years; three would have bothered him less.

In any case, everything of major importance had been decided. Washington at last had a complete and negotiable SALT position. Within hours after the May 1 meeting, NSDM 164 was issued. It outlined an SLBM freeze, using both the "Moscow numbers": 62 boats and 950 tubes (even though the latter still made no sense). It also accepted the one-plus-one arrangement, thus aligning Moscow and Washington on ABM's.

The front and back channels had merged. The contours of an ABM treaty and an interim agreement on offensive missiles had been accepted by both governments, and in Washington they had the support, or in some cases the acquiescence, of the appropriate agencies. These were contours, however. The completed *oeuvre* would require a few more weeks. The delegations in Helsinki would perform the larger part of it; their principals would pencil in the last critical details and then sign.

Smith left for Helsinki the day after the meeting in the President's office. On arriving, he immediately got down to business with the Soviets. It was a hectic moment, for much remained to be done. Although the ABM treaty needed attention, completing the interim agreement was now the central problem. Washington had not yet abandoned hope for prohibitions on land-based mobile missiles and on silo modification. And there were other issues, of which the most intractable, and menacing, concerned the SLBM freeze.

Washington accepted that the Soviets could have 62 boats and 950 tubes, but not without paying a price: in this case, retiring old missiles. In May, 1972, U.S. intelligence estimated the Soviet submarine force at between 41 and 43 boats, either deployed or under construction. The freeze on missiles was expected to hold the Soviets to that level; now it was proposed that only by "cashing in" old missiles and submarines could the Soviets build toward 62 boats and some near equivalent of 950 missiles. Thus, the new SLBM's would be replacements, not additional elements. Washington had counted about 310 vintage Soviet missiles, of which 210 are ICBM's and 100 SLBM's. Retiring them all could theoretically earn Moscow 19 or 20 additional submarines.

The Soviets accepted the replacement condition, but not the

American calculations of their own submarine strength, nor the American assumptions about which old missiles, or how many, would have to be retired. The equation was mind bending, but not the issue. Washington quite simply was trying to maximize the number of old Soviet weapons to be retired, Moscow to minimize this figure. In Helsinki, the Russians abruptly laid claim to an SLBM program of 48 boats. This was 5 to 7 more boats than the Americans had counted. To accept the Russians' count also meant accepting that they were that much closer to the magic numbers 62 and 950 and would not be obliged to replace nearly as many old weapons in reaching these totals. American technicians called this the "free ride" issue.

Rarely if ever had the Soviet delegation quoted a precise number in discussing its country's nuclear weapons. Challenging the number was obviously difficult; as Kissinger said in a press conference in Moscow on May 26: "The Soviet estimate of their program is slightly more exhaustive. They, of course, have the advantage that they know what it is precisely."

Disputing the number of Soviet submarines and SLBM's was not the most efficient use of the three weeks remaining to the delegations before Nixon's arrival in Moscow. They made a try, but the replacement issue had become the last major agenda item and was the last to be settled. They did dispose of other problems, most of them on Monday, May 22, the day the presidential party arrived. It was then, for example, that the Soviets finally agreed in principle to locate their second ABM site east of the Ural mountains. They rejected the language "east of the Urals," but Garthoff and Kishilov worked out a compromise (formally approved in Moscow the following day) which provided that each side's ICBM defense site must be located "no less than 1300 kilometers from its NCA site." The distance from Moscow to the back of the Urals is 1300 kilometers.

Also on May 22, the delegations settled the old issue of silo modification by agreeing that ICBM silos could not be "significantly increased." This hazy language offered little comfort to those in Washington for whom protecting Minuteman by limiting the size of Soviet missiles was a top priority.

Obviously, the Soviet leaders hoped to settle as many non-critical issues as possible before opening talks with Nixon and

Kissinger on the larger questions. Still, they didn't want to settle them without giving the U.S. delegation every chance to make some concessions, which explains why May 22 was such a busy day in Helsinki. An especially nice surprise for the Americans turned up when the Soviets changed course and agreed to ban all large ABM-type radars, other than the few allowed by the treaty. The Americans had been on the verge of writing off this goal by unilaterally proclaiming its desirability. That they got an agreement was due mainly to the persistence of Nitze, who had argued forcibly against yielding. A ban on very large radars should reassure people on either side who suspect the other of plotting a clandestine ABM buildup. In any case, the SALT agenda had been cleared of the last in a procession of radar issues.

The silhouette was acquiring body and tone. As each item was disposed of, the delegations put it into the formal language of international agreement. By the time Nixon and Brezhnev had their first talk about SALT on Tuesday afternoon, the delegations were well along in drafting the ABM Treaty, the interim agreement, and a number of agreed interpretations. Garthoff and Kishilov had been taken off the point and made chiefly responsible for the drafting, as well as for thrashing out the inevitable last minute technical problems.

The Nixon-Brezhnev meeting had flair and panache. It reversed the form of earlier summit conferences by ending happily, though in a kind of vertiginous confusion reminiscent as much as anything else of the Keystone Cops. In some ways, it resembled an American political convention. Most people didn't sleep much. Meetings lasted into the small hours. The pace was hectic. A number of agreements were reached, most of which had been worked out in advance. An exception was SALT, the main event. Unlike a political convention, which, however divided, will ultimately agree on a candidate, it was only probable not inevitable (as most people thought) that the Moscow talks would produce a SALT agreement. The affair nearly foundered on the SLBM replacement issue.

Brezhnev was under pressure, how much no one in Washington can say. The two weeks preceding Nixon's arrival had been for Soviet leaders at least as intense as the five following days, probably more so. First, on Monday, May 8, Nixon had thrown down the glove by announcing that North Vietnam's coastal waters would be mined, thus closing them to Soviet shipping and catalyzing the stiffest internal challenge to his authority that Brezhnev had faced. During most of that week, nobody in Washington, whether in the White House or elsewhere, was wagering that the Moscow summit would actually happen. The betting was the other way, with most people expecting a cancellation. Diplomats and others theorized that Nixon preferred a cancellation to the possibility that the Moscow negotiations would coincide with a dramatically worsening military situation in South Vietnam.

As always, the details of Moscow's internal struggle were hidden. Cryptic press reports offered a few hints, but hard evidence appeared when a senior and powerful figure, Petr Shelest, was demoted during an extraordinary meeting of the members and candidate-members of the Central Committee three days before Nixon's arrival. Shelest was removed from his job as party leader in the Ukraine, transferred to Moscow, and replaced by an old protégé of Brezhnev. Shelest is regarded as an ultra-hard-liner and the tone and nuance of some of his speeches convinced Kremlinologists he opposed both the treaty with Bonn and the SALT agreements. Almost certainly, he opposed proceeding with the summit after Nixon's May 9 speech.

Although the scope and significance of the Shelest affair cannot be measured, Brezhnev had obviously won a major battle; the people in Nixon's party left Moscow in no confusion about who was calling the tune, whether on SALT, Vietnam, or any other large issue. Indeed, Brezhnev used the meeting to dramatize Soviet foreign policy and to parade his authority. His room for maneuver with the Americans was somewhat extended three days before Nixon's arrival when the West German parliament finally completed ratifying the treaties with the Soviet Union and Poland. Nixon may have embarrassed the Kremlin by mining the harbors of North Vietnam, but matters of more direct and lasting importance to Brezhnev were falling into place.

Nixon and Brezhnev discussed SALT for more than two hours on Tuesday afternoon, May 23; they met again that evening and talked for another three hours, mostly about SALT. At that point, they left the subject to their advisers, but kept in close touch with it. Kissinger, of course, briefed Nixon at every stage, and it is believed that his Soviet colleagues were reporting directly to Brezhnev.

Negotiating for the Americans, besides Kissinger, were Helmut Sonnenfeldt, who had been with him on the April trip, and William Hyland, another member of the NSC staff who works with Sonnenfeldt on Soviet and European affairs. A third staff member took notes.

The Russians fielded an impressive team. There were Foreign Minister Gromyko, Ambassador Dobrynin, and a man whom the Americans had never seen and didn't expect to see, but who did most of the talking on his side of the table. He was Leonid Vasil'yevich Smirnov, and, as one of the Americans put it, "he came right out of the blue." Smirnov is a Deputy Premier and a member of the Central Committee. But his real job is directing the manufacture of Soviet missile systems and other modern weapons. He is Chairman of the Military-Industrial Commission and quite clearly exercised a good deal of influence on the Soviet SALT position.

For the Russians, there remained only to reach agreement on SLBM replacement. For the Americans, there were two additional issues: mobile land-based missiles and missile size. The United States wanted to ban the mobile missiles and obtain more restrictive and precise language on missile size than had been agreed to in Helsinki.

As in Helsinki, the Soviets said no to banning mobile ICBM's. On Tuesday night, after some discussion of the issue, Nixon finally told Brezhnev that deployment of mobiles by the Soviets would be regarded as grounds for abrogating both the ABM treaty and the interim agreement. (The U.S. delegation said essentially the same thing in Helsinki.) The problem, of course, is that mobile missiles, if deployed, could not be reliably counted by reconnaissance satellites and would frustrate the verification process.

The Americans fared little better in dealing with missile size, an issue that contained two persistent difficulties: silo modifications and the famous sublimit on very large missiles. The Soviets did agree to embellish the restriction on "significantly increasing" silo dimensions by specifying that any such increase would not exceed 10 to 15 per cent. They were not conceding much. A missile of far greater power than any other could be placed in SS-9 silos increased by 15 per cent. As for the sublimit, language worked out in Helsinki probably assures adequate protection against any increase in the number of missiles in the SS-9 class; but it is nonetheless a bit vague and incomplete, lacking, for example, a definition of what constitutes a "heavy" missile. The Soviets were determined to keep it that way. And they did. Still, any violation of the spirit of this language, let alone the letter, would probably oblige the United States to withdraw from the agreements. Moscow understands that.

After Tuesday night, Nixon and Brezhnev turned to Vietnam and other more temporal problems, leaving the abstractions of SALT to Kissinger, Smirnov, and company. The parties were still well apart on the contentious SLBM-replacement issue. They had a long session on Wednesday, met again that night, and wrestled the problem until 4:00 Thursday morning. They resumed Thursday evening, following a performance of *Swan Lake* at the Bolshoi Theater. When this penultimate session broke up at 3:00 Friday morning, the issue was still unresolved.

Some of the meetings were held in Gromyko's office in the Soviet Foreign Ministry, others in St. Catherine Hall in the Kremlin Palace, where the American party was staying. Smirnov was a tough and skillful negotiator, but showed little sensitivity to the political stakes in the enterprise. Gromyko intervened often to prevent a stalemate.

Unlike anyone else on either side of the table, Smirnov had a technician's grasp of the issue. Kissinger, Sonnenfeldt, and Hyland, while fully familiar with the ins and outs of SLBM's, were political animals. Kissinger's technicians—Philip Odeen, Colonel Jack Merritt, and Barry Carter—were in Washington, and a steady stream of cables and phone calls passed between them and the Kissinger team in Moscow. Some of the calls were made on open lines from the Kremlin. Since the conversations dealt with Soviet submarines and SLBM's, the American negotiators felt that they could not be revealing anything the Russians didn't already know. Hyland, in fact, took a Washington call from Carter at the Bolshoi Theater in the middle of the first act.

Dobrynin may have felt some fulfillment of the hope he'd expressed a year earlier: that one day Henry Kissinger, now seated across the table in Moscow, would find himself negotiating at a distance several thousand miles from his power base. Kissinger's staff in Washington had the job of preventing any erosion of support for the White House position within the government. This meant keeping key officials and Congressional figures informed of what was happening in Moscow and assuring their continued support for the agreement. Most important, it meant holding in line skeptical elements in the Pentagon. With a seven-hour time difference between the two cities and meetings in Moscow lasting into the small hours, a number of Washington bureaucrats found themselves working almost around the clock. The pace was frantic.

In Helsinki, the delegations, like everyone else, awaited a breakthrough. Their joint drafts of the ABM Treaty and the Interim Agreement were in place. They had only to write a protocol to the Interim Agreement solemnizing whatever could be worked out on the replacement issue. An American plane had been sent to bring the delegation to Moscow with the completed documents. The suspense was terrific. The delegates were losing as much sleep as their colleagues in Moscow and Washington.

In Moscow, the dispute hung on two points: the number of SLBM's the Soviets actually had, and the number of old missiles they would be obliged to retire in order to reach the agreed totals of 62 submarines and 950 tubes. The Americans were clear and hard, saying in effect: We've agreed that you will have more boats and more missiles, but not for free. You must earn each new SLBM by retiring an old missile.

Had Nixon and Kissinger been tempted to waver, the message from home might well have stopped them. The cable and telephone traffic from the White House reported solid opposition throughout the government to any major concession. Washington, in short, was "hanging tough" on the replacement issue, though well aware that the SALT agreements themselves lay in the balance.

The Russians quietly dropped their claim to 48 submarines. Both sides, it appeared, wanted to bury the embarrassing conflict over the number of Soviet submarines. They shifted the argument away from boats to tubes (SLBM's), with the Russians claiming a total of 768 either operational or under construction. Washington's estimate of their SLBM strength was 640. Both numbers applied to "modern" SLBM's deployed on Russia's Polaris-type submarines, known in Washington as "Y" class. The Soviets also have some older submarines, known as "G" class and "H" class. The more numerous "G"-class boats are diesel powered and have a combined total of 70 SLBM's. The nuclear-powered "H"-class boats have a total of 30.

Agreement existed on a single point: that the 210 old Soviet ICBM's would be subject to retirement. Otherwise disagreement was complete. The Americans insisted that the "G"- and "H"-class missiles also be placed on the retirement list, but the Russians flatly refused.

The U.S. "Moscow delegation," as some called it, went as far as it could go during the session ending Friday morning. Fortified by a stream of recommendations and admonitions from Washington, Kissinger offered a compromise, some parts of which had been discussed in Helsinki. Although lacking the virtue of simplicity, it was ingenious. The proposal arbitrarily split the difference between 640 and 768 by settling on the number 740. This was called the "baseline" number—the point at which the Russians could start building toward the agreed maximum of 950 SLBM's *provided* they retired one older missile for each new one. At first glance, the White House gambit seemed to give the Russians the better of it by splitting the difference in their favor. The Russians didn't think so, though, and neither obviously did the Americans. The U.S. compromise sought to dispose of the 30 "H"-class missiles by including them in the 740, thus confronting Moscow with a strict choice of keeping these older weapons or replacing them. The "G"-class issue, involving about 70 SLBM's, was treated differently. The proposal gave the Russians a choice of hanging onto these even older weapons, retiring them, or modernizing them. Any that *were* modernized, however, would count toward the grand total of 950. Here the Americans were having it both ways. They expected the Soviets to retire most of the "G"-class force, in any case, as the boats are old and noisy, the missiles short of range. (As confusing as all this may seem, it was only slightly less so to the experts themselves. After the White House party returned to Washington, several meetings of the Verification Panel were spent largely in trying to establish exactly what had been agreed to on SLBM's and what precisely it all meant.)

At 3:00 A.M. on Friday, May 26, it looked as if Nixon might leave Moscow without the SALT agreements that he and Brezhnev were to sign in just twenty hours. The issue that had built up around 100 old Soviet SLBM's still eluded settlement. The Russians had accepted 740 as the "baseline" number, but were unwilling to mix their "G"- and "H"-class missiles into the brew that Washington had confected.

They were eyeball to eyeball, as Dean Rusk might have put it. Nixon refused to budge and seemed prepared to accept the consequences. Brezhnev must have perceived this, and he was apparently less prepared to accept the anticlimax of a failure on SALT. Early Friday morning, Gromyko called a meeting for 11:30 A.M. As Kissinger would tell the press immediately after the signing ceremony, at that point "it began to break. By noon, I called Ron [Ziegler] and told him that it was beginning to break, and at 1:00 we had it settled."

Shortly after the 11:30 meeting began, the Russians said, in effect, that everything was agreed to. The issue of the "G"- and "H" class weapons would be settled on the American terms. They also said that the agreements would have to be signed that day. This seemed virtually to amount to a condition. The Americans didn't understand why Brezhnev was moving in such haste, and worried that the delegations would not have time to draft the protocol on SLBM's and get to Moscow in time for the signing ceremony, scheduled for 5:00 P.M. As it became clear that this could not be done, the signing ceremony was rescheduled for later that evening. The Americans tried to gain more time by moving back the dinner the President was giving at Spaso House for his hosts—from 7:00 to 8:30.

It was 12:30 P.M. in Moscow when messages reached Washington and Helsinki that the breakthrough had been made. The delegations were instructed to draft the protocol and get themselves and the completed documents to Moscow as soon as possible. Kissinger thought, as he would say in his press conference, that "it was the first time in the history of Soviet-American relations that joint instructions were sent to two delegations so that no misunderstandings could occur and where we were kept informed by the Soviet side about meetings going on in the Soviet delegation in order to speed up the drafting process. . . . All we did this morning was arrive at the general framework. The delegations then had to put it into language that will be put before you soon.

"So a tremendous amount of work was done by the delegation, and it showed how rapidly things could move in diplomacy when both sides want to move."

His words captured a little but scarcely all of the flavor of the events that followed the midday success. The delegation got the 12:30 message by telephone, but a written account of the SLBM settlement didn't reach the Americans in Helsinki until 2:30. The Soviet delegation got theirs much sooner. Garthoff, Kishilov, and Oleg Grinevsky, a Soviet delegate from the Foreign Ministry, immediately began drafting the protocol and conforming the relevant section of the Interim Agreement. They labored through the afternoon while the delegates worked on agreed interpretations of some parts of the agreements.

They left for Moscow as soon as the protocol was written and typed in English and Russian. The signing ceremony was now scheduled for 11:00 that evening. Most of the Soviet delegation accompanied Smith, Nitze, Allison, and Garthoff on the American plane, where, as someone put it, the last plenary was held.

The play within the play began when the plane landed at 9:00 P.M. The Russians sent a car to meet Smith, who raced off to the Kremlin with a motorcycle escort. He arrived to find no one there, as the ceremonial dinner at Spaso House was under way. The other three Americans—Nitze, Allison, and Garthoff—headed for the VIP lounge, assuming correctly that the Embassy must have sent people to meet Smith. At the airport lounge, they found only the air attaché, who was there to collect Allison; the two Embassy staff members instructed to meet Smith had leapt into their car to give chase when they saw him scooped up on the tarmac by the Russians. Nitze went directly to Spaso House, where he was supposed to dine. Allison, after changing into uniform, followed him.

Garthoff was carrying the documents. He had forehandedly arranged to have an IBM electric typewriter crated and sent along on the airplane, having guessed there might be typos or other mistakes in the documents: if true, it would mean retyping them before the signing ceremony. He'd been right. Mistakes had been discovered on the plane. A preposition was missing from Article

III of the Interim Agreement. Another error did violence to convention: Each country's name should have preceded the other's throughout one English-language version and one copy of a Russian-language version. But in the case of the Protocol to the Interim Agreement, the United States of America was named before the Union of Soviet Socialist Republics in both English versions. Finally, the words "of America" that normally follow "the United States" were missing from another document. All this would mean a good deal of retyping in Moscow.

Garthoff walked back to the plane, uncrated the typewriter, and drove off to the Soviet Foreign Ministry with some of his fellow plane passengers. He was taken to the Ministry's Office of American Affairs, where he called the Embassy for a typist. There wasn't much time. The power in that section of the Foreign Ministry had been turned off, so the electric typewriter was transferred to the treaty office and plugged in. Garthoff waited. The typist didn't appear. There had been a misunderstanding; instead of going to the Foreign Ministry, she had gone to the Ministry's guest house. Garthoff could not wait for very long. He had to take the documents—the ABM treaty, the Interim Agreement on offensive missiles, and the related protocol—to St. Vladimir Hall in the Kremlin for the signing ceremony.

By the time Smith reached Spaso House, the dinner was over. Nixon was preparing for the signing ceremony, and Kissinger was in the Embassy cafeteria about to begin the first of two press conferences he would hold that evening. Smith, who had been working since 5:00 A.M. and had not eaten all day, arrived in time to take part. He wearily told the American press that he and Semenov had continued their labors on the plane. "So," he said, "this is about the freshest treaty that I have ever talked about." The reporters pressed him for details of the morning agreement, specifically for details in the numbers of Soviet submarines and SLBM's. Such information would have allowed them to make reasonable evaluations of the agreement, and most were frankly irritated by the secrecy that continued to obscure SALT. Smith declined to talk about Soviet submarines. The Embassy cafeteria suddenly became quite tense. Kissinger broke in and tried to offer some guidance on Soviet SLBM's without using precise numbers.

One reporter responded with a *cri de coeur:* "Could I make a plea to you and Ron [Ziegler] as well? It has taken 30 months to get this treaty. The Senate of the United States wants to know what is in it. There is an argument about it. We have been out of our hotel an hour and a half. We get ten minutes of questions and to-morrow it is going to be our fault for screwing it up and creating political trouble. Can somebody else pass up the champagne [i.e., the signing ceremony] and let's keep this going?"

It was 10:55, time to leave for the signing ceremony, but Ziegler announced that Kissinger would be available for an extended session with the American press afterward.

Meanwhile, Nitze and Allison had managed to reach Spaso House before the dinner was over, but only Allison pierced the security network around the Embassy compound. Allison had been instructed to appear at the signing ceremony in uniform, presum-ably to symbolize the support of the Joint Chiefs of Staff for the agreements. Thus, he had no difficulty with security. Nitze, on the other hand, was not admitted and was even detained for a brief time. This former Security of the Navy and Deputy Security of Defense was unable to persuade U.S. security types that he had, indeed, been invited to dinner by the President. Fortunately, Nitze was recognized by a Soviet Foreign Ministry official, who ob-ligingly drove him to the Kremlin and maneuvered him through the security cordon there into St. Vladimir Hall.

It went off without incident. Scarcely anyone knew that Nixon and Brezhnev were signing imperfect documents. The following morning these would be retyped at the White House command post in the Rossiya Hotel. Nixon and Brezhnev would then go through a second and private signing of the corrected documents.

The day had been long and had provided surprise, suspense, drama, confusion, pith, and moment. It was not over yet. There remained Kissinger's second press conference; in setting and tone, it ended the proceedings with a fittingly bizarre flourish. The time was 1:00 A.M. The place was the dimly lit "Skylight Sky Room," a nightclub in the Intourist Hotel. Against a background of cham-pagne buckets and while gazing over a raised dance floor, Kissinger sought to cope with a group of disgruntled reporters, who were becoming progressively unhappier, partly because nobody had been able to supply texts of the agreements. In fact, there existed only the copies that had been signed and these had not been Xeroxed, probably because of their imperfections.

In mollifying the press, Kissinger cited figures on Soviet missiles and bombers. Almost certainly, no Moscow nightclub act ever played to an audience more bemused by its surroundings or the implausibility of what it was witnessing. It struck Kissinger as well. After noting at one point that "the Soviet Union has been building missiles at the rate of 250 per year," he added, "if I get arrested here for espionage, gentlemen, we will know who to blame."

Kissinger stressed repeatedly that the SLBM deal suited American interests. It did, he conceded, literally freeze a Soviet numerical advantage in boats and SLBM's. But the alternative to an agreement freezing the Russians at 62 boats, he said, might well be a Soviet submarine fleet of 80 or 90 boats within the five-year life of the agreement. Answering the charge that "the United States got stuck with a submarine deal," he said, "That is an absurdity. . . . It was the United States which insisted that submarines be included. The United States was in a rather complex position to recommend a submarine deal since we are not building any and the Soviets were building eight or nine a year, which isn't the most brilliant bargaining position I would recommend people to find themselves in."

Not surprisingly, most of the questions were about the struggle over SLBM's. It had deadlocked the talks and might have blocked agreement. An aura of mystery and no little confusion obscured the essentials of an already elusive issue. Kissinger gave a good bare bones briefing of the dispute and even sketched in some detail. His audience learned a fair amount, but the complexity of the subject guaranteed that not much of it would creep into the daily press.

It was no time for a rigorous discussion of the two agreements. Everyone was exhausted. By 1:45, the newsmen had no more questions, and the incongruous nightclub press conference ended.

The last person to reach his bed in the Rossiya Hotel was probably Garthoff. Along with the rest of the delegation, he was due to return to Washington via Helsinki early in the morning. Sometime after the signing ceremony, he suddenly remembered the typewriter in the Soviet Foreign Ministry. His last contribution to the day's events was retrieving the typewriter in the dead of night.

It was all over. The ABM Treaty had at last been signed, with each side renouncing the defense of its society and territory against the other's nuclear weapons. That is the treaty's historic essence. Thirteen of its sixteen articles are designed to prevent any deviation, clandestine or otherwise. A joint Standing Consultative Commission that will monitor compliance with both agreements was created by Article XIII. The Commission, already known as the SCC, will allow each side to challenge the other's activities and to obtain explanations of any questionable or ambiguous events in the other's territory.

As for verification, each side will rely entirely on its own national systems to monitor the other's compliance with both agreements; each formally agrees to forbear interfering with the other's surveillance systems, or to conceal those of its activities to be monitored.

The treaty embodies considerable compromise (especially on radar controls), much of it achieved with some pain. Only one element, though, is likely to cause trouble—at least, for the Americans—and even here probably only in the short run. The one-plus-one arrangement may well mean two Soviet ABM sites and one American, since Congress is unlikely to approve funds for NCA. Probably, the White House could have arranged something else, either a one-and-one arrangement, leaving each side with just one site, or two-and-two, leaving the United States with both Safeguard sites, the Russians with Galosh and one ICBM defense site. It is a measure of Safeguard's disrepute (as other than a bargaining chip) that nobody in Washington really wanted the second site, whereas a number of people did want NCA, however doubtful its chances on Capitol Hill.

So it was, curiously enough, that NCA crept back into SALT. The Americans, after proposing NCA, labored hard to bury the idea, only to let it resurface as part of a formal agreement. Much of the SALT bureaucracy preferred the simpler one-and-one solution, which would have precluded a second Soviet site and meant fewer radars and other ABM impedimenta to worry about. But, again, this source of so much bureaucratic wrangling is likely to be rather quickly forgotten, especially as SALT's second phase churns up new issues to quarrel about.

Most of the bureaucracy has little to complain about in the Interim Agreement, which froze all strategic missiles as of July 1, 1972. Everyone wanted SLBM's in the agreement. They are there. Almost everyone favored a hard position on the replacement issue, and the hard position carried the day. Admittedly, the Soviets will have more offensive missiles, but this was the price of agreement. And, of course, they would have had more missiles than the United States with or without agreement.

All the Americans involved in SALT were disappointed about not getting tighter restrictions on the size of Soviet missiles and on the number of very large missiles. Still, Moscow *did* accept special limits on the big weapons for which it has always had a strong preference, and accepting them almost certainly set off a considerable internal struggle. Whether Soviet performance in meeting the spirit of the restrictive language stands the test of time may depend on relations with Washington and the progress of SALT itself.

Knowing what and how to think about SALT is no easier after agreement than before. Paradox and contradiction continue to agitate the enterprise. Some serious people worry that the agreement limiting offensive missiles will promote not stability and economy but more strategic offense and the spending that goes with it as each side presses for improved systems not affected by the agreement. And then, consider that those who fought against ABM deployment in 1966 and 1967 had the stronger case; the same could be said of Safeguard's original critics. Yet who could foresee that Soviet fears of a system that could not perform its major function—defending Minuteman sites—would become the blue chip on the American side of the table? Or, for that matter, that a trip to China would give the talks a final burst of impulsion that may have been essential to the kind of agreement that was reached?

Critics say that Washington could have worked out a one-plus-one ABM deal at least a year before the Moscow agreements. Possibly so, but the Interim Agreement on offense could not itself have been pushed any faster. That argument leaves critics as it finds them. Although they rejoice in having an ABM Treaty, they see the Interim Agreement as a cover for an expanded arms race, as a "hunting license for new weapons," as one of them put it, or as "worse than nothing," in the words of still another.

They worry that the ABM problem cannot be judged as safely behind us, because the MIRV problem is still before us and might unhinge the treaty. With numbers of weapons no longer at issue, the military and technological bureaucracies, by this reasoning, will focus their efforts on refinement and innovation. If the critics are right, the Interim Agreement carries a heavy penalty.

Hawkish critics of the Interim Agreement complain that it will not stop the Soviet Union from doing anything it wants to do. Some solid technical analysis can be deployed behind their arguments. But, as is often the case, such analysis misses a larger political point, for SALT has a heavy political component. In doing a deal with the Americans on offense, Brezhnev was influenced much less by strategic calculation than by the politics of his foreign policy. Nixon and Kissinger were right to insist that he accept a link between offense and defense.

To have accepted Moscow's preference for a simple ABM agreement would have cost the White House the support of largish parts of the bureaucracy and Congress and perhaps even some members of the Administration itself. With justice, Nixon would have been charged with yielding America's prime source of bargaining strength in return for exactly nothing.

In a sense, the Interim Agreement, as some critics complain, can be seen as legitimizing improvements and modernization of offensive weapons, but it should not inspire them. With or without agreement, the Soviet Union would reach for a MIRV capability, while Nixon in any case would have moved toward ULMS, a follow-on strategic bomber, and, sooner or later, the Trident submarine as well.

Those who object to the Interim Agreement should judge it in relation to the ABM Treaty, to which they do not object. The great powers were unwilling—they may yet be—to put hobbles on the process of refining offensive weapons until they had set limits on ABM's and numbers of offensive missiles; the negotiating history shows as much. With that accomplished, either of the two parties, if it chooses, can argue plausibly that both the American and Soviet peoples are defenseless, and there is thus no need to improve offensive capabilities. Each society is unambiguously a hostage to the destructive power of the other. And then, each side can now also argue that a parity of sorts has been acknowledged. The Interim Agreement leaves the Soviet Union with something like a three-to-two edge in numbers of missiles and at least three times as much strategic megatonnage as the United States, which in turn has more than twice as many deliverable nuclear warheads (about 5,700 against 2,500) as the Soviet Union.

Most of the criticism comes from those who see too few restraints or from others, like Senator Henry Jackson, who see too many. The former argue that neither side is inhibited by the Interim Agreement, while those of Jackson's turn of mind worry that it inhibits the United States, but not the Soviet Union. So far, Jackson is a somewhat lonely figure in that his allies are not especially articulate or even visible. That could change. In time, Jackson's position could be overtaken. It could be carried beyond the Senator's concern about disparities in numbers of missiles and into a generalized alarm that the Administration had shamefully allowed the United States to drift from sufficiency to insufficiency, thus presenting the Soviet Union with a clear claim to strategic supremacy and all the political cards that go with it.

If these politically troublesome disparities are not somehow narrowed during SALT's second phase, the Administration could run into serious trouble, not least with its own most tried-and-true constituency. More exactly, by 1975 or 1976, perhaps even before, an aging Administration may find itself saddled with an aging bomber force and a submarine force said to be aging by hawkish critics, but with no new weapons as replacements. Neither ULMS nor a new strategic bomber will be ready before 1978 at the earliest. By then, the Russians already may have started MIRV'ing their giant missiles; at the least, they may have begun testing a workable MIRV. At that point, the old question of Minuteman vulnerability, to date a mostly arcane internal argument, could blossom into a full-blown and contentious political issue, one that could perhaps even bring pressure on the Administration to abrogate the ABM Treaty so as to be able to defend Minuteman. Fashions change quickly in the United States. A growing tendency to think about security chiefly in terms of reducing defense spending could be submerged by renewed cries of a missile gap and heavy pressure from Congress to deploy new or improved weapons with all possible speed.

Little imagination is needed to supply a scenario that could catalyze such a convulsion in the public mood. One or two political reversals for the United States, most likely in Europe, could provoke a closely reasoned statement by some prominent member of the defense community, perhaps in the form of an Adelphi Paper published by the prestigious International Institute for Strategic Studies, proclaiming a sharp decline in America's political and strategic power. Unlike most such papers, which reach a small specialized audience, this one might turn up on page one of *The New York Times*, as good a launch pad as any for a heated congressional debate. The author, probably to his own astonishment, could then find himself a guest on one of network television's late evening talk shows. Perhaps more certain, he would wind up before a Congressional committee.

Critics of more dovish or liberal (to use a word they may prefer) leanings should remember that the American public is unused to running behind the Soviet Union and might be far less impressed by the heavy U.S. advantage in warheads than Washington experts; in any case, the warhead advantage can scarcely be considered permanent if one assumes, as most experts do, that Moscow will one day MIRV its long-range missiles.

Those among the critics who figured in the effort to launch SALT in 1967 and 1968 might also recall that the Moscow agreements achieve essentially what they themselves were preparing to propose in the summer of 1968: A limit on ABM's and a freeze on both land-based and sea-based offensive missiles. The big difference is that since 1968 the United States has lost its lead in numbers of missiles. Equally, all critics of the Interim Agreement should note that by freezing the number of big Soviet land-based missiles, while allowing the Russians to build a larger number of submarines, the Interim Agreement does help to encourage the movement toward the more-stable sea-based systems, the sea being an environment in which the United States has natural operating advantages as well as better weapons. In that light, the agreement is consistent with the thrust of Washington's position since the start of the negotiations.

Dovish critics are untroubled by superior Soviet numbers. They know that whatever happens, the strategic forces of the United States will remain more than adequate for the deterrence-assured destruction role. The edge in quality, they also know, could be a permanent—certainly, a long-term—advantage. Still, peoples of the world neither think nor react in entirely rational ways. Some or many of them may draw the wrong conclusions from the putative Soviet advantages in numbers and size of weapons; America's technological superiority is a considerably less-conspicuous asset. If and when the warhead gap is erased, Soviet politicians, diplomats, and generals may proclaim an existing and growing strategic superiority. And the world might listen. Or it might not listen. But the risk that it will is there, and it is one that American leaders could scarcely ignore. Even parity is, for the Soviet Union, as much a political as a strategic value.

Moscow wanted an ABM treaty, but had little reason to negotiate on offensive weaponry, since the Americans were not building more strategic weapons. Granted the Soviets didn't negotiate seriously until they had established a big lead in the number of offensive missiles they possessed. Still, for the Russians to have entered the Interim Agreement was a political event of capital importance. That they did showed an affinity for the SALT process that existed apart from their obvious incentive to contain the ABM. The Interim Agreement inhibits their natural source of strength, very large ICBM's. They can now have 313 of these, but no more. Almost certainly, they will eventually stack MIRV's on all of them, perhaps erasing the heavy American advantage in warheads.

With time, however, Moscow may see little sense in maintaining 313 superbrutes, let alone a total force of between 1400 and 1600 ICBM's. If so, Washington would surely be pleased to begin discarding some portion of its 1000 Minuteman missiles. A strategic weapon's invulnerability, like a Victorian lady's good name, is its most precious asset. Because Minuteman will one day be vulnerable, its future is uncertain. The Russians may develop a similar unease about their own land-based missiles. The accuracy of the American MIRV's will improve, not necessarily by design, but through the inevitable refinements that accompany continued testing and tinkering.

With *both* sides now betting most heavily on sea-based forces, they might one day—perhaps before the end of the decade—jointly agree that the land-based ICBM is a dangerous relic of the middle age of nuclear strategy. Washington might even decide on its own that the celebrated triad—ICBM's, SLBM's, and strategic bombers—is more an indulgence than a strategic requirement. SALT poses a question that the government has not answered: Does the United States really need three different strategic forces, each capable separately of doing the second-strike job? No agency or institution of government has ever stated a need for the triad. Nor has any Administration given it the cachet of formal policy. The government has always favored redundancy, but that is a far cry from what has been deployed. Moscow, while not eliminating strategic bombers altogether, has been steadily moving away from them. The United States could eventually follow suit one day, reducing or supplanting the Minuteman force in some fashion that did not alter the strategic balance.

In pressing to limit ABM's and accepting a hold on its biggest missiles, the Soviet Union may be a convert to the macabre doctrine of assured destruction, even though there is no equivalent Soviet term, not yet anyway. What needs next to be said is that nuclear-force planning is one thing, nuclear-war planning quite another. Assured destruction is really just a tool for modeling forces and isolating the heresy of outright nuclear superiority. America's strategic forces are built around a capability to destroy some given part of Soviet urban society and industry; yet perhaps the most intriguing of the ironies of SALT—certainly the most reassuring—is that while assured destruction appears to have become the solemn dogma of strategy, it is unthinkable that (short of a massive nuclear attack) an American president actually *would* retaliate instantly against the aggressor's cities, thereby inviting the destruction of his own. And there is no reason to assume that Soviet leadership is less rational on this point than American.

Like most of what passes for strategic doctrine in the nuclear age, assured destruction is an abstraction, not reality. Reality lies closer to the endless scenarios devised by planners, in which the accidental or limited use of nuclear weapons against the United States (or Western Europe) would presumably be met with a selective and limited response that would seek to avoid population centers and rapid escalation.

Bureaucracy speaks of SALT in phases. The first seven rounds were Phase I. We are now in Phase II. It is tempting to say that the Phase I agreements were a major contribution. They may prove to be so, but it is probably too soon to measure the gains of Phase I. The returns may not be in for years. The scope of the achievement will depend on what the two sides do in future about SALT, which in turn will depend in large part on what they do about otherwise unrelated problems affecting themselves and other countries. SALT, like all large projects of history, is linked, however imperceptibly, to many other events and forces.

No one can say which issues will most influence the talks over the years ahead. Most likely, the arguments will become more, not less, complicated, especially as the emphasis shifts away from quantity to quality. New and no less foreign acronyms will emerge. For now, it would be unwise to look upon SALT as other than a semipermanent part of great-power relations: at times a real negotiation, at times a dialogue carried on just to sustain the process. Most people want arms-control negotiations to succeed, especially when nuclear weapons are involved. Within and beyond the government, people have reacted to the twists and turns of such negotiations by allowing themselves to be whipsawed by their fears or misled by their expectations. SALT should help to contain our fears and to hedge our expectations.

Agreement reached for its own sake and affecting little is probably worse than no agreement. Agreements, like those reached in Moscow, that arise from serious negotiation and exact some mutual restraint should become a useful base on which to build. Still, it is well to be cautious. The United States presently has little left to bargain with, save FBS and a threat to withdraw from the ABM Treaty after five years if progress toward a broader agreement on offensive weapons is not achieved.

Both the critics and the SALT bureaucracy, most of which likes the Moscow agreements, take a pessimistic view of the immediate prospects for Phase II. The Soviets will revive the FBS issue. And they will try to avoid being talked into yielding much of their numerical advantage in missiles. They will doubtless reject any proposal to limit MIRV testing, assuming such a proposal is made. The Americans will seek reductions in ICBM's in order to reduce the Soviet advantage in "throw weight," or megatonnage. And Washington, while perhaps ready for a deal of some kind on FBS, will try to minimize its concessions on this very hard issue.

No one expects progress toward a MIRV testing ban, the issue that most interests the arms-control community. At best, it may be possible to limit the number of MIRV's on each ICBM. More than half the Minuteman force will have three MIRV's. Conceivably, the Soviets might accept the same limitation on their big land-based missiles, though only in return for major concessions from the Americans. Whether Washington would pay a heavy price for such a limitation cannot be predicted. Probably neither side will limit the number of MIRV's on their SLBM's, but this is not worrisome, since only the larger and more accurate land-based missiles offer a first-strike threat.

To write off the prospect of setting some limits on innovation and refinement is premature, if not cavalier. After all, a number of so-called qualitative controls were built into the ABM Treaty. Radars were limited in size and power as well as in number. And banning exotic future defensive systems was an enormous contribution. It was also an achievement. Governments sometimes but not often renounce weapons that do not exist.

Skeptics should also understand that SALT is a moderating political force, but one whose effects are neither immediate nor obvious. SALT is likely to affect other things, but slowly. The arms race is not impelled by technology alone, or by technology in tandem with the notorious action-reaction cycle. Both these forces are partially shaped and balanced by politics, by the relations between the powers, by the attitudes and policies of political leaders who may or may not actively seek to improve these relations, for whatever purpose. Normally, it is harder to justify increased military spending during a period of *détente* than in a period of cold war. This would be especially true if *détente* appreciably moderated political difficulties between the great powers —reduced the level of their confrontation in Europe, say, and their indirect confrontation elsewhere. Moderating such difficulties in turn would sharpen incentives to apply greater resources to more useful and productive pursuits than improving strategic missiles.

Many Soviet experts, while acknowledging some pressure on Brezhnev to reorder priorities, doubt that it is enough to affect weapons policies. Perhaps. We don't know. We do know that as General Secretary of the Soviet Communist Party, Brezhnev is the boss, but not the chief of state. President Nikolai Podgorny, who is, would normally have signed agreements of this scope and character. Hence, we also know that in choosing to sign the Moscow agreements himself, Brezhnev was proclaiming his identification with SALT, which has become an instrument of his foreign policy—for now, a very much *détente*-oriented policy.

More and more, the issues that might touch off a political crisis or direct recourse to nuclear weapons are reaching the green baize tables. Fred Iklé, an authority on negotiation, worries that it "has acquired the nimbus of salvation," and warns against the notion that negotiation "will protect the world from destruction and eventually deliver it from the terrible engines of war."[14]

In the West, negotiation is seen as useful because it is a means of working out differences and reaching agreement; negotiation is supposed to force up compromise and settlement. Further east, especially in the Soviet Union, negotiation is often a balloon put into the air, useful only so long as it doesn't come down. In the past, many Soviet offers to talk were designed to buy time, becloud the issue, and acquire propaganda advantage and, hopefully, political leverage.

SALT, so far, appears to be a serious process, as well as a continuing one. But the talks rely on the intent and negotiating style of the parties. The record established over seven rounds of talks, along with the Kissinger-Dobrynin conversations on the margin, is neither reassuring nor disappointing; it is inconclusive. A modest interim agreement has been achieved. From the start, the two sides have engaged in a frank, open, nonpolemical dialogue on the weapons most vital to their security. That itself is a watershed. Certainly, it is not to be taken lightly or for granted.

On the other hand, neither side has really learned much about the other's purposes. The suspicion of each government that the other will use SALT in a self-serving way has not been appreciably narrowed by either the agreements or the process itself.

Negotiating with the Russians requires patience and consistency. In the early rounds of SALT, the Americans often showed neither. After an initial period of studied caution, they did a great deal more talking than listening. In effect, America did the running, too often at the expense of consistency. Washington knew from experience in other negotiations that only by holding to the core of a position would useful agreement emerge. This was the case with the Austrian settlement, with the recent Berlin negotiations, and with other arms-control agreements. But in Vienna and Helsinki, American proposals were sometimes thrown up like pasteboard figures, withdrawn at the first sign of resistance, and replaced by other equally perishable offers.

In fairness, the seemingly chaotic and inconstant character of the talks arises in part from their complexity. Unlike most arms-control negotiations, a basic SALT proposal can have many combinations and permutations; each variant may have merit. The difficulty is that Russian suspicions of entrapment are aroused by this kind of versatility. Americans may understand what they are doing, but Moscow does not. The Soviet leadership normally reacts to unconventional tactics by hardening its own position.

Negotiating against a deadline is always risky. But by arranging to sign a SALT agreement in Moscow, that is what Nixon elected to do. In effect, he placed himself in what French diplomats call the worst of positions: *demandeur*. It is hard for the other side to react to a self-anointed *demandeur* other than to exploit him. Yet, as it turned out, nobody seems to have been exploited. Brezhnev wanted, and apparently felt that he needed, the agreements as much as Nixon.

On May 26, 1972, Nixon and Brezhnev signalled their political constituencies and the world that limiting strategic arms was no longer a rhetorical matter but a fully operational problem. They showed a considerable *sérieux*, as the French would put it, and did so at some risk. Brezhnev, like Khrushchev before him, is seen by Shelest and other Soviet hard-liners to have mounted a high-risk foreign policy. Nixon's triangular politics is popular at home, but worries America's allies and therefore could do some violence to that web of special interests that America has with Western Europe and Japan.

SALT was well served by the Nixon-Kissinger system, which is suited to problems of surpassing sensitivity and long lead time. The back channel is a good place for dealing with rival powers, but allies, like bureaucrats, resent being left out: It is too soon to balance the undoubted gains of a secret trip to China against the long-run effects of not alerting the Japanese.

Triangular politics is useful, if only because the greatest single source of instability in the years ahead probably lies in the relentless hostility that sets China and the Soviet Union against each other. China draws a measure of security from triangular politics, while the United States gains some maneuverability vis-à-vis Moscow and Peking. Moderating its difficulties with the West permits Moscow, however, to focus attention on China. Embedded as it is in triangular politics, SALT cannot be divorced from Moscow's concern with China or Washington's uneasy relations with Japan and Western Europe.

As a political force, SALT has a double edge. It may moderate relations between the great powers, but, depending on how it is handled and what is agreed to, it could also hasten the disrepair of NATO, a prospect to which Moscow must be sensitive. Concessions on the FBS issue could go down badly in Europe. America's forward-based aircraft are the politically credible offset to the Soviet missiles aimed at European cities.

And SALT is the only major East-West transaction that has lacked European participation. Because they are left out, European governments feel more dependent on America and hence more vulnerable. Their security, they know, is as much at stake as America's. Triangular politics, they fear, will restore the world of Palmerston's England, which had "no allies, only interests." Or before him, Metternich, who told Talleyrand: "Don't speak of allies. They no longer exist."[15]

The choices in Phase I involved numbers of missiles and types of ABM defense. The choices in Phase II will be subtler. The lesson of Phase I was the desirability of restraint. Both sides satisfied themselves that they had more than enough strategic launchers, and so they accepted an equivalent of parity. The lesson of

Phase II may be the desirability of measure, balance, and proportion. Washington will confront a need to reconcile SALT with other primary interests. It will be a more consciously political negotiation.

Because it is wrapped in the theology and other kindred abstractions of strategy, SALT is an obscure, certainly an elusive, enterprise. Politics, nonetheless, lies at its heart. There is much more to SALT than meets the eye of many a systems analyst. Settling the SLBM replacement issue was not the most important event of the May, 1972 summit conference; nor perhaps was the signing of the SALT agreements themselves. The importance of the conference, coming as it did on the heels of Nixon's closure of North Vietnam's ports, lay in the fact that it was held at all.

Appendix

TREATY BETWEEN THE UNITED STATES OF AMERICA AND THE UNION OF
SOVIET SOCIALIST REPUBLICS ON THE LIMITATION OF ANTI-BALLISTIC
MISSILE SYSTEMS

The United States of America and the Union of Soviet Socialist
Republics, hereinafter referred to as the Parties,

Proceeding from the premise that nuclear war would have devastating consequences for all mankind,

Considering that effective measures to limit anti-ballistic missile
systems would be a substantial factor in curbing the race in strategic
offensive arms and and would lead to a decrease in the risk of outbreak of war involving nuclear weapons,

Proceeding from the premise that the limitation of anti-ballistic
missile systems, as well as certain agreed measures with respect to the
limitation of strategic offensive arms, would contribute to the creation
of more favorable condition for further negotiations on limiting
strategic arms,

Mindful of their obligations under Article VI of the Treaty on the
Non-Proliferation of Nuclear Weapons,

Declaring their intention to achieve at the earliest possible date the
cessation of the nuclear arms race and to take effective measures
toward reductions in strategic arms, nuclear disarmament, and general
and complete disarmament.

Desiring to contribute to the relaxation of international tension and
the strengthening of trust between States,

Have agreed as follows:

Article I

1. Each Party undertakes to limit anti-ballistic missile (ABM) systems and to adopt other measures in accordance with the provisions
of this Treaty.

2. Each Party undertakes not to deploy ABM systems for a defense
of the territory of its country and not to provide a base for such a
defense, and not to deploy ABM systems for defense of an individual
region except as provided for in Article III of this Treaty.

Article II

1. For the purposes of this Treaty an ABM system is a system to counter strategic ballistic missiles or their elements in flight trajectory, currently consisting of:

(a) ABM interceptor missiles, which are interceptor missiles constructed and deployed for an ABM role, or of a type tested in an ABM mode;

(b) ABM launchers, which are launchers constructed and deployed for launching ABM interceptor missiles; and

(c) ABM radars, which are radars constructed and deployed for an ABM role, or of a type tested in an ABM mode.

2. The ABM system components listed in paragraph 1 of this Article include those which are:

(a) operational;

(b) under construction;

(c) undergoing testing;

(d) undergoing overhaul, repair or conversion; or

(e) mothballed.

Article III

Each Party undertakes not to deploy ABM systems or their components except that:

(a) within one ABM system deployment area having a radius of one hundred and fifty kilometers and centered on the Party's national capital, a Party may deploy: (1) no more than one hundred ABM launchers and no more than one hundred ABM interceptor missiles at launch sites, and (2) ABM radars within no more than six ABM radar complexes, the area of each complex being circular and having a diameter of no more than three kilometers; and

(b) within one ABM system deployment area having a radius of one hundred and fifty kilometers and containing ICBM silo launchers, a Party may deploy: (1) no more than one hundred ABM launchers and no more than one hundred ABM interceptor missiles at launch sites, (2) two large phased-array ABM radars comparable in potential to corresponding ABM radars operational or under construction on the date of signature of the Treaty in an ABM system deployment area containing ICBM silo launchers, and (3) no more than eighteen ABM radars each having a potential less than the potential of the smaller of the above-mentioned two large phased-array ABM radars.

Article IV

The limitations provided for in Article III shall not apply to ABM systems or their components used for development or testing, and located within current or additionally agreed test ranges. Each Party may have no more than a total of fifteen ABM launchers at test ranges.

Article V

1. Each Party undertakes not to develop, test, or deploy ABM systems or components which are sea-based, air-based, space-based, or mobile land-based.

2. Each Party undertakes not to develop, test, or deploy ABM launchers for launching more than one ABM interceptor missile at a time from each launcher, nor to modify deployed launchers to provide them with such a capability, nor to develop, test, or deploy automatic or semi-automatic or other similar systems for rapid reload of ABM launchers.

Article VI

To enhance assurance of the effectiveness of the limitations on ABM systems and their components provided by this Treaty, each Party undertakes:

(a) not to give missiles, launchers, or radars, other than ABM interceptor missiles, ABM launchers, or ABM radars, capabilities to counter strategic ballistic missiles or their elements in flight trajectory, and not to test them in an ABM mode; and

(b) not to deploy in the future radars for early warning of strategic ballistic missile attack except at locations along the periphery of its national territory and oriented outward.

Article VII

Subject to the provisions of this Treaty, modernization and replacement of ABM systems or their components may be carried out.

Article VIII

ABM systems or their components in excess of the numbers or outside the areas specified in this Treaty, as well as ABM systems or their components prohibited by this Treaty, shall be destroyed or dismantled under agreed procedures within the shortest possible agreed period of time.

Article IX

To assure the viability and effectiveness of this Treaty, each Party undertakes not to transfer to other States, and not to deploy outside its national territory, ABM systems or their components limited by this Treaty.

Article X

Each Party undertakes not to assume any international obligations which would conflict with this Treaty.

Article XI

The Parties undertake to continue active negotiations for limitations on strategic offensive arms.

Article XII

1. For the purpose of providing assurance of compliance with the provisions of this Treaty, each Party shall use national technical means of verification at its disposal in a manner consistent with generally recognized principles of international law.

2. Each Party undertakes not to interfere with the national technical means of verification of the other Party operating in accordance with paragraph 1 of this Article.

3. Each Party undertakes not to use deliberate concealment measures which impede verification by national technical means of compliance with the provisions of this Treaty. This obligation shall not require changes in current construction, assembly, conversion, or overhaul practices.

Article XIII

1. To promote the objectives and implementation of the provisions of this Treaty, the Parties shall establish promptly a Standing Consultative Commission, within the framework of which they will:

(a) consider questions concerning compliance with the obligations assumed and related situations which may be considered ambiguous;

(b) provide on a voluntary basis such information as either Party considers necessary to assure confidence in compliance with the obligations assumed;

(c) consider questions involving unintended interference with national technical means of verification;

(d) consider possible changes in the strategic situation which have a bearing on the provisions of this Treaty;

(e) agree upon procedures and dates for destruction or dismantling of ABM systems or their components in cases provided for by the provisions of this Treaty;

(f) consider, as appropriate, possible proposals for further increasing the viability of this Treaty, including proposals for amendments in accordance with the provisions of this Treaty;

(g) consider, as appropriate, proposals for further measures aimed at limiting strategic arms.

2. The Parties through consultation shall establish, and may amend as appropriate, Regulations for the Standing Consultative Commission governing procedures, composition and other relevant matters.

Article XIV

1. Each Party may propose amendments to this Treaty. Agreed amendments shall enter into force in accordance with the procedures governing the entry into force of this Treaty.

2. Five years after entry into force of this Treaty, and at five year intervals thereafter, the Parties shall together conduct a review of this Treaty.

Article XV

1. This Treaty shall be of unlimited duration.

2. Each Party shall, in exercising its national sovereignty, have the right to withdraw from this Treaty if it decides that extraordinary events related to the subject matter of this Treaty have jeopardized its supreme interests. It shall give notice of its decision to the other Party six months prior to withdrawal from the Treaty. Such notice shall include a statement of the extraordinary events the notifying Party regards as having jeopardized its supreme interests.

Article XVI

1. This Treaty shall be subject to ratification in accordance with the constitutional procedures of each Party. The Treaty shall enter into force on the day of the exchange of instruments of ratification.

2. This Treaty shall be registered pursuant to Article 102 of the Charter of the United Nations.

Done at Moscow on May 26, 1972, in two copies, each in the English and Russian languages, both texts being equally authentic.

FOR THE UNITED STATES OF AMERICA:

RICHARD NIXON

President of the United States of America

For the Union of Soviet Socialist Republics:
   LEONID I. BREZHNEV
      General Secretary of the Central Committee
      of the CPSU

INTERIM AGREEMENT BETWEEN THE UNITED STATES OF AMERICA AND
THE UNION OF SOVIET SOCIALIST REPUBLICS ON CERTAIN MEASURES
WITH RESPECT TO THE LIMITATION OF STRATEGIC OFFENSIVE ARMS

The United States of America and the Union of Soviet Socialist
Republics, hereinafter referred to as the Parties.

Convinced that the Treaty on the Limitation of Anti-Ballistic Missile Systems and this Interim Agreement on Certain Measures with
Respect to the Limitation of Strategic Offensive Arms will contribute
to the creation of more favorable conditions for active negotiations
on limiting strategic arms as well as to the relaxation of international
tension and the strengthening of trust between States.

Taking into account the relationship between strategic offensive and
defensive arms.

Mindful of their obligations under Article VI of the Treaty on the
Non-Proliferation of Nuclear Weapons,

Have agreed as follows:

Article I

The Parties undertake not to start construction of additional fixed
land-based intercontinental ballistic missile (ICBM) launchers after
July 1, 1972.

Article II

The Parties undertake not to convert land-based launchers for light
ICBMs, or for ICBMs of older types deployed prior to 1964, into
land-based launchers for heavy ICBMs of types deployed after that
time.

Article III

The Parties undertake to limit submarine-launched ballistic missile
(SLBM) launchers and modern ballistic missile submarines to the
numbers operational and under construction on the date of signature
of this Interim Agreement, and in addition to launchers and submarines constructed under procedures established by the Parties as

replacements for an equal number of ICBM launchers of older types deployed prior to 1964 or for launchers on older submarines.

Article IV

Subject to the provisions of this Interim Agreement, modernization and replacement of strategic offensive ballistic missiles and launchers covered by this Interim Agreement may be undertaken.

Article V

1. For the purpose of providing assurance of compliance with the provisions of this Interim Agreement, each Party shall use national technical means of verification at its disposal in a manner consistent with generally recognized principles of internatonal law.

2. Each Party undertakes not to interfere with the national technical means of verification of the other Party operating in accordance with paragraph 1 of this Article.

3. Each Party undertakes not to use deliberate concealment measures which impede verification by national technical means of compliance with the provisions of this Interim Agreement. This obligation shall not require changes in current construction, assembly, conversion, or overhaul practices.

Article VI

To promote the objectives and implementation of the provisions of this Interim Agreement, the Parties shall use the Standing Consultative Commission established under Article XIII of the Treaty on the Limitation of Anti-Ballistic Missile Systems in accordance with the provisions of that Article.

Article VII

The Parties undertake to continue active negotiations for limitations on strategic offensive arms. The obligations provided for in this Interim Agreement shall not prejudice the scope or terms of the limitations on strategic offensive arms which may be worked out in the course of further negotiations.

Article VIII

1. This Interim Agreement shall enter into force upon exchange of written notices of acceptance by each Party, which exchange shall take place simultaneously with the exchange of instruments of ratification of the Treaty on the Limitation of Anti-Ballistic Missile Systems.

2. This Interim Agreement shall remain in force for a period of

five years unless replaced earlier by an agreement on more complete measures limiting strategic offensive arms. It is the objective of the Parties to conduct active follow-on negotiations with the aim of concluding such an agreement as soon as possible.

3. Each Party shall, in exercising its national sovereignty, have the right to withdraw from this Interim Agreement if it decides that extraordinary events related to the subject matter of this Interim Agreement have jeopardized its supreme interests. It shall give notice of its decision to the other Party six months prior to withdrawal from this Interim Agreement. Such notice shall include a statement of the extraordinary events the notifying Party regards as having jeopardized its supreme interests.

Done at Moscow on May 26, 1972, in two copies, each in the English and Russian languages, both texts being equally authentic.

FOR THE UNITED STATES OF AMERICA:
    RICHARD NIXON
        President of the United States of America

FOR THE UNION OF SOVIET SOCIALIST REPUBLICS:
    LEONID I. BREZHNEV
        General Secretary of the Central Committee
        of the CPSU

PROTOCOL

TO THE INTERIM AGREEMENT BETWEEN THE UNITED STATES OF AMERICA AND THE UNION OF SOVIET SOCIALIST REPUBLICS ON CERTAIN MEASURES WITH RESPECT TO THE LIMITATION OF STRATEGIC OFFENSIVE ARMS

The United States of America and the Union of Soviet Socialist Republics, hereinafter referred to as the Parties,

Having agreed on certain limitations relating to submarine-launched ballistic missile launchers and modern ballistic missile submarines, and to replacement procedures, in the Interim Agreement,

Have agreed as follows:

The Parties understand that, under Article III of the Interim Agreement, for the period during which that Agreement remains in force:

The US may have no more than 710 ballistic missile launchers on submarines (SLBMs) and no more than 44 modern ballistic missile submarines. The Soviet Union may have no more than 950 ballistic missile launchers on submarines and no more than 62 modern ballistic missile submarines.

Additional ballistic missile launchers on submarines up to the above-mentioned levels, in the U.S.—over 656 ballistic missile launchers on nuclear-powered submarines, and in the U.S.S.R.—over 740 ballistic missile launchers on nuclear-powered submarines, operational and under construction, may become operational as replacements for equal numbers of ballistic missile launchers of older types deployed prior to 1964 or of ballistic missile launchers on older submarines.

The deployment of modern SLBMs on any submarine, regardless of type, will be counted against the total level of SLBMs permitted for the U.S. and the U.S.S.R.

This Protocol shall be considered an integral part of the Interim Agreement.

Done at Moscow this 26th day of May, 1972.

FOR THE UNITED STATES OF AMERICA:
>   RICHARD NIXON
>   President of the United States of America

FOR THE UNION OF SOVIET SOCIALIST REPUBLICS:
>   LEONID I. BREZHNEV
>   General Secretary of the Central Committee
>   of the CPSU

Notes

Chapter 1

1. Harold Nicolson, *The Congress of Vienna* (New York: Harcourt, Brace and Company, 1946), p. 187.
2. *Ibid.*, p. 176.
3. *Ibid.*, p. 176.
4. Robert S. McNamara, Commencement Address given at Ann Arbor, Michigan, June 16, 1962.
5. Robert S. McNamara, Testimony before a combined session of the Senate Committee on the Armed Services and the Senate Committee on Appropriations, January 23, 1967.
6. Testimony during the Hearings before the Senate Subcommittee on Arms Control, International Law and Organization of the Committee on Foreign Relations, 1970, pp. 227–231.
7. Amron H. Katz, "Hiders and Finders," *Bulletin of the Atomic Scientists,* December, 1961.
8. Henry A. Kissinger, *A World Restored* (New York: Grosset & Dunlap, Universal Library Edition, 1964), pp. 145, 163.
9. Harold Nicolson, *op. cit.*, p. 154.
10. Alain C. Enthoven and K. Wayne Smith, *How Much Is Enough?* (New York: Harper & Row, 1971), p. 208.
11. Testimony during the Hearings before the Senate Subcommittee on Arms Control, International Law and Organization of the Committee on Foreign Relations, 1970, p. 223.
12. Testimony during the Hearings before the Senate Subcommittee on Arms Control, International Law and Organization of the Committee on Foreign Relations, 1971, p. 179.
13. General John D. Ryan, Address before the Air Force Association in Washington, D.C., September 22, 1970.
14. Hearings before the House Subcommittee on National Security Policy of the Committee on Foreign Relations, 1970, p. 300.
15. Testimony during the Hearings before the Senate Preparedness Investigating Subcommittee of the Committee on the Armed Services, 1968, pp. 140, 148.
16. *Ibid.*, pp. 60–61.

17. V. V. Larionov, *S. Sh. A.*, No. 3, 1970 (Moscow: *S. Sh. A. Ekonomika, Politika, Ideologioa*).
18. Testimony during the Hearings before the Senate Subcommittee on Arms Control, International Law and Organization of the Committee on Foreign Relations, 1971, p. 13.
19. Senate Committee on the Armed Services, Report 92-359 Authorizing Appropriations in fiscal year 1972 for Military Procurement, Research and Development, for the construction of facilities for the Safeguard Anti-Ballistic Missile System, reserve component strength, and for other purposes, 1971, p. 17.
20. Henry Kissinger, *op. cit.*, pp. 326, 327.
21. *Ibid.*, pp. 326, 327.
22. Henry A. Kissinger, Report for the Security Studies Project of the University of California. Reported in the *Washington Post*, January 30, 1972.
23. Leslie H. Gelb and Morton H. Halperin, "Diplomatic Notes," *Harper's Magazine*, November, 1971, pp. 28–30.
24. Henry A. Kissinger, *A World Restored*, p. 29.
25. Harold Nicolson, *op. cit.*, p. 120.
26. Lieutenant-Colonel C. Ivanov, *Kommunist Vooruzhennykh Sil*, August, 1969, pp. 9–16.
27. *The New York Times*, September 12, 1969.
28. N. I. Krylov, *Sovetskaya Rossiya*, August 30, 1969.
29. V. V. Larionov, *op. cit.*, pp. 28–31.
30. Charles L. Schultze, *et al.*, *Setting National Priorities in the 1972 Budget* (Washington, D.C.: Brookings Institute, 1971), p. 117.
31. *Ibid.*, p. 50.
32. Testimony during the Hearings before the Senate Subcommittee on Arms Control, International Law and Organization of the Committee on Foreign Relations, July 13, 1971, p. 212.
33. Testimony during the Hearings before the Senate Subcommittee on Arms Control, International Law and Organization of the Committee on Foreign Relations, April 14, 1970, p. 247.
34. Testimony during the Hearings before the Senate Preparedness Investigating Subcommittee of the Committee on the Armed Services, April 23, 1968, p. 52.

Chapter 2

1. Robert S. McNamara, Posture Statement delivered before a combined session of the Senate Committee on the Armed Services and the Senate Subcommittee on Department of Defense Appropriations on the fiscal year 1965 Defense Budget, January, 1964, pp. 31–32.

2. Hearings before the Senate Preparedness Investigating Subcommittee of the Committee on the Armed Services, April 23 and 26, 1968, p. 60.
3. Alain C. Enthoven and K. Wayne Smith, *How Much Is Enough?* (New York: Harper & Row, 1971), p. 170.
4. *Ibid.*, p. 177.
5. Chalmers Roberts, *The Nuclear Years* (New York: Praeger, 1970), p. 87.
6. Alain C. Enthoven and K. Wayne Smith, *op. cit.*, p. 178.
7. Robert S. McNamara, Posture Statement delivered before the House Subcommittee on Department of Defense Appropriations on the fiscal year 1967 Defense Budget, January, 1966, p. 59.
8. Robert S. McNamara, Posture Statement delivered before a combined session of the Senate Committee on the Armed Services and the Senate Subcommittee on Department of Defense Appropriations on the fiscal year 1966 Defense Budget, 1966–70 Defense Program, January, 1965, p. 55.
9. Hearings before the Senate Subcommittee on Arms Control, International Law and Organization of the Committee on Foreign Relations, June 16 and 17, 1971, p. 86.
10. *Ibid.*, p. 87.
11. Morton H. Halperin, *The Decision to Deploy the ABM: Bureaucratic and Domestic Politics in the Johnson Administration* (Washington, D.C.: Brookings Institute, 1971), pp. 11–12.
12. *Ibid.*, p. 21.
13. *Ibid.*, p. 22.
14. Henry L. Trewitt, *McNamara* (New York: Harper & Row, 1971), p. 127.
15. Hearings before the Senate Committee on Appropriations, January 26, 1967, p. 239.
16. *Ibid.*, p. 48.
17. *Ibid.*, pp. 249–250.
18. Chalmers Roberts, *op. cit.*, p. 86.
19. *Ibid.*, p. 87.
20. Albert Wohlstetter, "The Implications of Military Technology in the 1970's," *Adelphi Paper No. 46*, March, 1968 (London: The Institute for Strategic Studies), p. 4.
21. *Life*, September 29, 1967, p. 28c.
22. I. F. Stone, *Polemics and Prophecies, 1967–1970* (New York: Random House, 1970), p. 158.
23. *Life, op. cit.*, p. 28c.
24. *The New York Times*, September 29, 1967.

25. Robert S. McNamara, Posture Statement delivered before the House Subcommittee on Department of Defense Appropriations on the fiscal year 1969 Defense Budget, January, 1968, p. 53.
26. *Ibid.*, p. 55.
27. Hearings before the Senate Preparedness Investigating Subcommittee of the Committee on the Armed Services, April 23 and 26, 1968, p. 244.
28. Testimony during the Hearings before the Senate Preparedness Investigating Subcommittee of the Committee on the Armed Services, May 4, 1971, part II, p. 1927.

Chapter 3

1. *Pravda*, June 28, 1968.
2. Malcolm Mackintosh, *Juggernaut* (New York: Macmillan Co., 1967), p. 289.
3. Lawrence T. Caldwell, "Soviet Attitudes to SALT," *Adelphi Paper No. 75*, February, 1971 (London: The Institute for Strategic Studies), pp. 15–16.
4. Hearings before the Senate Preparedness Investigating Subcommittee of the Committee on the Armed Services, May 1, 1968, p. 186.
5. *Ibid.*, p. 17.
6. *Ibid.*, p. 118.
7. *Ibid.*, p. 119.

Chapter 4

1. Chalmers Roberts, *The Nuclear Years* (New York: Praeger, 1970), pp. 92–93.
2. *Ibid.*, p. 94.
3. George M. Reedy, *The Twilight of the Presidency* (New York: New American Library, 1970), p. 31.
4. Henry A. Kissinger, *A World Restored* (New York: Grosset & Dunlap, Universal Library Edition, 1964), pp. 11–12.
5. Hearings before the Senate Subcommittee on International Organization and Disarmament Affairs of the Committee on Foreign Relations, March 28, 1969, p. 331.
6. Richard M. Nixon, *Documents on Disarmament* (Washington, D.C.: U.S. Arms Control and Disarmament Agency, 1969), p. 255.
7. *Ibid.*, p. 255.
8. *Ibid.*, p. 253.
9. The *Washington Post*, August 13, 1969.
10. Chalmers Roberts, *op. cit.*, p. 113.

Chapter 5

1. *The New York Times,* November 18, 1972.
2. Senate Committee on the Armed Services, Report Authorizing Appropriations for fiscal year 1971 for Military Procurement, Research and Development, for the construction of facilities for the Safeguard Anti-Ballistic Missile System, reserve component strength, and for other purposes, July 14, 1970, p. 19.
3. *Ibid.,* p. 19.
4. The *Washington Post,* July 24, 1970.
5. *Ibid.*
6. Henry A. Kissinger, Congressional Briefing at the White House, June 15, 1971.
7. Gerard G. Smith interview in *U.S. News & World Report,* December 14, 1970.
8. *The New York Times,* December 24, 1970.
9. Henry A. Kissinger, *A World Restored* (New York: Grosset & Dunlap, Universal Library Edition, 1964), p. 156. He cites Wilhelm Schwarz, *Die Heilige Allianz* (Stuttgart, 1935), p. 13.
10. The *Washington Post,* June 1, 1971.
11. Harold Nicolson, *The Congress of Vienna* (New York: Harcourt, Brace and Company, 1946), p. 133.
12. *The New York Times,* January 9, 1972.
13. The *Washington Post,* October 17, 1971.
14. Fred Iklé, *How Nations Negotiate* (New York: Harper & Row, 1964), p. ix.
15. Duff Cooper, *Talleyrand* (Stanford, California: Stanford University Press, 1968), p. 253.

Index